BORN
TO PUNT
MY BETTING YEAR

ACKNOWLEDGMENTS

Thanks to ace photographer Zachary Culpin for taking some excellent shots of me roaming around Weymouth for the book, thanks to my family and friends for putting up with me during my spells of betting-fuelled misery and, most of all, thanks to the *Racing Post* readers for their enthusiastic support during my quest to win retirement. I'll keep trying – I'm just not feeling as optimistic as I was ten years ago!

Take care, comrades, and be lucky, Steve.

BORN
TO PUNT
MY BETTING YEAR
STEVE
PALMER

RACING POST

First published in Great Britain in 2011 by
Racing Post Books
Axis House, Compton, Newbury, Berkshire, RG20 6NL

1 3 5 7 9 10 8 6 4 2

A catalogue record for this book is available from the British Library.

ISBN 978-1-905156-83-2

Cover designed by Jay Vincent
Interiors designed by Fiona Pike

Printed and bound in Great Britain by the MPG Books Group

www.racingpost.com/shop

CONTENTS

FOREWORD

By Bruce Millington

The question I used to be asked most as editor of the *Racing Post* was 'so do you get loads of good tips?' And then Steve Palmer started writing his weekly betting diary and now the one thing people want to know above all else is 'what's Steve Palmer like?'

The fascination with Palmer extends to every type of *Racing Post* reader, not just the hardcore punters for whom he's become a cult hero. Owners, trainers, administrators, sportsmen, MPs. They're all fascinated by the man who is the embodiment of the wild, devil-may-care punter we'd all like to be in our more frustrated moments.

But it's not just as a gambler who is prepared to part with his final penny that Palmer strikes a chord with so many people. His diary also reveals him to be a multi-layered character with a lust for heavy-drinking, a disdain for the thoughtless and the ill-mannered and a touching vulnerability that makes him a compelling read whether he's sweating on a golfer holing a six-foot putt to make him five grand or despairing that the women of Weymouth seem attracted to flashy, muscular men rather than more deep-thinking types like him.

I've had the pleasure of working with Steve for ten years and as well as being a superbly talented writer, whether regaling readers with tales of desperately bad betting luck or via his authoritative golf previews, he is also a model professional, a highly proficient production journalist and a hugely popular member of the *Racing Post* team.

It was a source of great joy to us all that Steve's talents were recognised when he won the title of sports betting writer of the year at the Sports Journalists Association awards in both 2009 and 2010.

And finally I'd like to put one annoying myth to bed once and for all. No, Steve doesn't make any of it up. Yes his bets are all genuine. And, yes, there are people who bet as prolifically as that. There is, however, only one person who bets as wildly and can write about it as entertainingly. And that's Steve Palmer.

INTRODUCTION

Steven John Palmer was born in Weymouth, Dorset on June 26, 1978, son of Roy and Lynne, and younger brother of Susie.

He quickly became obsessed with sport, in particular football. And after showing abundant promise for the Radipole Primary school team he planned a career playing for Liverpool, the dominant force in the English game at that point, in the full expectation that he would be the midfield maestro who would carry the mighty Reds on to further glory.

Those plans were hindered in 1988, though, when the family moved to Perth, Australia seeking the Neighbours/Home And Away lifestyle. A traumatic year followed for Steve, who was forced to play cricket every day at his new school, with football (or soccer as it was known Down Under) rarely on the curriculum.

His natural sporting prowess allowed him to rapidly become a decent cricketer, which only served to annoy the locals, the rivalry between Australia and England seemingly reaching its peak in the late 1980s. England had been in command of the Ashes for a decade and any 'pommy bastard' who had the temerity to walk on to Australian shores was not in for a warm welcome.

Steve suffered regular physical and mental abuse after any matches in which he had taken the wickets of (or scored plenty of runs off) the school's star cricketers and his love of sport was waning as a result. The euphoria of winning the annual Ironman Championship was soon extinguished by further punishment in the changing rooms afterwards.

After a year, the Palmer family gave up on the idea of successfully settling in Australia and returned to Weymouth, where Steve soon made waves in the local cricket leagues for various clubs (recording record-breaking bowling figures of eight wickets for four runs off four overs in one match for Martinstown) and was one of 22 trialists for Dorset CCC ("they picked all the posh lads – I never stood a chance," he said).

Realising his dream of becoming a professional sportsman was set to remain nothing more than fantasy, Steve switched his focus to sports journalism, becoming Snickers/Channel 4 Young Sports Broadcaster of the Year in 1996 after a national competition which was judged by legendary football commentator Kenneth Wolstenholme.

Breezing through Weymouth College, with little interest in the Communication Studies, Sociology or Politics A-levels he was supposed to be studying, Steve devoted the vast majority of his free time to watching sport and upon turning 18 he decided it was time to employ his expertise more productively.

On the way back from an early-morning car boot sale, where he had been selling as many of his possessions as possible to bolster the meagre wages he was earning from various jobs, he walked into a betting shop for the first time and tentatively opened dialogue with the cashier.

Steve said he wanted to back Michael Atherton to be England's top runscorer in the first innings of the Third Test against India at Trent Bridge, but because Atherton was already 21 not out at the close of day two, the cashier explained that the market was not running any more.

"I was annoyed I couldn't get involved," said Steve, looking back on his early foray into the punting world. "So I asked instead for odds on Richard Krajicek winning Wimbledon, which had reached the semi-final stage. The bloke behind the counter realised I didn't have much money to play with, though, telling me Krajicek was even-money and not worth bothering with, so again I was left frustrated."

But Steve had one other fancy for that weekend – Steve Collins to beat Nigel Benn in the big boxing bout – so he asked for a price on the Irishman.

"I got another head-shake from the cashier because Collins was also too short for a teenage peasant like me to consider backing," said Steve. "But he suggested I pick a round for Collins to win in, and after 30 seconds' thought, I opted for round four."

Steve was quoted 40-1, handed over £2 and finally went on his way.

Over the next few days, Atherton went on to compile a top-scoring innings of 160, Krajicek cruised to Wimbledon glory and Collins had Benn on the ropes in round four at the Nynex Arena in Manchester on the Saturday night.

"I was absolutely buzzing in my bedroom as the Dark Destroyer wobbled," said Steve. Benn sustained an injury to his ankle and was unable to continue, so Collins won by technical knockout in round four.

Having written down 'Collins to KO Benn in round four' on his betting slip, Steve started fretting about whether a TKO counted for betting purposes, but when he was handed £82 on his return to the shop he realised he was on to a winner and so began his passionate – and tempestuous – love affair with betting.

Steve's punting gradually increased. "Graham Thorpe was my favourite batsman and he won me plenty for a little while," he recalls. "Then I started nailing a few football accumulators and never looked back."

The betting habit only intensified when Steve went to Bournemouth University to do a Multi-Media Journalism degree. Joining forces with housemates Luke Tredget, who has since gone on to become a golf odds compiler for Betfred, and Richard De Melim, a Derby County-obsessed character who in Steve's words "accidentally impregnated an Italian woman and was forced to move to Bari to marry her", young Palmer spent three years punting enthusiastically in a Coral shop with his comrades.

The journalism degree took a distant back-seat to the betting. Greyhound racing was the staple diet of the three young scholars, with Friday the most eagerly anticipated time of the week. Backing Monmore to have more winning favourites than Swindon at a shade of odds-on was described by Steve as "like a licence to print money", providing a full afternoon of entertainment "while the rest of the journalism class worked on pointless shorthand and did pretend work for their pretend radio stations".

Losing streaks impacted heavily on the group, with regular trips to

Cash Converters to pawn possessions for punting funds, but the three betting amigos progressively honed their technique. The final weeks of 'study' put all three under severe pressure – the punting distractions meant there was a distinct possibility of them walking away from three years of expensive education without any qualification to show for it – but some last-gasp through-the-night dissertation sessions meant they did just enough.

"I scrambled a 'Desmond Tutu' despite being by far the most talented journalist in the year," chuckles Steve, who is clearly not a fan of the university system. De Melim did likewise, while Tredget happily settled for a third.

Work experience stints on various newspapers and radio stations followed for Steve, whose growing passion for golf was taking over his life, and without any obvious paths opening up for full-time employment, he got a job as the assistant professional at Came Down Golf Club in Dorchester, swiftly getting his handicap down to just nine by taking to the course each day in the hour before sunset.

Steve could usually be found, though, watching golf on TV behind the counter in the club shop, avidly following his bets. "I remember being in the process of landing a nice touch on Gary Orr in the Portuguese Open when I spotted a mini-bus full of visitors pull up in the car park," said Steve. "I quickly locked the shop door so I could watch Orr sink the winning putt in peace. I was only on £25 a day, so the punting was much more important."

It was while reading the *Racing Post* during a quiet spell between selling Mars Bars that Steve spotted an advertisement for a sports journalist's position at the paper. The Editor was looking to bolster the sports desk on the eve of the Euro 2000 football championship and Steve sent off an application form the following day.

A phone call came from then Sports Editor Bruce Millington a few days later to arrange an interview, but with Steve distracted by the golf, confusion reigned as to the date that was set for their meeting.

"Bruce said I should come up to London next Tuesday," said Steve. "And as we were speaking on a Friday, I presumed 'next Tuesday' meant a week on Tuesday. Surely he would have just said 'come up on Tuesday' if he meant the impending Tuesday which was only four days away?"

Steve turned up 11 days later to discover Bruce was in the Lake District and then Deputy Sports Editor Paul Kealy greeted the Weymouth raider with the words: "He thought you were coming up last Tuesday – you've missed the boat son."

Determined not to waste the trip, Steve and the pal who had joined him on the voyage north decided to embark on an impromptu tour of London, eventually ending up blind drunk in a boat bar on the River Thames (he didn't miss that boat), where they befriended two Canadian girls who were travelling around Europe.

A dejected Steve decided that having blown his chance of a career in sports journalism, he would join the Canadians on the Eurostar to Paris and forge a new life on the continent, but his friend physically restrained him from boarding the train to France and forced him back to Weymouth.

Millington was informed of the mix-up on his return from holiday and re-scheduled the interview, eventually getting a chance to grill the youngster on a range of sporting issues. Steve's assertion that Nicky Butt should be the first name on the England team-sheet did not go down well with his potential new boss, but tipping France to win Euro 2000 certainly did, and before long Palmer had joined the *Racing Post* sports desk as a fresh-faced 21-year-old.

He moved to lodgings in Chislehurst, Kent, before switching down the road to Sevenoaks, then spent seven years commuting to Canary Wharf from Brighton, before being allowed to work from home in Weymouth from the start of 2010.

Steve took over the sports desk's Pick Of The Day column at the end of 2000, a quirky look at the day's events which became a big hit with readers, and he also made a name for himself among his peers with a cavalier approach to punting.

Sitting opposite Kealy, now the *Racing Post* Betting Editor, Steve would typically bet on every dog race with his colleague, one often ending the session owing the other thousands of pounds, and a spell spread betting on Barking Bananas (the winner's trap multiplied by the runner-up's trap multiplied by the third-placed hound's trap) eventually sent both men barking mad.

Focusing on golf was always Steve's most successful course of betting action, and during a particularly glorious run of winners in 2004, he was close to reaching the £30,000 bank balance he has since targeted as the amount with which he could consider becoming a full-time professional gambler.

When Retief Goosen won the European Open that year, Steve was able to fork out £10,000 on a new car, the biggest investment of his life. A couple of years later, some more golf successes allowed him to go on a £5,000 holiday to Barbados with his then girlfriend, and he had got a taste for big wins.

A few times he has won in the region of £9,000 on a single bet and he bagged more than £10,000 in a day in 2008 and again last year when his confidence in the Spanish national football side contributed to two hugely profitable 24-hour periods.

Steve has suffered serious setbacks too – he lost £4,800 on the 2009 Masters having wrongly assumed it was a two-horse race between Tiger Woods and Phil Mickelson – and his punting journey has often been derailed by recklessness.

Over the years, he has frequently been massively disillusioned, shattered by setbacks in his personal life, hating his commute to England's capital city, living in places where he hardly knew anyone and drinking heavily to quell the pain.

He has twice quit the *Racing Post* – a loathing of London and a general lack of ambition being the main contributory factors – and he once enjoyed a three-month spell as a professional gambler. But he has always returned to writing work having run out of money.

Steve's desire is to win enough from betting to become a full-time professional gambler and £30,000 is the figure he has often touted as a foundation from which he could build a satisfying existence for himself ("I think it's impossible for me to lose £30,000," he once said).

In recent years, Steve has upped his stakes in a bid for freedom, and in April 2008 he wrote his first *Betting Week* column, which detailed every wager he struck in a seven-day period. Steve's betting diary became a regular feature of the *Racing Post on Sunday*, cementing his status as a cult figure among Post readers and users of its racingpost.com website. He has won the Sports Journalists' Association Betting Writer of the Year award ever since its inception in 2008.

Steve has attacked bookmakers with gusto. He has often ended up skint, desperately muddling through to payday on the 15th of each month to replenish his ammunition supplies, but has also been on wonderful runs that have put him close to that magical £30,000 figure.

En route, ever haunted by an addictive personality that sees him regularly succumb to powerful urges for fried chicken, lager, young blonde women and various other dangerous pursuits, he has frequently found himself distracted from the task of winning money.

At the age of 32, Steve is still hoping to earn a responsibility-free, pro-punter lifestyle, but friends paint the picture of an often troubled individual is as high as a kite one day and as low as a submarine the next, and whose mind wanders too easily on to other things for him to become a clinical and consistently successful betting machine.

This book includes every one of his *Betting Week* diary entries from 2010, 12 months in which he went for the jugular on a number of occasions in his quest to win freedom. This is the story of a year in the life of Steve Palmer – a man born to punt.

CHAPTER 1

ARRERS ANGUISH

Raymond van Barneveld

Friday, January 1

New year, new start, new Steve. I am quitting booze for January, going to slowly but surely crank up an exercise regime, and I expect to be resembling Steve 'Bronzed Adonis' Beaton some time around Valentine's Day.

Healthy body, healthy mind – that's my new catchphrase. And a healthy mind is more equipped to identify winners than an unhealthy one. Healthy body, healthy mind, unhealthy bookmakers, healthy bank balance, etc.

Saturday, January 2

I was starting to feel amazing as the last few drops of New Year's Eve rum passed out of my body and I was building an enormous lust for life in general – that was until I foolishly killed five minutes looking at Facebook around high noon.

There is nothing quite like a social networking site to suck morale from a man's heart, and I was subjected to approximately one million pictures of 'friends' doing all sorts of 'wacky' things as they saw in 2010.

It seems that many people now like to spend their entire New Year's Eve taking photographs – even taking photographs of people taking photographs – so they can show everyone on Facebook what a great time they had taking photographs on New Year's Eve.

What happened to living for the moment? Living for the moment when you get to show everyone else how wonderful a previous moment was seems to be the standard way of thinking nowadays.

Facebook, like football betting, binge-drinking, depression and psoriasis, is something I'm looking to rid myself of in 2010, but old habits die hard.

In fact, Betfair was the next website I visited that afternoon to place a wager on the football. Moderate drinking, joy and perfect skin might be easier to achieve this year than a world without the twin evils of FB and FB.

I had to support Tottenham, though, to add to Peterborough's away-day woes in the FA Cup, and I was hugely confident that Spurs would comfortably manage to notch the four goals necessary to land my £200 on any unquoted scoreline at 7-4.

Once I had that investment in place, I got my BDO World Championship darts bets on (£150 on Scott Waites at 4-1 and £50 on Ted Hankey at 13-1) and then I lost a five-leg arrers match of my own 3-2 against a pal in his garage (missing about 100 doubles in the process).

Anyone who says darts is not a sport (this is the time of the year such nonsense is often heard) is a moron. What Phil Taylor does (projecting a slither of tungsten into a tiny target from seven feet, nine and a quarter inches) is a greater example of sporting prowess than what someone like Titus Bramble does (bundling people over and hoofing a ball into Row Z), but no-one questions football's status as a sport.

After my arrers defeat, it was nearly 5pm and injury-time was being played at White Hart Lane with Spurs three goals up. I was calling myself all sorts of nasty names for slipping off the football-betting wagon again (idiot, dickhead, mug, knob, dumbo, dipstick, spanner, plonker, prat, prick, loser, numbskull, sausage, etc) and wondering whether I'll ever develop the quality of willpower.

But then good old Jeff Stelling suddenly popped us back to the Lane on Soccer Saturday and Robbie Keane had nailed the decisive fourth with the last kick of the game. A positive last-gasp goal? What's that all about then? That just doesn't happen in the real world, does it? I'm sure all last-gasp goals are supposed to bust coupons and spread misery.

Had I been playing a game of cards at this stage (my second least favourite activity behind wrestling stinging nettles), I would have been mulling over whether to stick or twist. I had banked £360 from Spurs, but Reading and Liverpool were just about to kick off in the TV tie, so I could play up some of the winnings.

I managed to stick until Liverpool's equaliser just before half-time, but then I was twisting like Shakin ruddy Stevens thereafter, having £40 at 11-2 on a 3-1 Liverpool win, then £60 at prices ranging from 11-4 to 9-4 on 2-1 as the Reds continued to splutter.

Those spur-of-the-moment correct-score bets were the epitome of the type of wasteful, impulse gambling that ends up leaving men sleeping in cardboard boxes on the street. In all seriousness, I must find a way of curbing these urges. With the weather as it is at the moment, all the cardboard in the world wouldn't keep you warm at night. It's a swift transition from the cardboard box to the coffin box.

Anyway, the £100 Liverpool loss would pale into insignificance if Raymond Van The Man Van Barney Van Barneveld could see off Simon Whitlock in the semi-finals of the PDC World Championship. With a £200 each-way at 12-1 Barney voucher in my possession, I could pick up £1,400 if the five-times world champion progressed past the waddling weirdo from kangaroo country.

Laying off (by backing Whitlock to win the match) definitely crossed my mind because my finances are not in terrific shape at the moment, but I could not believe the so-called Wizard was favourite, and I was not prepared to invest a bean at odds-on. So instead of playing it safe and securing more than £600 whatever the outcome, I settled down for what turned into my most stressful night of 2010 thus far.

Barney cruised into a 4-2 lead before losing 6-5 and I was left looking skywards as I tried to make sense of it all (I'd written 'You should definitely have had a saver on Whitlock' on my bedroom ceiling).

A desperate man, I immediately turned to Phil 'The Saviour And Redeemer' Taylor for solace, having £190 at 2-1 on Europe's greatest sportsman beating Mark Webster 6-0. Watching The Power surgically destroy the Welshman with unwavering tungsten control was like enjoying a full-body massage from a Swedish princess – calming, soothing, entrancing, with a deeply satisfying finale.

Sunday, January 3

Had a swim at the spa with my mate to get over the Barneveld disappointment, frightening a couple of old ladies with my aggressive butterfly stroke. If you want to clear a pool quickly, get to work on some butterfly.

As I was leaving the pool I noticed a list of banned behaviour. Butterfly wasn't on there but from top down it read: No diving, no bombing, no heavy petting . . .

What kind of killjoy wrote that list? Heavy petting is the third most heinous crime one can commit in the pool? Does that mean full, penetrative sex is allowed? It's not on the list.

While sprinkling some talc on my thighs in the changing room, it hit me how much I wanted Taylor to do a demolition job on Whitlock in the arrers final. It had become an England versus Australia contest in my eyes and I thought about driving straight to the Ally Pally armed with several flags of St George and demanding a front-row seat from the Ladbrokes boys to hurl Ashes-related abuse at Whitlock.

The icy roads meant police were urging people not to travel unless "absolutely necessary", though, and I couldn't justify my Aussie-bashing falling into that category.

So it was more TV tension ahead and, although Webster provided some relief by beating Barney in the third-place play-off (I had £150 on the much more motivated Webster at 11-4), the Taylor correct-score wagers I had placed in the morning (£175 on Taylor to win 7-0 at 11-2 and £205 on 7-1 at 9-2) went horribly awry.

When Whitlock went 2-1 up, my betting interest was ended, but not for one minute did the possibility of a Taylor defeat enter my thinking. After the 14-times champ levelled at 2-2, I had £110 on Taylor to win 7-2 at 9-2 before he rattled off four sets on the spin to go 6-2 up.

Game over? No, Whitlock hit double-one (madhouse) to make it 6-3, creating an even madder location between my ears.

Monday, January 4
Assessed finances. Frowned a lot.

Tuesday, January 5
Invested every penny I had at my disposal on the golf, placing £200 on Richard Sterne to win the Africa Open at 12-1, £90 on Dustin Johnson to win the SBS Championship at 23-1, the same stake at the same price on Angel Cabrera, £80 on Nick Watney at 20-1 and £40 on Rory Sabbatini at 41-1.

Wednesday, January 6
With no money to bet with and a no-drinking-until-February rule in operation, at least the snow provided some entertainment. My nephew kept trying to say, "Let's make snowballs!" but he can't pronounce the first s. I told him he should try to get in the England cricket team if he wants to make them. He didn't seem to get the joke.

Thursday, January 7
Sterne was top of the Africa Open leaderboard when I tuned in for coverage at 8.30am and I was hopeful of a one-bet, one-winner start in the first golf tournament of the year.

Friday, January 8

I had re-nicknamed Scotty 'Too Hotty' Waites to Scotty 'I Should Be Bent Over Someone's Knee And They Should Smack My Botty' Waites after his feeble final-set performance against Martin Phillips at Lakeside. After Hankey's 5-4 defeat the previous night, I was feeling like the unluckiest man in the world.

But then I remembered the chap I saw begging on the streets of Malawi a few years ago who had no arms and no legs, and immediately stopped feeling sorry for myself. It's easy to lose perspective when immersed in the punting game, but if you can afford to punt in the first place, you have almost certainly been born a very lucky bugger.

CHAPTER 2

ROCKET GROUNDED

Ronnie O'Sullivan

Saturday, 9 January

When your first wager of the day is a £10 reverse forecast on some Brough Park action, you know you're short of betting options, but after watching Sterne drop away in the third round of the Africa Open, I popped forlornly into a Coral shop for a change of scenery.

Blue-shirted staff with 'Think 21' badges on (I wish I could remember what it was like to be 21 to be perfectly ruddy honest), frustrated men tickling FOBTs, frustrated men gathered round dog form, frustrated men staring into their cups of tea, frustrated men talking to other frustrated men about how frustrated they are – yep, the scenery hadn't altered much from the last time I had visited.

I switched my attentions to the Masters snooker, having £150 on Ronnie O'Sullivan at 3-1 and £50 on Stephen Maguire at 11-1, then headed off to play snooker myself to take my mind away from the sports betting world for a few hours.

You know you're getting old when the snooker club feels more like a youth club. My pal and I, both 31, must have been in the top five per cent of the 50 or so people in attendance in terms of seniority.

It was amusing to watch a teenage blonde girl, who had a touch of the Anna Kournikovas about her, playing pool with about 15 lads surrounding her table. The number of cues in the club was doubling every time she bent over to play a shot. If I ever become a parent, I so desperately want to have a son rather than a daughter. If my daughter chose to spend her Saturday afternoons hanging out at the snooker club with 15 hormone-fuelled lads for company, I think I would be forced to buy the club and turn it into a block of flats.

I won my match 5-1, then headed off to KFC for a Family Feast, enjoying the usual hilarity when the cashier asks how many cups are needed for our 'family' to drink the bottle of Pepsi that goes with the chicken, chips and beans mountain.

"Four? Five?" asked the nice chap behind the counter. "No, two mate," replied my pal Trifleface, with his non-related binge-eating partner Steve salivating behind him.

On the way home, via Coral for a successful £40 on Trap One at 6-4 in the 7.43 at Monmore, I made a trip to the bank to evaluate my finances and elected to have all the remaining cash in my account (£250) on Charl Schwartzel to win the Africa Open at 4-1.

Sunday, January 10

Schwartzel soon took control and I bought my nephew a Transformer (robot in disguise) to celebrate the much-needed bag-of-sand cash injection.

In the US golf, Sabbatini was clear at the top of the leaderboard after a birdie at the 17th hole and no doubt trading very short on the exchanges, but getting out of bed and turning on the computer to lay off in the early hours of a chilly morning did not appeal, so I suffered the anguish of his par five at the 18th knowing it had probably blown my chances of a £1,680 return.

I was ridiculously tired as Geoff Ogilvy edged Sabbatini by a shot

– the 3am finishes from Hawaii had taken their toll – and the bags ended up under my eyes rather than in my Betfair account.

I turned over to Celebrity Big Brother Live during one advertisement break in the golf and the camera was trained directly on Katia's peachy buttocks as she slept in her pyjamas. For three minutes solid the camera didn't move – it just had a close-up of Ronnie Wood's ex-girlfriend's arse.

I realise these celebrities are getting paid plenty of money for such intrusion, but it must be hard to sleep peacefully while knowing your backside is being screened for the inspection of the nation.

Monday, January 11

Possibly the most incredible thing I've ever seen in my life occurred over the last week or so. Let me explain.

I purchased a remote-controlled tarantula about a year ago (it's five times as big as a real tarantula) and it's been sitting in the corner of my bedroom. A few days into the new year, I noticed a real spider (not a tarantula but quite a big one) crawling across my carpet in the direction of the remote-controlled tarantula, then it paused just before reaching it, spent about a minute admiring the magnificent specimen towering over him, before nestling underneath the tarantula's front legs.

I thought that was amazing enough (a real spider being attracted to a fake one), but when six or seven days later the real spider was still dutifully paying homage at the feet of the giant lump of plastic he thought was a remarkably large member of his species, my jaw was starting to drop. I gently prodded the spider to see if I could convince him to abandon his position, but several prods later it became obvious he had died.

The spider was clearly convinced he had found some sort of God-like figure, wanted to be near him, and was so in awe of him he was prepared to starve by his side. Mindblowing.

Tuesday, January 12

Had another £125 on O'Sullivan for the Masters at 13-8, along with another £25 on Maguire at 12-1, then I watched Kevin And Perry Go Large on ITV2 in the evening, which is officially the third-best film ever made (behind Top Gun and Happy Gilmore).

Wednesday, January 13

Had £210 on Sterne to win the Joburg Open at 15-1, £125 on Edoardo Molinari at 22-1, £10 each-way on Martin Maritz at 300-1, £105 on Sabbatini to win the Sony Open at 27-1, £55 on Stephen Ames at 45-1, £65 on Brian Gay at 39-1, £65 on David Toms at 37-1 and £35 on Stuart Appleby at 79-1. I also weighed in with a £25 each-way double on Sterne (14-1) and Sabbatini (25-1) and a score at 55-1 on Chad Campbell to be first-round Sony leader.

Come the evening, I decided that given I had actually watched a few episodes of Celebrity Big Brother, and had an intimate knowledge of Katia's posterior, I could justify a betting interest, so I had £105 at 11-8 on Vinnie Jones (no nonsense), £25 at 16-1 on Nicola Tappenden (adorable little princess) and £20 at 26 on Dane Bowers (surprisingly decent bloke).

Thursday, January 14

The fast starts in Joburg of Schwartzel and Darren Clarke, two of the very last names eliminated from my shortlist so I could have proper stakes on Sterne and Molinari, left me fuming.

Friday, January 15

Oh cripes, I've got to move house.

Saturday, January 16

Moving house is not straightforward, is it? I think it's definitely one of the most challenging tasks a human being can face. I would say creating another human being (the giving birth bit, not the preliminaries) is probably the only assignment one can face that is more traumatic than moving house. I'm so glad I don't possess a womb.

My move was made slightly more bearable, though, by the fact my dad works for a funeral directors, so we could use a big van that usually transports dead bodies around to shift my treasured possessions to their new home. Not only did this speed up the process but it also provided much comedy value as curtains twitched manically while my concerned new neighbours tried to work out who the coffin carrier had come to pick up.

To confuse the onlookers further, the first item I removed from the hearse was the life-size and realistic cuddly-toy tiger I purchased from Longleat a few years ago.

"Who's died, Doris?"

"Not sure, love, but they've just taken out a dead tiger to make some extra room. Maybe it's Tubby Turner from No. 24."

Once I had reassured the locals that none of their friends had passed away, I downed tools to watch the Masters semi-final between O'Sullivan and Mark Williams, which turned out to be one of the best snooker matches in the history of the sport. I probably wouldn't have taken that view had O'Sullivan lost, but watching him edge through 6-5 in a thriller was the highlight of my year so far.

Unfortunately, Mark Selby beat Maguire in the second semi-final, so I couldn't count any chickens yet.

Sunday, January 17

Schwartzel's Joburg Open win was a crippling blow. I noticed he had drifted to 10-1 on the eve of the tournament despite having impeccable credentials, but I wanted a chunk on Sterne, so had £210 at 15-1. Why didn't I have £110 on Schwartzel and £100 on Sterne?

Because I've got a mental problem, of which I'm fully aware, yet seemingly powerless to overcome. When it comes to outright golf betting, a little devil inside my head always tells me any return of less than £2,000 is not worth the trouble. The devil insists that if I successfully predict the winner from a massive field of golfers, then I should get at least two bags for my efforts.

But if you win £1,000 a week, that's £52,000 a year, and you wouldn't need to work for a living. I know I should put my eggs in more baskets, but the "get rich quick" devil is forever residing between my ears to stop me doing so.

After Schwartzel's comfortable triumph, my mood dipped further when the clutch on my car snapped as I was moving some more stuff to my new flat, leaving me stranded on a dual carriageway. O'Sullivan winning the Masters suddenly became even more important with the cost of a new clutch looming over me.

The Rocket secured a 5-3 advantage over Selby after the first session and then went 9-6 up in the first-to-ten-frames final in the evening, so it was looking like a trying weekend was going to end on a high.

But then Ronnie lost the plot, took on a ludicrously tough green left-handed, and Selby went on to win 10-9. The Jester from Leicester, eh? Yep, he's hilarious.

The match ended just before midnight and I found myself as depressed as I've been in a long while. Another Rocket-backer texted to inform me that O'Sullivan traded at 1-20 on Betfair. I often wish betting exchanges had never been invented – losses were always much easier to swallow when you knew you hadn't had any chance to avoid them.

Still, the final round of the Sony Open golf was to come, and I had Sabbatini and Steve Stricker (£110 at 8-1 after round three) in contention. I stayed up until 3.30am to watch a Mr Palmer end the night a winner. He was a golfer called Ryan, though, not Steve, and I was awash with sadness.

CHAPTER 3
HOPE SPRINGS ETERNAL

Tim Clark

Monday, January 18

I was short of funds and morale, but I knew I needed to try to get my brain around the golfing week ahead because the Abu Dhabi Championship had been a lucky tournament for me in the past (I had £125 on Martin Kaymer at 66-1 when he won in 2008 and £200 on Paul Casey at 28-1 when he won in 2009), so I ignored the plight of my stricken car and weighed in with three Abu Dhabi wagers (£125 on Kaymer at 16-1, £45 on Alex Noren at 47-1 and £30 on Alvaro Quiros at 69-1).

I later made three Bob Hope Classic investments (£75 on Tim Clark at 25-1, £65 on Justin Leonard at 28-1 and £40 on Gay at 41-1) and had a £100 double on Kaymer (14-1) and Clark (22-1).

Tuesday, January 19

Unfortunately, I found myself in front of a TV screen as the line-ups for the Manchester derby Carling Cup first leg were announced, and with midfield destroyers everywhere I could not resist having £90 on under 1.5 goals at 3-1.

The match provided a perfect illustration of why football betting is bonkers. United's opening goal was entirely down to Craig Bellamy slipping over as he went to challenge Antonio Valencia – it was a goal so soft it should be used to advertise cotton wool – and then just before half-time Man City were awarded a penalty for a foul outside the box.

When I placed my bet, I hadn't factored in Bellamy might be wearing the wrong studs in his boots and that the referee wouldn't know one of the most basic laws of Association Football. Silly me.

Wednesday, January 20

Lesson learned? Evidently not, because 24 hours later I had the teams for Liverpool versus Tottenham in front of me and had £50 on Spurs at 5-2. Tottenham's line-up was superior to Liverpool's in every position bar goalkeeper, but Liverpool won comfortably. It's a mad sport.

I immediately switched to a much safer betting medium – Celebrity Big Brother – laying Jones and pressing up on Bowers and Tappenden.

Thursday, January 21

Kaymer, Noren and Quiros all made superb starts in Abu Dhabi and I was left wishing I could have made larger investments. The Thursday night Bob Hope coverage was rained off, so I had to find some alternative television, and I stumbled across Slumdog Children Of Mumbai on Channel 4. It was one of the most harrowing programmes I've ever seen and had a seriously deep impact on me.

A seven-year-old girl, who was once poisoned when a rat chewed off one of her toes while she was sleeping in the slums, was working a 15-hour shift during the monsoon season, dodging traffic as she tried to sell flowers to more fortunate souls. She made the equivalent of 40 pence for that shift, then went back to the slums to help her gran care for her younger siblings. Her dad died years ago, before her mum abandoned her.

And yet despite enduring such hardship, she was so cheerful and courteous to the Channel 4 team as she guided them through life in the slums, steadfastly refusing to wallow in self-pity. There are a lot of spoilt brats I see on my travels around England who could learn a lot from this poor girl.

It was an instant dose of perspective for me. I made a vow at that point to never feel sorry for myself again. There are so many people worse off than you and I – we should not be getting downcast about any of the comparatively trivial matters we have to deal with when children are starving to death on the same planet as us.

Friday, January 22

While moving house you find all sorts of strange things you never knew existed. A newspaper cutting of me posing as a dashing 17-year-old after being awarded the Snickers/Channel 4 Young Sports Broadcaster of the Year honour had me cursing the ageing process, while an 'official matchday programme' I had compiled in 1993 left me utterly bemused as I was clearly under the impression back then that I was the manager of Northwich Victoria. I had even written a 'View From The Dugout' for Victoria fans in a 22-page programme!

No wonder I've never amounted to much if at the age of 15 my greatest ambition was to manage Northwich Victoria.

Saturday, January 23

I finally completed the house move before spending all day and all night watching golf on my own. Kaymer and Clark were going jolly well.

Sunday, January 24

Yeeeeeeeeaaas Martin, as Graham Taylor once famously screamed after Martin Keown had converted a penalty kick in training. Kaymer held his nerve and Fred Done owed me £2,125.

I felt like I was back in business and after casting an eye over the latest Bob Hope prices I had a further £200 on Clark at 10-1, meaning I would make £40,000 from the weekend if the little South African could finish atop the leaderboard the following night.

By now word was spreading on the *Racing Post* sports desk that I was on a course for a 'facespitter' (a winning bet so large that you can spit in the face of your boss because you don't need a job any more) and I was regularly receiving texts of support and encouragement from colleagues.

Monday, January 25

I quickly evaluated the Welsh Open snooker, having £140 on John Higgins at 15-2 and £60 on Ding Junhui at 19-1, but it was hard to think about anything but the possibility of landing a £40,000 booty from the golf.

Most Monday nights are pretty dull, but thanks to weather delays in the Bob Hope, this was going to be the most manic Monday of my life. The final round was being staged on the Palmer Course, which I had convinced myself must be a strong omen for good, and even though Clark, one shot behind, was trading fractionally bigger than 3-1 on Betfair as play was about to commence in California, I was confident enough to let the bet ride. I had, though, placed some savers on Matt

Kuchar (£150 at 18-1) and Mike Weir (£150 at 14-1) as I considered them the biggest threats.

Just as the man carrying my hopes and dreams was about to tee off, a ladybird landed on my chest, and again my fluffy mind marked this down as The Lord's way of saying this was going to be my night. I didn't have any windows open in my flat so was stunned to find an insect had forced its way inside. In my excitement I picked up the ladybird and circled it around my head a few times. I know it's money spiders with which you're supposed to do that, but I didn't have one of those to hand, so I thought I'd take my chance as the next best thing had presented itself.

I played some Pan-Pipe Moods on the stereo to calm myself down as Clark scrambled a par at the first, but even downing a tumbler of sedatives would have had no soothing effect on me after he missed a four-foot birdie putt on the second.

Clark putted like an elephant on the front nine, spurning countless birdie chances, so I was pleased my Rod Lavers (Kuchar and Weir) were making strong headway up the leaderboard. Bill Haas and Bubba Watson were the only real bogeys in my punting nostrils as the event turned into a five-runner affair.

Clark's chip-in for birdie at the fifth kept him hot on the heels of the leaders and for the first time my thoughts turned to the possibility of doing a spot of trading. But it is only rich men who can trade these positions properly anyway – I haven't had more than £20,000 in my bank account since a particularly glorious run in the summer of 2004 – so all I could think about doing was to lay off the potential Clark winnings on Betfair (about £3,700) and mess about with another few hundred quid. The real meat of the potential winnings was sitting in Bet365's vaults waiting to be presented to me once the double had copped.

Clark slowly eased his way into the thick of things on the back nine and the £40,000 dream remained alive, but I felt compelled to get further involved with Kuchar, who was looking the likely winner as he boarded the tee at the penultimate par-five. I had £500 at even-money, which left me winning almost £5,000 on the weekend if Kuchar won and almost £40,000 from a Clark triumph.

The following hour or so will live long in my memory. My new neighbours must have been disappointed with the latest addition to their block of flats when I greeted Clark's successful birdie putt at the 15th hole with a huge outpouring of emotion.

I was extremely touched by the messages of support that were flooding underneath my blog on racingpost.com – I felt like Happy Gilmore trying to win the US Open (anyone who hasn't seen the film will not know what I mean) and Haas was playing the role of Shooter McGavin.

Didi Hamann, a contented man having just backed a winner in the Charlton-Leyton Orient game, even phoned to offer his support as Clark was standing over his birdie putt on the 17th. I think I scared the ice-cool German with my passionate reaction to that one finding the bottom of the cup.

I hadn't felt so alive and engrossed by the world since falling into a midwife's arms 31 long years ago. For once it seemed that I was actually playing an important role on planet Earth, landing a significant blow for the humble punter right on the nose of the mighty bookmaker.

It was all looking so rosy – Clark and Kuchar were sharing the lead – £40,000 or £5,000! It was like being a contestant on Deal Or No Deal. Kuchar was on the 18th green putting for birdie, while Clark was in the centre of the 18th fairway waiting to hit his second shot.

I was thrilled when Kuchar missed his putt (looking back now that was the opposite emotion from what I should have been feeling) because it meant all Clark needed to do was knock a fairway wood on or around the green of this par-five, take two more shots from wherever it landed, and seize the lead on his own at 30 under par.

But then everything went from looking very rosy to looking very, urm, thorny. The final few moments of the tournament are a bit of a blur, but when Haas holed for birdie at the 17th to make it a three-way tie for the lead and then Clark pulled out a seven-iron with which to lay up at 18, my world fell apart and I dived into some frantic last-gasp trading.

As soon as Clark elected to lay up, I knew he had left the door wide open for Haas, so desperately tried to salvage something from the week. A look back at my Betfair records show that in the space of about five minutes I got £103.97 on Haas at 11-8, £419.03 on Haas at 6-5, laid £500 of Clark at 2-1, had £477 on Haas at 11-10, then laid £61.25 of Clark at 13-8.

This may just sound like sour grapes, and yes, my grapes have never been so sour, but laying up was a stupid decision by Clark. If he didn't know about Haas's birdie at the 17th and that knowledge would have influenced the lay-up decision, then the caddie should be sacked forthwith. But even if Clark was oblivious to the threat of Haas and thought 29 under was going to qualify him for a play-off, surely he should have been pulling out all the stops to make birdie anyway to reach 30 under par and win in regulation play.

He only had about 220 yards to the green for goodness sake. I could have got it on the green with a five-wood and I've never been to a gymnasium before!

With his natural draw he wouldn't have needed to fly it over the water on the left – a three-wood aimed right of the green, drifting gently towards the putting surface would have done the job. An up-and-down from around the green or a long two-putt was always going to have more chance of success than a pitch from distance, no matter how good he is with his wedge. But timid Timothy couldn't get the water out of his mind. Most golfers carry bananas in their bag for sustenance on the way round, but I think Clark prefers to eat fairycakes.

I'm extremely proud with the way I dealt with the disappointment once Haas had birdied the last to win by one. In times gone by, such a savage blow might have left me in a dangerously dark mood, but I couldn't stop thinking about the slumdog children of Mumbai, who would happily have swapped places with me at that point.

I put an REM album on, nibbled on a pot of Muller Rice, and then turned my mind to the Qatar Masters, placing £200 on Quiros at 30-1 in the early hours, confident another chance to win big would not be too long coming.

CHAPTER 4

BACK ON THE BIKE

Alex Reid

Tuesday, January 26

I woke up in terrible pain. I had a thick head, a sore throat and was going through Kleenex like nobody's business (not in a good way). It was the most sudden arrival of severe man-flu I have ever encountered and I wondered whether the mental trauma of the previous night had resulted in this physical meltdown. Suffering seemed to be literally oozing out of my body.

I turned my phone on to find all sorts of texts – 'hope you took a decent profit', 'did you lay off a big chunk?', etc – which didn't aid my recovery. I know I could have guaranteed thousands of pounds but my loathing of laying off meant I let the whole lot ride almost all the way to the finish. Even with the O'Sullivan debacle fresh in the memory, my natural instinct was to take the gamble. I don't think I've got a trading bone in my body.

To take my mind off the Clark calamity, I fiddled with my CBB position on Betfair, meaning I won £400 on Bowers, £300 on Tappenden, £200 on Alex Reid and lost £250 on anyone else.

In the golf, I had £100 on Noren for the Qatar Masters at 54-1, £70 on Soren Hansen at 35-1, £50 on Johan Edfors at 84-1, £15 on Ricardo Gonzalez at 299-1, £310 on Phil Mickelson for the Farmers Insurance Open at 13-2, £60 on Charles Howell at 35-1, £50 on John Rollins at 37-1 and £45 on Brandt Snedeker at 41-1 – and I had a £100 double on Quiros (28-1) and Mickelson (13-2).

Wednesday, January 27

I was still feeling very ill. I would advise against getting yourself in a position to win £40,000. It's not good for your health.

Thursday, January 28

Just for the ruddy hell of it, I pressed up with another £35 on Gonzalez, who was still trading as high as 399-1 despite lurking in 25th place.

Friday, January 29

Quiros finished tamely in Qatar on just three under par at the halfway stage. At least that means I can probably forget about my double and won't be waking up with a fresh bout of misery-fuelled man-flu on Monday morning.

I pocketed £200 from Reid winning Celebrity Big Brother, having backed him at the point where he got completely naked and allowed fellow housemates to spray fake tan all over his body. Joe Public loves that sort of caper.

If Reid had worked out a cure for cancer while inside the Big Brother house or a masterplan to end the worldwide recession, he might not have won, but by parading a pair of muscular buttocks in front of the nation and charging around like an orange version of the Incredible Hulk, he triumphed by a landslide.

Gordon Brown now knows exactly what is required if he is going to halt his slide in the opinion polls. Jeremy Paxman could be in for a shock during the next edition of Newsnight.

While Reid was in the process of being crowned champion, I also had a couple of wagers on Stephen Warnock and Kieran Richardson to make the England World Cup squad, having heard a few whispers about John Terry and Wayne Bridge not being the best of friends anymore.

I had £150 on Warnock at 9-4 and £50 on Richardson at 10-1 on the basis that they provide the best options for left-back cover with Bridge likely to be staying at home wondering if he can trust anyone but his dog.

Saturday, January 30

Had £300 on Roger Federer at 4-6 to beat Andrew Murray in the Australian Open final – I was expecting to see something like 1-5 when I took a casual glance at the prices and nearly strangled my mouse in my haste to place the bet. This Murray chap is just a poor man's Tim Henman in my eyes.

Quiros had moved into contention after the third round of the Qatar Masters and I was hopeful for my £100 double with Mickelson as I sat down with almost £30 worth of Chinese takeaway and my mate Trifleface to watch the evening's sporting action.

Trifleface could not believe how much my mood depended on the scorelines that were rapidly changing in front of us. With Adrian Lewis, my main Players Championship darts wager (£95 at 18-1), looking like he was heading for a second-round defeat to Andy Hamilton at the Circus Tavern, John Higgins losing to O'Sullivan in the snooker semi-final and Mickelson making a poor start to his third round at Torrey Pines, I was glumly struggling to find the motivation to force another slice of sesame prawn toast through my crestfallen lips.

But then Lewis rallied to edge past The Hammer, Higgins fought back to win 6-4, Lefty made eagle at the 13th hole to propel himself back into the thick of things, and suddenly I was gayly tossing sweet and sour chicken balls into the air, catching them on my zestful tongue as they fell, and all was right with the world once again.

Later in the evening, with Trifleface safely returned to his pregnant wife (she decided it was the only way she could become as big as him), I re-evaluated the Qatar Masters, having a £110 press-up on Quiros at 15-1 and a £200 saver on Lee Westwood at 3-1.

Sunday, January 31

I watched Federer toying with Murray, although I had switched over to the golf by the end of the second set, and I'm told I missed seeing the losing finalist burst into tears.

Yep, Murray got just over a million Australian dollars for finishing runner-up. You have to feel for him. It must be so tough to keep the waterworks under control when you realise you're only being given about £550,000 for spending the week running around in the sun. I'm surprised he didn't flood Melbourne with his tears after a setback like that.

Quiros finished second in Qatar and Westwood finished third, so I was close to welling up too. An unscheduled visit from my sister and nephew did not help matters and I was given a dressing down in my dressing gown for swearing in front of the little fella as Robert Karlsson kicked clear at the top of the leaderboard. I think mothers tend to overplay how much a kid picks up from what you say in front of them, but if my nephew gets into trouble at nursery for calling someone an "annoyingly consistent lanky Swedish arseface", I might revise my opinion.

I emptied the contents of my main Betfair wallet (£174.34) on to Karlsson at 1-100 after he had birdied the 17th hole, thinking I might as well use the money-buying opportunity to pay for my *Racing Post*, and despite Quiros's near-miss I was in good spirits. I had backed Gonzalez ante-post at 400 and he finished ninth – in no other sport can you back genuine title contenders at such fancy prices and I was excited about my golf-betting future.

With Premier League basement boys Portsmouth looking a club in complete disarray, I had to have a couple of football tickles on Man City (£200 to win to nil at 10-11 and £100 on any unquoted scoreline at 4-1) and then it was on to the final round of the Farmers Insurance, where Ben Crane was topping a curious leaderboard.

I was hoping ante-post selections Mickelson, Howell, Snedeker and Rollins might challenge from slightly off the pace, but I had £100 on rising Aussie star Michael Sim at 8-1 when he started looking like Crane's biggest rival.

Sim soon set about closing the gap between himself and Crane, so I was pleased with my investment, but I got distracted by switching channels to check on the darts. Taylor had just gone 9-7 behind in a first-to-ten-legs Players Championship semi-final against Paul Nicholson and I launched £100 on The Power to win the match at 4-1. He hauled himself to 9-9 and I mentally banked the £400 winnings – Taylor was throwing first in the deciding leg and was long odds-on to emerge victorious – but then Nicholson hit double-five with his final dart (with The Power waiting on 40) to leave me in pieces.

I tried to get my £100 straight back by having £200 on Mervyn King to win the final at 1-2 on Betfair, but nasty Nicholson edged another tight match.

Snedeker narrowly missed a birdie putt at the par-five 18th which would have got him into a play-off, while Sim laid up on the same hole (I think Tim Clark was on the sidelines giving him some instructions), also made a par and finished tied with Snedeker for second place. I've already had four ante-post win-only golf wagers finish runner-up this year (at 41-1, 25-1, 30-1 and 41-1). Maybe I need to say the words "each" and "way" a little more often.

Fortunately, Higgins crushed Ali Carter in the Welsh Open final to land me a bag of sand and keep me ticking over nicely.

Monday, February 1

Had some Dubai Desert Classic wagers (£120 on Quiros at 22-1, £95 on Ross Fisher at 28-1 and £25 on Gonzalez at 199-1), £90 on Ernie Els for the Northern Trust Open at 26-1, £55 on Howell at 45-1, then I marched to the town centre to have my first alcoholic beverage since January 1.

I was so excited that my self-imposed month-long drinking ban had been lifted and was ready to savour my first sip of Carling Black Label. But, tragically, the pint tasted more like washing-up liquid than lager – the publican clearly had some issues with his pipes – and every mouthful was an ordeal.

I have never really thought about this until now, but canned lager is so much greater value than draught, don't you think? Canned lager never lets you down – the lager just goes straight in the tin and is always of good quality – whereas draught lager has so many more potential dangers to pass through (dirty barrels, slimy pumps, etc) before it is put in your glass (which may have been used directly before you by a chap with ten coldsores on his lips). Yet draught lager is much more expensive than canned.

I downed my pint of Fairy and purchased some cans from the off-licence to drink at home instead. If you're trying to find something to deliver guaranteed satisfaction, you know a can can. You've got to be daft to drink draught.

Tuesday, February 2

Munched on some out-of-date crumpets – a bit of mould never hurt anyone eh? – while I put £145 on Stricker to win the Northern Trust Open at 16-1 and £70 on Sabbatini at 33-1. I also had £215 on Kaymer at 11-1 for Dubai, £65 on Soren Hansen at 39-1 and a £120 double on Kaymer (11-1) and Els (25-1).

I popped down the snooker club for some baize action and was staggered to find a pair of Germans playing on the neighbouring table. They were not just Germans – a nationality I had never before seen represented in a snooker hall – but they were extremely noisy Germans. In fact, they never shut up, and when I was on the verge of a 30-up (a massive break at my level of snooker) I was furious with their constant jibber-jabber.

If I went to a snooker club in Germany (I'm not even certain they exist), I would be as quiet as a mouse. I'm not a violent person, but I thought about punching one of them in the face just to remind them of the standard practice that if you're in a foreign country (particularly one with a history of warring against your own), it is not really the done thing to act like you own the joint.

When I missed a black off the spot, I felt like putting some black in their eyes, but fortunately my peaceful instincts held me back and I did my bit for Anglo-German relations by allowing them to loudly jest around their table. I expect one of them is an up-and-coming player known as the Jester From Leverkusen.

Wednesday, February 3
Spurs will win easy, won't they? Leave it, Steve, leave it.

Thursday, February 4
Off we go again. Four days of torture before the golfers I back all finish second.

Friday, February 5
Try to get that pecker up, you miserable bastard.

CHAPTER 5
STRICKER DELIVERS

Steve Stricker

Saturday, February 6

I woke up a little dejected having devoted the previous evening to attempting the notorious Mentos-Coke trick. I remembered my old mate Dave (everyone's got a mate called Dave, haven't they?) once told me it was possible to create a spectacular firework-like display by putting a few Mentos (little mints) into a bottle of Coke.

But all I ended up with when taking on the job with my mate Keith in a deserted car park (not so many people have got a mate called Keith) was sticky shoes and a feeling that after 31 years playing the game of life I should probably have found better ways of spending my Friday nights than trying to get cheap thrills from mint-Coke explosions.

Anyway, I comforted myself with the fact my golf bets were going well – Quiros and Kaymer were in contention in the Dubai Desert Classic and Stricker was dominating proceedings in the Northern Trust Open.

There really was no need to do any more betting – those three wagers were going to make for an absorbing weekend – but I got a late-morning text from my old football corners guru who was getting excited about Portsmouth getting a six-and-a-half start against Man United in a corners match bet. He said the market was framed like an England versus Andorra game and Portsmouth had been grossly underrated.

Hmmmm, football betting, eh? I ended up having a tentative £60 at 9-10, which could not in itself do any serious damage, but the text got me thinking about football again and I found myself having a cursory glance through the fixture list while I waited for a sofa to be delivered to my new flat.

Before long I had convinced myself Liverpool were a shockingly bad price for the lunchtime Merseyside derby and laid £150 of the Reds at 11-10.

Half-time at Anfield and there was still no sign of the sofa, but my spirits were high as ten-man Liverpool were looking woeful, and I decided the £150 was as good as in my bank. This misplaced confidence meant I did not hesitate in having £200 on Man City to beat Hull at 4-5 in a 3pm kick-off.

Come 5pm, after Liverpool had defied their sending-off with a 1-0 victory, United had won the corner count by about four million to one and City's playboys had succumbed to Hull, I was £419 down for the day on a sport I'm not supposed to be betting on and building an unhealthy rage.

My corners guru had dropped into the end of his initial text that

Aston Villa would probably rest a few players in the late kick-off at Tottenham because of forthcoming cup games, so without even looking at the line-ups I slapped my remaining Betfair balance (£392.33) on Spurs at 11-10 (trying to get all my money back) and marched up the pub for a few soothing pints of San Miguel.

Five minutes into the game, I turned to my mate Trifleface (very few people have got a mate called Trifleface) and said it had draw written all over it. He agreed with me and asked if I had put a bet on the draw. I told him I had put almost four hundred quid on Tottenham and he gave me one of those looks I've seen so many times before, which translates to: "Oh no, Steve's having another mental breakdown."

Spurs huffed and puffed to no avail, I was £800 down for the day, and quaffing lager like a thirsty ferret to quell my anger.

To compound my misery, later in the night Trifleface spilled an entire plate of spaghetti bolognese on my beige lounge carpet while trying to eat and study Zoo magazine simultaneously.

He felt terrible and wouldn't stop apologising, but I just laughed and told him I could probably buy a new carpet every week if I stopped betting on football.

Sunday, February 7

As I scrubbed the lounge carpet while watching the final round of the Dubai Desert Classic, it looked like Quiros was going to make sure I could quickly forget about Saturday's disappointments. The Spanish ace was one shot ahead and putting from short range for eagle on the 13th hole – the tournament was at his mercy and it seemed like £2,760 would soon be coming my way.

But the big-hitting maverick bashed the eagle putt a few feet by, missed the return, and then went to pieces over the closing holes, smashing a three-wood into water at the 18th to completely surrender his chance.

Kaymer finished fourth, I hadn't made a bean from the tournament, and suddenly my whole life was in the hands of Stricker, who had built a six-shot lead going into the final round of the Northern Trust.

Possibly the lowest my morale has been all year was during the American's stumbling start to round four (his six-shot lead was down to two in no time at all) and as I started out on a long journey to Gatwick Airport for a golf holiday, I was starting to wonder whether I would even be able to afford to buy myself a bag of tees on arrival in Spain.

Text messages from pals with Stricker news were read by eyes swollen with stress, but fortunately the long-time leader recovered his composure to get the job done. Dear Steve, I love you, love Steve.

Monday, February 8

I've seen some things in my time but watching the Welsh Ladies Golf Union work on their short games on the practice ground at Desert Springs Golf Club in Almeria may well be the most gainful employment my eyes have ever had.

These multi-talented young princesses in tight-fitting shorts were displaying incredible technique, leaving my playing partner Steve Davies and I feeling humbled on the neighbouring putting green.

"They're half our age, they're girls and they're much better than us at golf. How does that make you feel, Steve?"

Despite the humiliation, those few hours certainly gave me an idea for a possible career switch, with the role of coach for the Welsh Ladies Golf Union an extremely appealing vocation. Two middle-aged blokes were in charge of about 16 budding Annika Sorenstams.

Standing beside a bunker in the sunshine, staring at a load of pert 18-year-old bottoms while offering occasional words of advice on stance, grip, swing, etc? How can a man actually get paid for that?

Tuesday, February 9

My opening drive of the holiday was a power fade with the Big Dog, which meant the par-five green was in range (did you see that, girls?), but I drew my three-wood approach too much and nearly killed a set of builders who were working on a house to the left of the fairway.

The wheels came off after that and I shot 104 on an extremely challenging course in 30mph winds. I tried to rouse myself for a strong finish before boarding the 11th tee but went back into my shell when I saw a sign that read: 'Beware snakes and scorpions'. It doesn't half put some pressure on your tee-shot when you know a hungry viper might be waiting for you in the rough.

When I got back to the sanctuary of the clubhouse, I turned my mind to the upcoming professional golf, placing three Pebble Beach Pro-Am wagers on Betfair, £100 on Dustin Johnson at 22-1, £50 on Watney at 43-1 and £30 on Davis Love at 74-1.

I tried to deposit some more money, but my Stricker winnings had clearly not gone into my bank account yet, so I had to spend a couple of hours texting friends in England to get my other bets in play. Various characters helped out and I managed to get £200 on Darren Clarke to win the Avantha Masters at 16-1, £100 on Shiv Kapur at 25-1, £75 on Gareth Maybin at 33-1 and a £145 win double on Johnson (22-1) and Clarke (14-1).

Wednesday, February 10

I nailed another great opening drive and hit a perfect five-iron lay-up, but Steve D's third shot then crashed into the builders on the left and they went bonkers. With abuse raining in, suddenly my serene progress up the first was threatened and I put my 'don't hit it left' swing into operation for fear of further winding up the building community.

My third shot drifted right into a greenside bunker, I thinned my fourth over the cliff edge, took a penalty drop, made a double-bogey seven, and we tip-toed past the angry builders en route to the second tee.

Anglo-Spanish relations improved greatly later in the round, when I realised I had left my pitching wedge by the side of the first green. I explained my plight to a greenkeeper and he raced off in a buggy to try to find the stricken wedge.

The language barrier between us was so enormous it made the Great Barrier Reef look like a slither of seaweed, but I gave him ten euros for his trouble and we were soon bestest friends. Pointing at my ball, he said in broken English: "Now in the hole!"

It was a beautiful moment. I didn't quite manage to hole out from 100 yards, but used the rescued club to hit a punch shot under the wind that set up a birdie, eventually shaving three shots off the previous day's round.

I had forgotten how physically demanding playing 18 holes on consecutive days can be and I hobbled off the course with so many aches and pains – my right shoulder was knackered, my legs were like jelly, my feet were covered in blisters and I even had some cactus injuries on my hands and shins (I would advise against attempting miracle shots from behind cacti).

Never has a hot bath been so welcome and as I lay in the tub I started to comprehend what all those pleasure-pain enthusiasts are so hooked on. I had never really understood their peculiar ways, but I suppose if you have someone pouring candle-wax over your nipples for ten minutes, it is going to feel wonderful when they finally start stroking them with an ice cube (even more wonderful than it would have done had you not gone through the initial candle-wax agonies). Anyway, it was the most satisfying bath I've ever had in my life.

Thursday, February 11

Back in Blighty just in time to watch some Premier League darts. I had £70 on James Wade to beat Barneveld at 6-5 on Betfair, which lost, and then £140 on Taylor to beat Whitlock at 1-2, which won. The Power at 1-2? I'll do well to place a better bet than that this year. I'm so ashamed by the paltry stake.

Friday, February 12

When I saw my Stricker booty had still not reached my bank account, I rang Victor Chandler to discover they have a new rule whereby you have to request winnings to be paid back to your bank (they don't return them automatically).

Oh yeah, great idea – you hang on to my £2,465 lads, I don't really need it. Let's see if I can bet it up to £100,000, then I'll take it off your hands. If not, just keep what's left for your Christmas party.

Saturday, February 13

Clarke put his second shot in the water at the 18th hole in India to get my day off to a shocker. Another yard or two of carry, he would have been putting from ten feet for eagle and had the tournament by the gonads.

Still, with Johnson leading at Pebble and Clarke only two shots behind going into the final round of the Avantha, there was certainly scope for clearing my scope of spittle all over my boss (a £55,725 return if they both won).

Sunday, February 14

Clarke was bang in contention until racking up a bogey six at the 14th hole, and I returned to bed knowing my retirement plans were back on hold. I later pressed up on Johnson with £212.05 at 11-10 and was pleased to see big Dustin birdie the final hole for victory.

Outrageously, having pocketed four-and-a-half bags in two weeks on the US Tour through Stricker and Johnson, I was feeling a little flat that I hadn't nailed a life-changer. Greed is such a disgusting sin.

Monday, February 15

Gathered my Accenture Match Play tanks on the lawn – £200 on Ross Fisher at 35-1, £200 on Kaymer at 22-1, £150 on Stewart Cink at 41-1, £150 on Ernie Els at 40-1 and £100 on Quiros at 45-1 – then had £100 on Howell to win the Mayakoba Classic at 21-1.

Tuesday, February 16

Had a £50 each-way double on Fisher (33-1) and Howell (20-1), then several pancakes.

Wednesday, February 17

Had some more pancakes for breakfast. My way of showing my love for The Lord is slightly different from the norm. Rather than fast through Lent, I eat pancakes every day to celebrate all that is great about his kingdom (pancakes, sugar, lemon juice, forks, etc).

Thursday, February 18

I had been offered front-row seats for the Premier League darts in Bournemouth but had to sit working in a steel tower in Canary Wharf instead. As soon as my transatlantic golf double motherload hits planet Earth, I'm going to spend every day doing as I please.

Friday, February 19

Oh Tiger, you've been such a naughty boy, haven't you? Am I going to have to get a new hero?

CHAPTER SIX
RICKIE FOWLS UP

Rickie Fowler

Saturday, February 20

I think the worst kind of hangovers are the ones where you do not deserve to be hung over. Sometimes circumstances conspire against you and, despite your best intentions, excessive drinking materialises without you being able to do anything to control the situation.

I was making my way home from the pub in a reasonable condition on Friday night, en route to the Chinese takeaway, but the temperature was so ridiculously low that anyone staying outside for longer than five minutes would almost certainly have died. My toes were attempting to get inside my feet and a large stalactite was forming in my pants.

So I had no choice but to dive in another pub for shelter, abandoning hope of making it to the Chinese alive, and by the time I returned to the icy streets of broken Britain my body had been so numbed by drink I could have gone skinny dipping with some polar bears in Alaska with a fair degree of comfort.

You know the drill, though. Such warm glows tend to turn to firm woes overnight, and it was with a view to watching the lunchtime fixture in the recovery position that I had £200 on Man United to beat Everton at 10-11.

Dimitar Berbatov's exquisite half-volley was just the tonic I needed, but my joy lasted only three minutes (I'm sure there are unsatisfied wives up and down the land who can empathise with me) before Everton equalised. Two more Toffee-coated kicks to the ribs later – Berbatov's flavoursome tonic had turned into a Bilyaletdinov-Gosling-Rodwell-conjured cow-crap casserole – and I was regretting my decision to consider football a potential healing aid.

The golf betting was not going well either. Cink was my only player left in the Match Play at the last-eight stage and he had a bang-in-form Casey to overcome in the quarter-finals. I felt it was time to add another string to my bow and I fancied Ian Poulter to come through the other side of the draw, so I had £300 on the cocksure Englishman at 9-2, hoping for a Cink-Poulter final.

I did not have time to watch the opening exchanges of the quarter-finals, though, as I had to make an extremely rare visit to a supermarket to purchase items for a long-overdue housewarming party I was staging in the evening.

Doing something you hardly ever do is never easy, is it? The phrase "unaccustomed as I am to public speaking" roughly translates to "this is going to be a rubbish speech" and I felt like putting a warning sign on my front door which read: I have never hosted a party before so don't get your hopes up – it's bound to be seriously lacking in one way or another.

As it turned out, the supermarket was by far the most challenging aspect of being the party host. It was packed to the rafters and I found safely guiding my trolley around other shoppers was tough enough without even worrying about what I was going to put in the ruddy thing.

Clearly annoying more seasoned campaigners with my lack of trolley etiquette, I must have used my catchphrase "sorry, I'm not a regular shopper" about 15 times, blazing my way around the store like I was at the wheel of an Asda Mazda.

Anything that looked remotely 'party-esque', I chucked in the trolley. Lots of stuff has the word party on it, so if you're shopping for a party you feel almost contractually obliged to buy them. I wonder if anyone has ever eaten a 'party sausage' while not being at a party? That would be extremely naughty, wouldn't it?

Even when you reach the checkout counter, you're not out of the woods, because putting your goods into carrier bags can provide a further headache. I learned the hard way, as a couple of custard slices were crushed in my desperation to get out of the firing line, that fragile items need to be allocated a bag of their own.

It was harrowing stuff. I took stock by a relatively quiet newsagents-like section of the supermarket as I steeled myself for the trolley-push to the car park, being drawn to a dinosaur magazine that appeared to be offering a free plastic replica Tyrannosaurus Rex skull with every purchase.

I was about to buy the magazine – I had always wondered about the exact dimensions of a Tyrannosaurus Rex skull – when an old man who can only be described as a mentalist appeared out of nowhere going bananas.

"Ooh, you don't want to buy that, son – it's a con. You have to keep buying the next part, then the next part, and they keep putting the price up each time. It's a con, it's a con . . ."

I threw the magazine back down and assured him I was not going to buy it, by now regretting my little trolley pit-stop, but he still kept shouting at me, "it's a con, it's a con . . .", tailgating my trolley as I tried to escape, clearly under the impression he could not emphasise the point enough.

I honestly believe at least one policeman should be stationed throughout the day at every major supermarket. Trolleys are more incendiary devices than any bombs known to man, while opportunist mentalists lurk in the supermarket undergrowth looking to prey on the weak.

I returned home to watch Cink defeated by Casey, but Poulter beat Jaidee and then Sergio Garcia to keep my spirits high enough for me to host a party.

Sunday, February 21

My flat resembled a landfill site when I awoke – the house had certainly been warmed.

Highlights included a wonderful argument between a husband and wife, the latter having been banned by the former from wearing a sexy black-lace dress she had originally put on (because he had deemed it "inappropriate" for the party). I offered her £20 to get a taxi home and return in all her glory, but the warring couple soon left.

It wasn't all fun, fun, fun for me, because at some point my toilet seat was broken beyond repair by one of the revellers (I'm calling it the Toiletgate scandal). I've got a prime suspect in mind (the bigger they are, the harder they fall) but it is not a crime that is easy to prove.

I popped out for a roast dinner before settling down for the golf, which proved a bad decision because Reg from the flat downstairs was waiting to give me all sorts of grief about the previous night, leaving the main door unlocked being the most serious misdemeanour.

I apologised profusely but throughout my dressing down I couldn't help wondering how long it would be before there is no-one on Earth called Reg. No-one christens their boy Reginald anymore, do they? So many great names appear to be falling by the wayside – Bernard, Harold, Herbert, Cyril, Stanley, Arthur, Dudley, Maurice, Percy, Adolph.

It's a shame. I might call my son Ian in tribute to Mr Poulter, who won me £1,380 by defeating Casey to keep my punting engine ticking over nicely.

Monday, February 22

I supped on an apple and raspberry j2o drink that a pregnant party-goer had left from Saturday (I wish I could get pregnant – they're delicious) while sorting out my Phoenix Open wagers.

With only one golf tournament to worry about, I didn't feel the need to shave my shortlist so much and I ended up with a Magnificent Seven. I had £540 on Mickelson at 17-2, £205 on JB Holmes at 25-1, £62 on Anthony Kim at 69-1, £56 on Steve Marino at 74-1, £55 on Ryan Moore at 74-1, £50 on Rickie Fowler at 109-1 and £32 on

Charley Hoffman at 129-1.

I noticed a sign had appeared on the flats entrance from the 'Management Committee' explaining the importance of locking the main door overnight. I wonder if Reg is related to that bloke from the supermarket? You've made your ruddy point, mate.

Tuesday, February 23

Coral had sent me a Champions League bet offer (place £25, get a £25 free bet), so I had it on draw half-time, Barcelona full-time for the Spaniards' match at Stuttgart. The price was 10-3 but when I had both £25 stakes on the same bet, it became a 13-2 chance (best at 7-2 elsewhere).

At half-time, with Stuttgart winning 1-0, I weighed in with £250 on under 2.5 goals at even-money and despite an early Barca breakthrough it ended 1-1. It felt great to get that footy-winner buzz back – every tackle, every wide shot, every stoppage was a joy to behold – and I could feel the addiction coursing through my veins again.

Wednesday, February 24

I struggled to get my head around the Inter-Chelsea game and ended up having a hopeful £300 on under 1.5 goals at 7-4. Three minutes gone, 1-0. Marvellous. At half-time, I had a £50 cover shot on the 1-1 draw at 5-1, then after Chelsea equalised and Inter went 2-1 up, I had a desperate £60 on Inter to win 3-1 at 11-2.

I managed to lose £410 on a game in which anything could have happened and on which anyone betting on it with anything more valuable than peanuts should have their own nuts removed as punishment for being so silly.

Thursday, February 25

I had £260.21 on King to beat Ronnie Baxter at 1-2 (lost), then £300 on Adrian Lewis to beat Terry Jenkins at 8-11 (won), then £165 on Barneveld to beat Whitlock at 6-4 (lost), then £500 on Taylor to beat Wade at 1-3 (won). Ho hum.

Friday, February 26

Gorged on some party leftovers – trifle, chocolate-filled crepes, meringue nests, Ferrero Rocher, etc – to forget about the previous night's arrers anguish. Tomorrow is another day, God willing.

Saturday, February 27

It was officially still winter according to the Meteorological Office, but I headed into the weekend full of the joys of spring.

It had nothing to do with budding bluebells, a red admiral flying past my face or witnessing a frog emerge from hibernation to plop into a pond, though. My joy stemmed from the fact I had more golfers in contention in the Phoenix Open than you could shake a ruddy seven-iron at – Kim, Moore and Fowler were all ten under par and one shot off the lead at the halfway stage.

I was in such a strong position and assumed I would be winning a fortune the following night. I made for the pub early, buying drinks for pals as if I had just become a lottery winner, gleefully ignoring the fact there were 36 holes to be played and about 36 other golfers who still had a chance to win.

Full of beans, I popped into an internet cafe to get some bets on Chelsea's lunchtime fixture with Man City, confident the 50 pence it cost me would be won back in spades by either a 1-0 home win (£90 at 7-1) or a goalless draw (£66.34 at 16-1).

I was disappointed to find a gaggle of City fans gathered around me for the match. One of them insisted on loudly shouting "Come on you blues" at regular intervals despite the fact Chelsea were playing in blue and City were in their white away kit.

I know his brain is probably programmed to instruct his mouth to bark "Come on you blues" whenever he is watching his team, but you'd think he would find a way of tinkering with the grey matter a little when City are playing against a side who are wearing blue.

Maybe I'm a pedant. Maybe he's a moron. Maybe we should all just try to get along – society won't work without tolerance I suppose.

At half-time, with the score 1-1, I spent another 50 pence having £50 on no third goal at 4-1, before giving up on the game completely from a betting perspective when City took the lead.

Not that the goals were ever the main talking point. I lost count of the number of times somebody in the pub dramatically announced "Ooh, Bridge and Terry are getting close, they're getting close" as our depraved nation yearned for a punch-up between former best friends.

The Wayne Bridge-John Terry saga certainly sparked some heated debate at my table.

"Would you shake my hand if I'd shagged your Mrs?"

"Well, when do we ever shake hands anyway?"

"Alright, would you talk to me if I'd shagged your Mrs?"

"Only to call you a **** before I headbutted you."

After City scored a fourth, I marched straight to Coral to have £400 on Sunderland to beat Fulham at their 5-4 coupon price, then had £60 on draw half-time, Arsenal full-time at 7-2 for the Gunners' trip to Stoke. Cesc Fabregas's late penalty meant I was level for the day, although Kim and Moore then dropped away in Phoenix, leaving Fowler as my only hope of a golf windfall.

Sunday, February 28

There were so many babies screaming away while I tucked into my roast dinner. I quite like the idea of becoming a father, but only if the midwife could guarantee to provide me with a baby that doesn't scream.

I was doing some screaming of my own when Sunderland failed to break through Fulham, but Rickie was going to come to the rescue, wasn't he? Fowler was 6-1 second favourite behind Snedeker, who I fancied to fold like a pack of cards from the front, and I pinpointed the chief dangers as Howell, Camilo Villegas and Hunter Mahan. I decided to go for the jugular again, with £150 on Howell at 33-1 the only bit of hedging I bothered with.

When Fowler eventually took the lead deep into the final round, the TV coverage became increasingly poor and my stress levels rocketed. But fortunately *Saving Private Ryan* was on Channel 4 at the same time, so during adverts in the golf I could get some instant perspective.

The golf became a straight match between Fowler and Mahan and I had some token bets on Mahan just so I would have some ammunition supplies for next week if Fowler botched the final few holes (watching Saving Private Ryan was pressing home the importance of ammo). I had £250 at even-money and £75 at 6-4, and with Fowler trading around the 4-5 mark I could have secured about £3,000.

But I didn't lock in the bags (because I never do) and when Fowler laid up from prime position on the par-five 15th hole my mood plummeted. I presumed my old mate Tim Clark had jetted into Phoenix and somehow bundled Fowler out of the way to take the shot for him.

Position A on the fairway, a perfect lie, no wind and 230 yards to the pin? A smooth four-iron to a soft green? My great grandmother could have hit that shot and she's been dead for 20 years! A power-packed, young go-getter who is averaging 290 yards for driving distance this season should certainly be taking it on.

I hobbled forlornly to the fridge (I was so crestfallen I couldn't even walk properly) to get some Stella Artois as Fowler's foul-up enraged me. Mahan took full advantage.

Still, at least I had *Saving Private Ryan* to remind me life could be a lot worse. If I had been born a few years earlier, I would have had to spend my time dodging bullets and tanks and wrestling with Germans who were trying to kill me. My generation don't appreciate how lucky they have been.

I used to get angry about the fact I had been born at a time that meant I was at university during the height of the Spice Girls boom – the Girl Power craze meant female students were not quite as liberal with their loving as they are these days – but I should be grateful for the 1978 birth date given the hell that others (like 1888 or 1918) would have brought me.

I wish I had guaranteed the three-bag return when Fowler was odds-on, but if he had won and I had not pocketed five-and-a-half bags, I would have felt like I had been robbed. I can't suddenly change my laying-off policy now – the horse bolted long ago.

And what is there really to be gained from becoming a trader, ekeing out a little profit here and there? There is a scene in *Saving Private Ryan* where a pathetic excuse for a man is crying like a baby on some stairs while his mate is getting knifed to death by a German above him. This tearful character was supposed to be supplying ammunition to his comrade but he was too afraid to help and will forever be remembered as a feeble disgrace.

I don't want to be remembered as a feeble disgrace. I want to die a hero. We are around for such a short time and you will quickly be forgotten if you die having spent your life negligently crying on staircases, trading for small profits on Betfair, etc.

The Fowler bet did not work out, but if I had won five bags on him, I could have had five bags on Mickelson to win the Masters, then 40 bags on Rory McIlroy to win the Open, then given 700 bags to Children In Need and died safe in the knowledge I was a hero.

Monday, March 1

A mate who had made a brief visit to my flat the previous night rang up to see if Fowler had won and weighed in with a very annoying question I have been asked many times before.

Him: "What could you have got for the each-way then?" Me: "20-1." Him: "Why didn't you do that then?" Me: "Goodbye."

Tuesday, March 2

For the Malaysian Open, I had £200 on Thongchai Jaidee at 10-1, £38 on Danny Willett at 64-1, £35 on Edfors at 69-1, £29 on Kapur at 84-1, £25 on Alejandro Canizares at 119-1, £19 on Danny Lee at 159-1 and £12 on Nicolas Colsaerts at 249-1, and for the Honda Classic I had £197 on Els at 26-1, £125 on Robert Allenby at 18-1, £85 on Padraig Harrington at 28-1, £28 on Mathew Goggin at 89-1 and £27 on DJ Trahan at 94-1. I also chanced a £40 each-way double on Kapur (66-1) and Els (25-1).

In the evening, I endured a swim, remembering this was the year I was supposed to be getting fit.

There is a designated slow lane, medium lane and fast lane, and a bit where kids just splash about.

I opted for the slow lane but still found myself getting lapped by old ladies. A lifeguard I got chatting to suggested I could use a float if I wanted to make it a bit easier. How did the 1988 Perth Junior Iron Man champion regress to this state? Ronald McDonald has got a lot to answer for.

I had so much momentum after the swim, though, that I went to have a peek at the gym. It didn't look a fun place to hang out – two musclebound men were stretching each other's calves between iron-pumping sessions and achieving that notoriously tricky macho-gay look – but I was guided to an office to speak to a girl called Danielle who was in charge of the gym membership.

Unfortunately, Danielle is the sort of girl you just don't say no to. I wasn't even listening to what she was saying as her glorious lips glistened through some sort of magical balm – I just kept saying yes and before I knew it I had signed up to a £33-a-month membership.

They know what they're doing in these places, don't they? If they had put a Daniel in front of me, I would have told him I had a life-threatening heart condition and been out of the door within seconds, but Danielle was always going to get the result they wanted.

Wednesday, March 3
Short of ammo, I had a token and joyless £30 on a 0-0 England-Egypt draw at 14-1.

Thursday, March 4
A £300 chunk at 5-6 on Taylor minus 3.5 legs against Barneveld was never in any danger of losing.

Friday, March 5
It is such a shame Taylor is almost 50 years old – he's the most

dependable betting proposition in world sport. Nothing lasts forever, though, eh? You only have to watch Saving Private Ryan if you need reminding of that fact. Lest we forget.

CHAPTER 7

THE BIG EASY

Ernie Els

Saturday, March 6

Every dog has its day! You can't beat a good saying, can you? I'm a big fan of sayings. How boring would it be if we all just went around using straight-laced, functional sentences without even attempting to jazz up our communications? Every dog has its day is my favourite saying at the moment because when a pal uttered those five words while we were studying the formguide for the 7.52 at Nottingham in a Coral shop the previous evening, it inspired me to forgive the fact that Trap One was still a maiden after no fewer than 18 races and have £30 on at 3-1.

I was so pleased for the little blighter as he cantered round the final bend well clear – you could almost lip-read him barking "every dog has its woofing day you sceptical formbook students" as he danced over the winning line in front.

It's so reassuring, isn't it? Has your life been miserable ever since you emerged from your mother's womb? Well, don't worry, because every dog has its day. You may not be a dog but don't let that worry you either – 'every life-form has its day' is a less well-known saying but is built on just as much truth. So look forward to your day. Today might be your day. Imagine that!

I decided I had better invest some of the dog winnings on a haircut, as I was starting to resemble a tramp again and had a fancy sports journalism awards bash to attend in a couple of days' time.

I have a private arrangement with a young lady (mate's girlfriend's sister), who is a former salon stylist, that allows me to get my barnet cut at her house at relatively short notice for £10. It's usually a good set-up and I prefer it to the hurly-burly of a public venue, but on this occasion her dog Poppy was being ridiculously unwelcoming.

Maybe Poppy was just over-excited about the success of Trap One in the 7.52 at Nottingham and bubbling over at the prospect of her 'day' arriving some time soon, but she seemed very eager to let me know she was the boss of the house.

I was feeling slightly nauseous anyway, with eight pints of Carling Black Label still swilling around inside me from the previous night, and having an enormous furball throwing itself at me while I was being groomed just added to my woes.

At one point, I thought I must have been hallucinating through distress as a female postman passed by the front window (sign of the times, eh?), then I cracked and had to request five minutes of fresh air to recover from Poppy's relentless perversions (what is it with dogs and their obsession with nether regions?) as the lawless beast threatened to end my hopes of fatherhood.

The "she's only playing" line made an appearance on many occasions. It disturbs me how owners always justify their dog's behaviour in this way. It's only when a limb or an eyeball is removed that 'play' seems to cross their line. You would never let your kid get away with screaming in the face of a stranger and then lunging at their genitalia, so why is it alright for your dog to do so?

After an hour of torturous trimming, I had to vacuum my locks off the carpet and some deeply ingrained dog hair came up too. The stench of mutt swept up my nostrils. Maybe this is a way to cure problem gamblers who are addicted to dog racing. I'm not sure I've got it in me to even look at another dog after vacuuming up the stale hairs of this rancid mongrel.

Later, having shipped £150 backing Tottenham to beat Fulham at 6-4, I popped round Trifleface's house and I got a real snapshot of married life. His pregnant wife was slumped on the sofa watching an Ant and Dec production, another stinking dog (this one was called Ted) was roaming free, and before long the wife's 14-year-old brother was banging at the front door begging to stay the night because he had drunk himself silly on alcopops and did not want to have to face his parents.

I felt sorry for Trifles. Surely it is only financial constraints that stop everyone living alone. I could understand the value in co-habiting in caveman times – the more club-wielders there were to fight off dinosaurs the better – but in the year 2010 (when the most dangerous animal alive is the dog) there is no need. Don't own a dog, live alone and, hey presto, you've got a safe and peaceful existence.

Sunday, March 7

Awoke to Malaysian Open heartbreak – Jaidee, Edfors, Canizares and Willett got close but no cigar. Well, Noh cigar to be more precise, as Korean teenager Seung-yul Noh was victorious.

I had intended to get stuck into some footy betting afterwards but I dipped into the pub for a lunchtime pint and got distracted. The barmaid called Sophie at my new local is definitely in the top five most beautiful human beings I have ever set eyes upon and she was gliding gloriously around the pub, lighting up the place with her smile as she served up the Sunday roasts.

I decided at that point that I spend so much time gambling in monetary terms, with varying degrees of success, I should not be afraid to do a bit of gambling in other walks of life, namely by gambling my dignity and risking the embarrassment of rejection by offering Sophie my phone number.

Sounds straightforward, doesn't it? Give her your phone number – five easy-to-say words – but for someone who is not exactly a star graduate from the Russell Brand School Of Seduction it was the equivalent of climbing five Mount Everests.

I attempted some 'banter' every time I ordered a pint, looking for a natural way of dropping the digits, but it was so tricky. Sometimes I would end up getting served by the barman (why does he have to be so ruddy alert?) and it would be a wasted trip. I was beginning to lose heart and about to abandon my plans, but then during another banter raid she mentioned her step-dad works in a Ladbrokes shop and I grew more confident.

"Gosh, we've got so much in common – I love betting, your step-dad works in Ladbrokes – when do you want to get married?" I didn't actually say that – I just nervously mumbled something far less extravagant and returned to my seat – but the fact she had said the word Ladbrokes somehow galvanised me and four or five ales later I had completed my mission.

It was a good job I didn't have any golfers in contention in the Honda Classic because I had endured enough stress for one day. What shall I do for my next non-monetary gamble? Jump off a cliff and see if I can avoid dying? Imagine the buzz if you walked away with nothing but a few cuts and bruises. You would feel invincible – you would be throwing your number at pretty girls willy nilly.

Monday, March 8

I consumed a KFC brunch with more caution than usual – one drop of mayo on my shirt or tie and my trip to the SJA Sports Journalism Awards would have been thrown into jeopardy.

It was hellish being back on the London Underground again.

Sensible people only go underground when they die, but I had no real choice if I was to make the awards venue on time.

Event sponsors Skybet had made me their 10-11 favourite for the Betting Writer of the Year award and I was finding the pressures of favouritism intolerable. I turned up last year expecting not to win and really enjoyed the night, but this year, even allowing for my natural pessimism, the odds-on quote meant I clearly had a strong chance of having to go on stage to do a speech.

I hate public speaking. I've been best man twice – once in a small Dorset village called Portesham and once in the African wilds of Malawi (it's a long story) – and I thought nothing could be worse than that. But awards ceremonies trump it and I was on edge all night.

I would probably have been buzzing after claiming the award had I beaten some people I dislike. But fellow nominees Kevin Pullein, a dear friend and colleague for ten years, and Derek McGovern, the Daily Mirror man who also seems like a tremendously good egg, are not the sort of characters you want to wave your gong at while blowing raspberries.

Once the champagne came out to bolster the two bottles of wine already inside me, I stepped into a different universe and was last seen explaining the virtues of punting to Terry Venables (who described betting as a vice he had never followed) while taking a wonderful trip down memory lane.

We were so close in '96, eh Tel? Oh, we were so, so close.

Tuesday, March 9

A quick McDonald's breakfast at Waterloo, then a train back south, getting my golf wagers sorted as soon as possible (£205 on Mickelson for the CA Championship at 10-1, £80 on Ogilvy at 27-1, £50 on Watney at 41-1, £40 on Els at 49-1 and £25 on Holmes at 84-1; £100 on Bryce Molder for the Puerto Rico Open at 20-1, £80 on Alex Prugh at 25-1, £30 on Carl Pettersson at 69-1 and £25 on Spencer Levin at 109-1).

I was too exhausted to speak to telephonists, so I had my double on my Paddy Power internet account, placing £70 on Mickelson (8-1) and Molder (18-1) for a potential £11,970 return.

Wednesday, March 10

A quick McDonald's for lunch (if I keep using the the word quick I don't feel such a glutton), then I endured my 'induction' at the gym. I don't like the word gym. I think I might end up hating everyone I know who is called Jim just through some sort of subconscious negative association.

Thursday, March 11

Stiff as a board (not in a good way). Jim'll Fix It, my arse.

Friday, March 12

Sophie has still not made contact. I must have written down an incorrect digit, eh? Yeah, that's right – it's definitely nothing to do with me coming across as the most peculiar customer ever to have set foot in the pub. Right, I need another gamble. Let's find a nice cliff.

Saturday, March 13

With pay-day still 48 hours away, I was down to my last £80 and facing up to a weekend with no betting activity whatsoever. My flat was fully kitted out at last, my car was firing on all cylinders again and I was completely debt-free, but the few notes in my pocket had to finance my activities until Monday morning.

There was no room for luxury items – only life's essentials – so I put aside £10 for food, £50 for lager and £20 for a Mother's Day present, then stayed in bed until late afternoon to kill some time.

Money was tight but the figure of Els was perched on my shoulder all day like a comforting angel (well, not really – he was actually in Florida playing golf) as the Big Easy made merry in the CA Championship.

As I made my way into town for some dinner, I found myself singing: 'Oh Ernie, you're so fine, you're so fine you blow my mind, hey Ernie, hey Ernie' as I skipped past strangers in the street. I wasn't singing at a volume that would breach noise pollution laws, but those unfortunate enough to be in my vicinity certainly crept by with a degree of caution.

I really enjoy playing the role of mentalist occasionally and when I'm a bit older I think I'm going to take up the job on a full-time basis. I reckon some of the people who 'normal' folk label as mentalists may not be bonkers at all – they just get a kick out of making others feel uneasy by acting deranged.

Anyway, who is to say that a man merrily expressing his love for another man in the street isn't normal? Those surly characters looking at me with concern on their faces must have been out-and-out homophobes.

I decided a nice shiny Betfred football coupon would make an extremely good Mother's Day present so I marked down home wins next to Man United v Fulham (2-9) and Barcelona v Valencia (4-11), and an away win next to Valladolid v Real Madrid (2-7), and handed over £20, only to be disappointed when I remembered betting shops these days transform coupons into much smaller pocket-sized slips once they go through their machines.

The gift, then, looked more pathetic than I had hoped, but that was the least of my worries when a melee broke out around me involving a Scottish fella who was refusing to pay for his dog bet. He was claiming the race had already started, so his wager should be voided, but the cashier had got him on in time, and an almighty rumpus ensued. The manager called the police as the adamant Scot continued to withhold payment.

Unfortunately for me, the potential criminal (I don't want to sound like Arsene Wenger but I didn't fully see the incident) was stopped from leaving by the manager locking the shop door and standing guard in front of it while he waited for law-enforcement officers.

I didn't want to get involved – I get myself into enough melees without having to join other people's melees – so I sat tight and pretended I was engrossed in Craig Thake's Big-Race Trends in my *Racing Post* while all hell broke loose around me.

Financial constraints meant I didn't have many plans for the weekend, but being held as a virtual hostage in a betting shop was certainly not high on my list of ways to while away the time.

I had always thought that if I ever ended up in a hostage situation and my life was in danger, it would be nice if there was a nubile young lady in the same predicament, so you could have a little cuddle and perhaps end your days on a high. But a cursory glance round the shop was enough to deduce that if the Scottish bloke started waving daggers around, a cardboard cut-out of Fred Done was about the most desirable cuddle companion I could hope for.

Several minutes later, after I had written inside my Mother's Day card and put the betting slip in the envelope, there was still no sign of the police, but the warring parties had somehow reached an agreement that allowed the raging Scot to leave the premises, so I escaped just behind him.

Sadly, I found myself in a slightly more sinister melee a few hours later, when I attempted to make a citizen's arrest after walking past a teenage boy who was urinating against the pavilion of Weymouth Bowls Club.

Sickened to my very core, I felt obliged to punish this outrageous behaviour and was looking to apprehend the villain while calling the authorities, but I suffered a torrent of abuse from the rest of the law-breaker's gang and my back-up was slow in coming, so I had to abandon my plans. As the poor manager of Betfred found to his cost earlier, policemen are very hard to come by when you actually need one.

I wasn't sure what the rules were regarding citizen's arrests anyway. I think the Government need to provide more clarification. Maybe all citizens who have never committed a criminal offence should be issued with handcuffs, so they can cuff offenders at any point during the day. I might email Jack Straw with that suggestion. Is he still the chap in charge of clearing our streets of feral youths?

I was so disturbed by the evening's events that I proceeded to drink myself into oblivion and was last seen drenched in Lilt at 3am in a fried-chicken outlet. By all accounts, it was not a good look. In fact, I think I should probably have been arrested.

Sunday, March 14

Ernie was tied for the lead with 18 holes to play, so I still looked on for a two-grand boost, but physically the day was proving a challenge.

My contribution to Mother's Day was seriously lacking and my present was received without much acclaim. But by the time Real Madrid had cruised to a 4-1 victory, I had my redemption. Almost £43 – what a great present, eh?

My sister thought she had trumped me as usual with a shiny pair of earrings, but you could probably buy two sets of ruddy earrings with £43. It's the thought that doesn't count.

When Els holed a long par putt on the 14th hole of the final round in Florida, I knew I was going to be in clover too. The putt encapsulated what betting is all about. For the average man, who is not going to score the winning goal in a World Cup final or make love to Melanie Slade, nothing gets close to punting in terms of getting one's juices flowing. You blew my mind, Ernie!

Monday, March 15

I ducked into my local independent bookies having popped out for a paper and ended up having £15 on Trap Two in the 4.18 at Swindon. It resulted in your classic dog-race disappointment. Trap Two led going round the final bend and then lost by half a nostril to the fast-finishing Trap One.

I've seen grown men punch walls, kick over rubbish bins and shout naughty words after backing dogs in a betting shop that lose by half a nostril, but as someone who has grown accustomed to life being a regular source of dissatisfaction, I just cheerily wished the turf accountant a happy Cheltenham and wended my way to the exit.

I could not resist supporting Liverpool after seeing they had named what is arguably their strongest possible side against shambolic Portsmouth – I had £200 on Liverpool half-time, Liverpool full-time at 4-5, £30 on 3-0 Liverpool at 8-1 and £40 on any unquoted scoreline at 4-1 – and enjoyed the Reds' 4-1 romp.

Tuesday, March 16
Got my Transitions Championship golf bets in play (£147 on KJ Choi at 39-1, £128 on Howell at 43-1, £115 on Cink at 49-1, £110 on Holmes at 54-1 and £100 on John Senden at 64-1).

Wednesday, March 17
Having ignored the opening day of the Cheltenham Festival, I bowed to temptation before the Champion Chase and had £120 on Master Minded at 5-6. I'd heard he was quite fast.

Come the finish, I was chastising myself for dabbling in a sport I know nothing about. A little bald chap connected with the winner was going bananas on the television, but I was going, urm, the opposite of bananas (sananab?) in my lounge.

I tried to get my money back on the next race with £14 on Deutschland at 9-1, working on the basis that among all the obvious love for Ireland at Cheltenham and the odd show of affection for the United Kingdom, there appeared to be no such clamour for all things German, so Deutschland may be an inflated price in the market.

And I thought Deutschland's jockey Ruby Walsh would be well up for it having just flopped aboard an odds-on favourite. Good analysis, eh?

No, the Germans went home disappointed and fortunately Channel 4 went off air to stop me chasing my losses any more.

Thursday, March 18
Watched golf all day and night while trying to resist the lure of Channel 4. If I get addicted to horseracing, too, I'm doomed.

Friday, March 19
Had a silly £200 on Kauto Star at 4-5 just before the Cheltenham Gold Cup. Sport of Kings, eh? Hmmm, I prefer Queens.

CHAPTER 8

DANGEROUS DISTRACTIONS

K J Choi

Saturday, March 20

Not for the first time in my life, a day began with an enormous sigh because my body was suffering from acute alcohol poisoning, which meant six or seven hours of rehabilitation lay ahead before I could re-enter the human race.

I'm certainly not the only one who goes through these challenges on a regular basis and it is fascinating how drinkers weigh up the pleasure/pain equation. I was probably out pleasuring myself (not like that, you perverts) for six or seven hours on Friday and that left me with six or seven hours of pain to deal with on Saturday. An hour for an hour then. Is that a value bet?

Maybe, as if often the case in the punting world, the 'no bet' option is the most sensible course to take. Don't drink, don't get hung over and use your time in God's Garden more constructively (sewing, baking, composing, etc).

But in the punting world the 'go all in' option is a constant attraction that offers the chance of serious riches. You won't end up with a nice patchwork cushion, a fresh honey and saffron loaf or a masterpiece to rival Beethoven's Fifth Symphony, but you might hit the fun jackpot if you make merry in a public house.

That was definitely the case on Friday night as my local was staging a hypnosis show, featuring notorious mindbender David Days, and he put on one hell of a performance.

I had never seen hypnosis in action before and am a naturally sceptical chap (I still believe the Earth's flat, for example), but it was all very convincing and friends of friends who ended up participating on stage assured me they would never have done the things they did had they not been under the control of Double-D (I'm afraid David Duval has had to relinquish his nickname to a better man).

Arguably the highlight of the show was when Double-D put a 20-something blonde under a spell that made her think he had the biggest plonker she had ever seen. The filthy so-and-so stared at his groin with her tongue out for the rest of the night. I wonder how easy it is to acquire these hypnosis skills?

Barmaid Sophie was working again and I was struggling to get any banter going, but after a few San Miguels I thought I had hatched a masterplan.

Me: "I'm gonna tell her she's the only one in here who is capable of hypnotising me."

Trifleface: "Don't say that. Honestly mate, don't say that."

A few minutes later . . .

Me: "You're the only one in here who is capable of hypnotising me."

Sophie: "That's not too cheesy, is it?"

Me: "Yeah, I suppose it is quite cheesy. Two pints of San Miguel, please."

Back at the table . . .

Me: "I said it."

Trifleface: "You dick."

Sunday, March 21

A mate texted to ask if I wanted to watch Man United v Liverpool with him in the pub, so I quickly assessed the line-ups, laid £210 of United at 5-6, and headed up there.

Sophie was working again, which meant my interest in the game was sporadic to say the least, although when United's winner went in I could think about nothing else but my dislike of the three young men who greeted the goal with ridiculously loud cheers. We were in Weymouth – you have to go to the Isle of Wight to get further from Old Trafford – but these lads were leaping around like they were born at the Stretford End.

Later, the Transitions soon turned into a Choi versus Jim Furyk shootout and when they were tied at the top of the leaderboard after six holes I could probably have guaranteed a couple of grand. But all concentration on golf was lost completely when Sophie rang me up, unbelievable drama considering I presumed she had thrown my number straight in the bin.

Furyk holed a birdie putt while she was on the line and I had to try to block out that anguish. The dour American eventually edged Choi by a shot, my potential £5,880 return turning to dust.

Oh well, I thought to myself, I would probably have paid £5,880 to get that phone call.

Monday, March 22

Choi's sad demise meant I couldn't go all guns blazing on the Arnold Palmer Invitational, settling for £78 on Watney at 27-1, £65 on Sean O'Hair at 33-1, £56 on Mahan at 37-1, £32 on Howell at 64-1 and £21 on Haas at 99-1.

Tuesday, March 23

Had a hot date with Sophie and placed some hot bets on the Andalucian Open – £50 each-way on Maybin at 50-1 and £40 each-way on Canizares at 80-1.

Wednesday, March 24
My £200 Tottenham to beat Fulham, Chelsea to beat Portsmouth double at 8-13 and 3-10 was a cracker.

Thursday, March 25
Introduced Sophie to the delights of Premier League darts (I know how to treat a lady) and fortunately the action from Birmingham was gripping. I had £200 on Wade to beat Jenkins at 8-11, £33.42 on Baxter to beat Barneveld at 3-1 and £427.38 on Taylor to beat Lewis at 1-3 to make the night even more enjoyable. My £200 on King to beat Whitlock at 5-6 was the only loser.

Friday, March 26
Is there a Gold Cup today? No? Thank goodness for that.

Saturday, March 28
It was with great relief that I cast an eye through the day's Premier League football fixtures and had the urge to bet on only two of them. There is nothing worse (well, obviously there are lots of things worse) than forming a strong opinion on several games and having to sprinkle stakes around like confetti (imagine sprinkling steaks around like confetti at a wedding – that would be a good laugh, wouldn't it?).

The only teams I could be convinced about winning were Tottenham (against Portsmouth) and Everton (against Wolves), so I had a £200 double at 2-9 and 11-10.

I didn't tune in to Soccer Saturday to follow every kick of the ball at White Hart Lane and Molineux (you can't affect the results, so what's the point?). I pottered around in the betting shop for a couple of hours instead, fiddling with a few doggies (having some greyhound bets, not tickling the chins of labradors), supping on a hot chocolate and generally winding down in my familiar and safe Coral cocoon.

Fish and various other marine life use coral to shield themselves from predators and the evils of the ocean, while armies of men use Coral as a peaceful retreat that protects them from the dangers of the wider world. It's a funny old game, Saint.

Everton's failure to score at Wolves rendered the day a losing one, but I had a 1980s party to look forward to at the local pub, so a couple of pals and I settled down with a crate of Budweiser in my flat to get ourselves in the mood.

It's a sad reflection on 2010 life that people yearn to go back 30 years, isn't it? Why don't we have a 2010 party? Because the 1980s were miles better than the 2010s. Billy Joel, Phil Collins and Feargal Sharkey or Usher, Dizzee Rascal and Lady Gaga? It's no contest, is it? Modern life is rubbish.

I would love to report what happened at the party, but with Weymouth's finest barmaid dressed as a young Madonna and me drinking Kronenbourg as if it was Evian, the night was an intoxicating blur of which I remember little.

Sunday, March 28

I woke up extremely drunk and decided to stay that way by walking immediately to the local, where I was reminded how difficult it is to buy strangers a drink. The first chap I offered a drink to said: "Why? Have you won the lottery or something?" I told him I was just in a great mood and wanted others to join me in a celebration of life, but he rejected the drink offer, as did another bloke a few minutes later.

I think this is a British thing. Scepticism is so rife on these shores. Why is this man offering to buy me a drink? What's the catch? Is he trying to get me drunk? What's he going to do to me? The truth was, of course, I would have paid for the drink, walked off and left them to enjoy it, but they ended up £3 worse off because they didn't trust me. And if they can't trust me – I've got a choirboy-like face so innocent I make Ronan Keating look like Hannibal Lecter – they won't be able to trust anyone in that same situation. It's very sad.

The £200 I placed on Blackburn to beat Burnley at 8-15 before heading to the boozer proved a shrewd investment and it meant I was happy to play the simple but riveting 'random phone call game' in which a pal and I occasionally partake.

You give a friend your phone, he or she scrolls down the names in your contacts list with eyes closed, then whichever name it lands on when they stop, you have to phone them. So even if it lands on someone you haven't spoken to in years, someone to whom you have absolutely nothing relevant to say or someone you would potentially have never contacted again in your life, you have to phone them.

The tension is always unbearable, but on this occasion I got lucky as I ended up with James Pyman, the notorious *Racing Post* Number Cruncher. I had not spoken to the Number Cruncher for several months, but I pretended I was interested in the percentage of winning favourites in two-mile handicap hurdles at Ludlow and managed to disguise the fact I was ringing him under duress.

The day rapidly worsened. I had laid £400 of Liverpool against Sunderland at 4-11 and Torres soon blew that bet apart, then Els, a player who I have backed more than any other this season but stupidly left alone for Bay Hill, took full control of the Arnold Palmer Invitational.

Monday, March 29

After three days of excess, I decided it was time to take stock and, after placing £500 on Man City to beat Wigan at 2-5, I went to the man-made hell-hole known as the gym.

It is soul-destroying to listen to 'personal trainers' patronising the people foolish enough to employ them. I was struggling on a rowing machine while one obese woman behind me was being told: "It's going to take time. The best way to measure progress is to take a picture of yourself now, then take another one in a couple of months, then . . ."

Yeah, great advice. In a couple of years' time, she will probably be looking at a picture of herself an inch thinner. Two years of pain in the gym for an inch? Good value?

It is like being back at school. My jumper was actually confiscated and put behind the reception desk because I had left it on the floor beside the running machine I was using rather than put it in a locker. When I asked if they had seen anyone take my jumper, I was informed of what had happened and rebuked for not following gym rules. I felt like punching her squarely on the jaw – I'm paying £33 a month to be treated like this – but as a natural pacifist I merely laughed in the face of this utterly pathetic conduct and made for the exit. Possibly never to return.

Tuesday, March 30
Sophie texted to inform me she was getting back together with her ex-boyfriend. Savage blow.

Wednesday, March 31
Had a late-afternoon round at the local nine-hole golf course to get away from it all and club professional Jon Bevan was running a Masters raffle (£2.50 a go to win 20 free rounds or £100 worth of range balls). I bought two tickets and was devastated to pick Nathan Green out of the hat first, but my second grab won me the services of Mickelson, so if Lefty gets the job done at Augusta next week I'll have no excuse for not sorting out my ugly swing.

In the evening, I had £100 at 100-30 on under 1.5 goals in Arsenal versus Barcelona and watched the game in a pub (obviously not the local). It looked a good bet at half-time but was, in fact, the worst bet ever struck.

I stayed in the pub longer than I really should have done, discovering a new lager, a Danish brew called Tuborg, to help me through my Sophie sorrows. I like the Danes – they make good bacon, they make good beer, they make rubbish Arsenal centre-forwards.

Thursday, April 1
McDonald's shouldn't be allowed to sell apple pies. Brown must act now to save people from themselves. I enjoyed watching King beat Jenkins (had £200 at 4-6) while eating several apple pies.

Friday, April 2
I'm trying not to go off the rails, but if I was a greyhound, I would

certainly have a W next to my name on the racecard. I'm short of motivation for life again, it doesn't look like I'm going to have a Masters war chest with which to go for a retirement wager next week, and the taste of Tuborg is the only thing keeping me going. Oh, fiddlesticks.

CHAPTER 9
MASTERFUL MICKELSON

Phil Mickelson

Saturday, April 3

I was in the midst of one of the longest booze benders of my life, but I had not taken my eye off the betting ball completely and was acutely aware that I needed a serious wager to be successful in order to provide ammunition for the Masters.

If I was going to get something close to resembling a Masters war chest, I needed to put all my eggs in one basket and then hope that the basket eventually yielded thousands of valuable objects (chickens, pounds, etc). So I put my thinking cap on, having removed my drinking cap for a few minutes, and mulled over the sporting weekend.

Wouldn't it be great if we each had a different cap for everything we did? It would make the world much easier to understand, wouldn't it?

What's that strange chap doing over there lurking by that collection of trees? Oh, don't worry, it's nothing sinister – I can see he's got his climbing cap on – he's just going for a good, old-fashioned climb.

My thinking cap helped me decide that I should put the remaining £400 at my disposal on Blackburn to beat Portsmouth in a double with Man City to beat Burnley. At 5-4 and 8-11, it returned £1,554.55, a pot large enough to throw some decent Augusta arrers.

I was being super disciplined – all my money was going on one bet. It was, as I used to bark at my five-a-side football team just before sending them on to the pitch, death or glory.

I sat in the local watching Soccer Saturday and Blackburn's inability to break through the basement boys was extremely irritating. The goalless draw was another dagger in my already crippled heart.

With half an hour to kick-off at Burnley, I was gloom-ridden. I rated Man City one of the best 8-11 shots I had ever seen but could not raise a bean to back them. Fortunately, when you're sloshed, all sense of shame goes out of the window and I didn't hesitate to get the begging bowl out to get some wedge on the Citizens. A colleague got me £400 at 4-6.

I watched the game in a different pub and before I had even drunk my first pint of Guinness, City were three goals up. I was pleased but could not help cursing Blackburn ruddy Rovers.

As half-time approached, a kid of about four or five, who was dressed in a full soldier outfit, kept pestering my pal and I with war talk, saying some truly staggering things about how he hated Germans and had been spending the day shooting them.

I know children tend to make a lot of things up and unless the Dorset Evening Echo missed the greatest story in the region's history this lad had not actually spent the day shooting Germans, but I could not believe a mind as young as his was able to feel hate towards a whole nation of people. I guess he must have been brainwashed to hate Germans at some point by a parent or guardian – it's tragic the way the next generation can be so heavily influenced by the previous one.

I think people should have to pass a fit and proper persons test before they are allowed to become parents, in much the same way as you have to if you are going to take ownership of a football club.

If you can't prove you can sustain the finances of Portsmouth FC, you will not be allowed to take charge at Fratton Park, but if you want to create a child and brainwash them into becoming a serial killer, no one will bat an eyelid. It just doesn't add up.

Later, with City about a million goals ahead, I returned from the gents to be told by Trifleface: "Looks like they're gonna call it off – waterlogged pitch." I presumed this was banter but then I saw Burnley manager Brian Laws telling the referee conditions were unplayable. Outrageous antics!

I dread to think what I would have done had the game been abandoned. I would probably have marched straight to Burnley to find Laws and broken several laws beating him around the chops.

As the full-time whistle blew, we made a trip to the bookies for a hot chocolate (it was time for me to eat something) and the dog action from Poole was being held up due to a problem with the hare.

I loudly quipped in as feminine a voice as I could muster: "Ooh, I'm having a bad hare day!" and it brought the house down. I think I could do stand-up comedy in betting shops – there is always a sympathetic audience on hand.

I did a spot of guffawing myself as Trifleface enthusiastically shouted "come on you Baggies" during every dog race, supporting trap six as if his life depended on it, merely because the hound was wearing the colours of his football team.

Laughter is the best medicine, eh? Or is it morphine? I always get those two confused.

Sunday, April 4

The constant boozing was befuddling my mind. I got chatting to a 77-year-old grandmother called Jean in the local (as you do) and she tried to give me some words of wisdom. While I pined for the barmaid, Jean told me to target fatter girls because they are superior 'home-makers'.

In return, I told Jean to back Black Apalachi to win the Grand National. I think both pieces of advice may have fallen on deaf ears (in her case, she had no choice).

I spent the afternoon on the seafront watching bands (God, I wish I had concentrated on being in a band when I was younger rather than my GCSEs), then I had a packet of pickled onion Monster Munch to freshen myself up a bit before foolishly returning to the local in the evening.

Monday, April 5

It was time to halt my descent towards alcoholism. I watched my recording of the Houston Open in a completely bewildered state. I was pretty sure I made a serious tit of myself in the pub the previous night, so I wallowed in a pit of self-loathing. For the foreseeable future, Diet Coke is my tipple of choice.

I rang up the mate who owed me £266 of Man City winnings and he kindly put it on Mickelson to win the Masters for me at 13-1. I was ducking and diving, as they say in Only Fools And Horses, trying to secure Masters funds. The borrow-now-and-pay-back-later-with-interest game can be beneficial to all parties – some people need money now, some people would rather have more money in a couple of weeks – so it is simply a case of linking up a trustworthy short-term needor (I think I've invented a new word there) with a trusting long-term investor.

By the end of the day, I had managed to scramble another £200 on Mickelson at 14-1, £106 on Poulter at 39-1 and £94 on Kim at 43-1, after which a power cut sent my flat into blackout for several hours. I was, quite literally, in a very dark place.

Tuesday, April 6

I was reduced to tears in the morning by The Jeremy Kyle Show, which featured two kids who have Harlequin ichthyosis disease. It was time to take a good hard look at myself. I had spent a week mourning the fact that a girl I've only known for a few months didn't want to romp with me any more, feeling ridiculously sorry for myself, at the same time as these two brave twins were going through their daily ordeal of having to scrub red-raw skin off their fragile bodies.

I consider myself to be an utterly pathetic character sometimes. How dare I be miserable about my trivial travails when other poor souls are dealing with stuff like Harlequin ichthyosis? Get a grip, son.

Later, I went out of my flat sober for the first time in ages and it was quite scary. The world seemed such a weird place. I complimented my betting-shop manager mate on his new haircut and he told me I had seen him twice already since his haircut and had already given it fulsome praise.

As I had some embarrassingly small bets on the dogs, I spotted a little boy gazing through the door of the bookies in wonder at the screens. He was holding a football. I expect plenty of promising potential Wayne Rooneys have been lost from the training pitch by the lure of the betting shop. How many England caps did Steve Claridge get? You don't need your thinking cap for that one, do you? How many England caps have I had? Same answer. It's probably no coincidence.

I tried to look like I was having a terrible time in the shop so as not to encourage the youngster.

Wednesday, April 7

I was chain-eating Easter eggs to keep me ticking over and with a little help from my friends I got another £160 on Mickelson at 15-1. I'm nowhere near the £5,000 potential facespitter I was hoping to place, but a total of £626 gives me an interest.

In the evening, just after Man United had gone 2-0 up against Bayern in the Champions League tie (bet that little German-hater was cheering), I got a text from Hamann urging me to back Bayern to qualify. I had £25 at 4-1 and Arjen Robben's goal was by far the highlight of my day.

The winner afforded me the chance to have a £50 double on Mickelson to win the Masters and Canizares to win the Madeira Islands Open (14-1 and 25-1).

Thursday, April 8

Popped to the shop for some milk and was provided with a stark reminder of the sheer futility of human existence. One woman was charging around her garden with a mower, trimming grass that had clearly been fully cut only two or three days previously. Another lady was eagerly wiping her already very clean windows with a cloth.

It was impossible to distinguish between the areas on the window she was about to wipe and the areas she had already wiped – it was a wholly inane act – but she obviously had nothing better to be doing with her time.

What is the point? Cutting that grass, wiping that window, writing this diary, living on this planet – can anyone think of a good reason why we are doing all this?

Friday, April 9

The Diet Cokes are on me if Lefty wins.

Saturday, April 10

As I browsed around a pet shop, I was on reasonably good terms with myself, with Poulter leading the Masters and Mickelson tied for third alongside Kim.

I'm a flawed character in so many ways, but since I started punting regularly from the age of 18, I've enjoyed consistently excellent results betting on golf and, with my three Masters selections bang in the thick of things at Augusta, I had the feeling another coup was in the offing.

It was during the second round of the Masters that I decided I should invest in a pet. I need a companion of some sort. Living alone and working from home can turn you into a bit of a nutcase. If talking to yourself is the first sign of madness, seeing how far you can stick a dart into your arm without drawing blood may well be the second.

I reasoned a pet might help. Amid the rabbits and the lizards, I was drawn to the Syrian hamsters, who I was staggered to find trading for just £8.50. I think it's outrageous that any lifeform can be purchased for just £8.50. If you were an absolute psychopath, there are all manner of things you could do with a hamster. There is a nature reserve approximately 50 yards from the pet shop. You could pay your £8.50, take your hamster over to the lake and feed it to a swan for some sort of depraved entertainment.

Don't shoot the messenger. I'm not an absolute psychopath and would never dream of doing something like that – I'm merely a borderline psychopath. But the likes of Freddie Starr and Richard Gere have reportedly treated hamsters with a serious lack of respect in the past and for £8.50 these poor little blighters could easily fall into the wrong hands.

I decided my moral code of conduct could not justify buying a hamster for £8.50, so I left empty-handed and bought some Unicorn Phase 5, Phil Taylor-endorsed, titanium shafts from the arrers shop round the corner instead. Guess how much they cost? Yep, £8.50. Three thin slithers of titanium go for the same amount as a living, breathing bundle of fluffy love. Crazy.

Taylor would make a good companion, wouldn't he? We could play darts all day and discuss the amazing advances in shaft technology that have taken place down the years. I'm not sure I would be able to fit him in a cage, though.

I had put aside some wedge to have on the Grand National, so once I had seen if the new shafts helped my game (nope, I'm still crap), I headed up a pub to see if my overnight investments on Black Apalachi (£60.53 at 18-1) and Comply Or Die (£40 at 27-1) would amount to anything.

Black Apalachi got near the front early doors and was jumping like a stag. As he approached every obstacle I crouched down like a slip-fielder and then leapt up in unison with my beloved black beast as he dived over it. He looked the likely winner for such a long way and my heart rate was increasing with every passing furlong. Now I know why my colleagues are always banging on about this ruddy sport, I thought to myself. This is one of the most exciting things I've ever seen.

But then a serious rival loomed large. And I mean large. Maybe I was imagining it, but is Don't Push It about double the size of Black

Apalachi? The wind quickly left my sails when they went side by side at the top of the run-in. It was like lanky Steve Cram against little Peter Elliott – Don't Push It opened his stride and Black Apalachi looked like a tiny foal that AP McCoy's mount had just popped out on the home straight (the sex education lessons at my school were very poor).

I was disappointed but as an experienced punter I got over it instantly. Friends who had spent all morning texting me for National advice, though, did not take the near miss so well. My pal Lee, a musclebound fireman, shed his macho image as he admitted Black Apalachi's loss had him welling up (hose down those tears big boy) as his only bet of the year (£50 at 16-1) failed by an agonising margin. He texted: I can see how you love the buzz. Let's get drunk and sulk.

I was on a self-imposed booze-ban, so I couldn't join Lee. I played with my nephew for a bit instead in the build-up to the Masters third round, providing an easy target at which he could fire one of his many huge water pistols.

I didn't mind getting soaked – I'll do anything to give the lad a laugh – but I couldn't help feeling incredibly guilty about how much water we were wasting. I tried to sit him down to explain that there were children his age in Africa who were dying because they did not have enough water to drink and that it made me feel uncomfortable that we were getting through bucket after bucket for nothing but a spot of tomfoolery.

You can't reason with three-year-olds, though. He reacted with a blank expression before squirting another litre in my face and running off shouting "accident, accident".

Sunday, April 11

Poulter and Kim had dropped slightly off the Masters pace, but Mickelson was one shot behind in second in what looked like a two-man contest with Lee Westwood. I managed to get £80 on Westwood at 15-8 to appease those characters who constantly abuse me for not trading. Have you laid off, Steve? Oh yeah, I've chunked on Westwood, mate. All bases are covered!

I went to the gym to let off some steam a few hours before Lefty was due on the tee, although five minutes proved enough to unload all the steam I had to offer. Going to the gym with Lee is a humiliating experience. After three minutes on the cycling machine, he made me put my fingers on a heart-rate monitor and it had me at 159, which was at least 60 higher than he said it should have been. So not only are you supposed to be shedding a million calories a second, you're supposed to do it while maintaining the heart rate of Alan Warriner-Little? How is that possible?

Disillusioned, I ended up bouncing around on a medicine ball thing as if it was a space hopper, getting a few frowns pointed my way, especially from Lee, who seemed embarrassed to be associated with me. Everyone is so serious in gyms. I suppose we're all there because we're unhappy with our bodies and bursting with insecurities, so I guess glum expressions should be worn at all times.

I expected my heart rate to bust 159 while watching the final round of the Masters, but when it started I felt in a no-lose position. If Mickelson won, I would win eight and a half grand and if he lost I could console myself with the fact that I wanted to stake five grand on him and would have been rolling around the floor in pieces had he blown a winning chance with £75,000 on the line.

Lefty played like the genius he is and I was calm throughout, only losing some control after his awesome approach from pine needles to the 13th green all but sealed victory.

I was pleased but I have to admit I'm feeling like I should have 75 bags in my Betfair account as I commence a cushy life as a pro gambler. Fowler and Choi, who blew great winning chances for me and finished second in events leading up to Augusta, have a lot to answer for. If one of them had triumphed, not to mention Sabbatini, Clark, Quiros and Snedeker, who all finished second when I had backed them ante-post in weeks prior, I would now have left full-time employment behind.

But you really have got to be an arse to be moaning after winning eight grand, so I'm trying to force those thoughts from my mind. Diet Cokes all round lads – let's rot our teeth instead of our livers!

Monday, April 12

The previous Monday, I woke up skint, my gums were bleeding because my body had been so ravaged by alcohol and I was so depressed by recent events I was questioning whether there was any point putting myself through the challenges of life any longer. This Monday, I woke up filthy rich, I was planning all sorts of expensive teeth-whitening procedures, and I cheerfully bounced out of bed with a lust for life that made Mr Motivator look like Victor Meldrew.

As Chinese philosopher Confucius once so shrewdly put it: Our greatest glory is not in never falling, but in rising every time we fall.

I was back in the game and wondering where to launch my next attack. I was brought up to fear anything and everything, taught to believe lacking ambition was a sensible and commendable trait, but I've thrown off these shackles as I've got older and become more adventurous. As Robert F. Kennedy once put it: Only those who dare to fail greatly can achieve greatly.

Right then – £8,000 on Swindon to beat Exeter in the live game at 1-2? No, I'll leave that one!

Tuesday, April 13

It dawned on me that I had enough to buy 1,000 hamsters, launch them all into the lake and watch the swans go into a feeding frenzy. Instead, I got my golf bets in place – £175 on Gay to win the Heritage at 35-1, £170 on Allenby at 33-1, £165 on Howell at 64-1, £145 on Stephen Ames at 39-1 and £105 on Cink at 49-1, along with £110 on Graeme McDowell to win the China Open at 28-1, £100 on Peter Hanson at 33-1, £80 on Willett at 40-1 and a £25 each-way double on McDowell (28-1) and Howell (60-1).

CHAPTER 10

PAIN IN SPAIN

Lionel Messi

Wednesday, April 14

Jetted to Camp Nou to watch Barcelona thrash Deportivo La Coruna.

Thursday, April 15

For the first time in the history of the universe, a volcano in Iceland stops people getting from Spain to England, and I'm in Spain wishing to get to England. I fear I may have used up all my luck ration from The Lord with Mickelson on Sunday.

Friday, April 16

Stranded in Barcelona for the foreseeable future. Cheryl Cole may be used to dealing with Ash-created misery but I'm not.

No planes, no trains (the ruddy French are on strike for a change), no driving licence (so no hire car option), the coaches are full up and a cab to Paris costs two bags (adios amigo). Oh well, at least I can spend another afternoon pottering around the FC Barca superstore. For just 18 euros they sell these wonderful teddy bears that play the club anthem when you touch their left paw. Every ash-cloud has a silver lining, eh?

Saturday, April 17

My eyes opened, I yawned heartily, did some calf stretches, then I grabbed my big megaphone and started playing with it.

That's not a euphemism for something that many young men like to play with in the morning – the FC Barca megaphone I purchased from Camp Nou is the new apple of my eye.

As a kid, you can get attached to all sorts of peculiar toys and never want them to leave your side. Grown men are supposed to know better, but I now like to have my FC Barca megaphone (which can play the club anthem at a ridiculously high volume as well as act as a standard loudspeaker) within touching distance 24 hours a day. It provides a comforting source of instant joy in an often troubling world.

On this particular day, I had every right to need a Cuski-like object on which to clutch, because my pals and I were still stranded in Barcelona due to the volcanic ash crisis and fast running out of basic requirements.

Pants, for example. Army commandos have been known to survive for long periods without pants, but my military training is limited and, having only packed for a one-night stay in Catalonia, a lack of fresh testicular support was becoming an issue.

I had attempted to avert the impending crisis by purchasing some crisp new FC Barca boxer shorts and slips from the Camp Nou superstore the previous day, but it was only when trying to put them on that I realised they were designed for boys rather than adults. Without wishing to brag, there wasn't room to land my chopper in base camp.

So Eyjafjallajokull, the erupting Icelandic volcano, was having a more serious impact than most people realised. Eyjafjallajokull? I think I used words similar to that when I found out another potential flight home had been cancelled.

With no flights, and trains to France all booked up, our party was mulling over various escape options and no route could be ruled out entirely. I now know that Lausanne in Switzerland is almost exactly half the distance from Paris that Barcelona is from Paris. It's knowledge I'm sure I'll put to good use when that ruddy volcano erupts again in 400 years' time.

For one euphoric moment, it seemed that some high-flyers (or low-flyers in this case) were going to let us on their private jet from Spain to Kent which could fly safely at an altitude under the ash cloud. We were saved!

The offer, though, turned out to be nothing but an elaborate tease and was withdrawn a few hours later. It was like being invited into a back room for a cuddle by a lap-dancer only to find a burly bouncer waiting to beat you up and steal your wallet.

We had no choice but to purchase tickets for a coach from Barcelona to Paris, which was departing at 9.30pm and arriving in the French capital at 11.30am. You do the math. I had once been violently ill on a football away coach that took five hours from Weymouth to Grantham, but that was child's play compared with Barcelona to Paris.

With 14 hours cooped up on a bus ahead, it was like being on death row waiting to be plonked upon the electric chair (well, probably not quite as bad as that, but you know what I mean).

The masterplan was to then get a train from Paris (Eurostar was fully booked) to Le Havre, followed by a ferry from Le Havre to Portsmouth. Trains and boats I can handle, but the coach was clearly going to be a struggle.

Fortunately, an obscure channel on my hotel room TV was showing Higgins versus Barry Hawkins in the first round of the World Championship, so I could take my mind off the challenges ahead.

I had placed £600 on Higgins to win the title at 5-1, so was watching with interest, although the German commentary was unhelpful, with Germany's answer to John Virgo regularly asking: "Wo ist der cueball gehen?"

After getting thrown out of the hotel (don't worry – I didn't disgrace myself – it was checkout time), I had £250 on Man City to beat Man United at 15-8 and watched it in an Irish bar in central Barcelona. It was very dark, I was sitting down, and I grew increasingly unhappy as time passed by – excellent preparation for the coach trip.

In the last few hours before boarding, I desperately tried to find a toy shop, so I could purchase a few items to entertain me while on the coach. A games compendium, something at which you would not look twice if you were at home with a TV and computer, suddenly became the holy grail. But toy shops were impossible to find. There were countless lingerie outlets selling all sorts of saucy things, but I could not locate a single toy shop.

I feel so sorry for the kids of Spain – they've clearly got nothing to play with apart from mummy's frilly knickers. No wonder Fernando Torres often looks so feminine – he probably spent his childhood dressing up in brassieres to quell his boredom.

The closest we could get to a toy shop was a sort of bric-a-brac store that sold lots of strange little things. There was no games compendium on offer, so instead I purchased a crucifix, which came complete with a stricken Lord upon it for just five euros. I was banking on it keeping us safe during the dangerous journey ahead.

"The Lord is my shepherd" became my new catchphrase as I stepped on to the coach, although I wondered if even the Lord had the power to guide me out of this predicament when I discovered there was no toilet aboard. A 14-hour journey with no toilet? These Spaniards must possess bladders the size of bulls, I thought to myself.

I'm shaking now as I recall the agonies of the pilgrimage to Paris. The last thing you need during an examination like this is to find a 'character' seated nearby – if everyone just suffers in silence it is more bearable – but sure enough there was a fat lad wearing a Man United training top a few rows down who was clearly under the impression he was the next Peter Kay.

I would rather have spent 14 hours French kissing Peter Beardsley than have to listen to this moron chuntering on.

Another bloke sitting to my left had a 'comedy' mobile ringtone that made the sound of a cockerel every time it rang. It was unquestionably disgraceful conduct to leave the mobile functioning through the night.

I mumbled "cock" loudly enough for him to hear every time it went off, but he must have been under the impression I was joyfully playing a game of 'name that animal sound' because he showed no inclination whatsoever to turn it off.

I resorted to eating biscuits and popcorn to ease the pain and texting people for sporting information. Howell was sharing the lead at the halfway stage of the Heritage and I thought I might have a ten-bag cash injection to perk me up on arrival back in Blighty.

But before long Howell started frittering shots away. I suppose with the Lord busy safely shepherding me 516 miles inside a lump of steel, he did not have time to be helping Chucky Three Sticks maintain his momentum on the Harbour Town Links.

My mood picked up slightly when Ames and Cink crept into contention, and Higgins' smooth passage into the second round at the Crucible was pleasing, but nothing could alleviate the distress caused by the cramped conditions.

I tried every position known to man in an attempt to get comfortable enough to sleep – I felt like I was going through the Kama Sutra on the back seat with my colleague Mark Langdon – but nothing would work. I felt like a goldfish, just staring dead-eyed through the glass, not asleep, not awake, possibly alive, possibly not.

At service station stop three or four (you'll have to forgive my hazy memory because I was deliriously unhappy at the time), I decided to raise my morale by employing my GCSE French D grade to full effect by asking if I could buy a chicken.

For some reason, je voudrais un poulet (I would like a chicken) is one of the only phrases I have remembered from my French lessons, and with cuddly toy chickens trading for a few euros I felt an urge to employ it.

I didn't really need to speak in order to purchase the chicken – I had already plucked it from the shelf and taken it to the counter – but I held it aloft and said "je voudrais un poulet" before handing over my money to the bemused cashier. Who says teaching French in English schools is a waste of time, eh?

Sunday, April 18

The coach finally rolled into Paris and the 'character' was still going strong, making some trademark Englishman abroad comments about how France is "a dump".

I thought I would be full of glee on alighting the coach, but I was in too much of a daze to feel any glee. I actually had to sprint back aboard to grab the poster I had bought at Camp Nou (it was the only No. 150 in a sea of single-figure numbers in the poster pot so I took a gamble despite not knowing what was on it) and the small pink travel cushion (crafted in the shape of a kitten) that I had acquired at the first service station.

With several hours until our train to Le Havre, we had the chance to take an open-top bus tour round Paris, a city that is home to some astonishingly beautiful women.

Unfortunately though, I was in no position to start any potential cross-channel romance in what is probably the fashion capital of the world. The blue tracksuit bottoms I had hastily purchased from a

Barcelona discount store for comfort on our epic journey did not co-ordinate well with my cream loafers (the only footwear I had brought on tour). I had a bulging rucksack on my shoulders, I was clutching my pink-pussy cushion in one hand and a mystery poster in the other. I looked like a patient who had escaped from a high-security unit rather than a James Bond-like smoothie from England.

The train to Le Havre and ferry to Portsmouth were a joy to behold in comparison to the coach and the next most demanding leg of my trek to Weymouth was a rattler from Portsmouth Harbour to Southampton Central, on which two inebriated 20-something girls decided to plonk themselves down opposite me.

They opened conversation with the rather peculiar question: "Can you tell us about all your long-term relationships please?" and at that point I realised I was in for a difficult 45-minute passage up the south coast.

I was not in the mood for banter. I had left my hotel room 35 hours earlier, I was knackered, I stank and I had bags under my eyes that made John Prescott look like a Russian beauty queen.

"I haven't had any long-term relationships," I replied, banking on that ending our dialogue, but incredibly the tete-a-tete continued through to Southampton, where they each picked up my phone and put their numbers into it.

As the old saying goes – treat them mean, don't wash or sleep for 35 hours, always wear the same pair of pants, look and talk like a serial killer, keep them keen.

Monday, April 19

In the early hours of the morning, my train finally reached Weymouth. I was so thirsty on the approach to Bournemouth but the buffet car had run out of everything apart from tonic water. I wasn't sure what tonic water tasted like on its own but took the gamble on it tasting similar to normal water and bought three cans.

It doesn't taste like normal water – it tastes like sewer water.

Ames, Cink and Howell all fell well short in the Heritage but I was

Steve rides a big bird with a smile on his face

Ooh, what price for the fat white one?

Possibly the happiest moment of Steve's life as he gets some Subbuteo floodlights for his birthday

When I grow up I want to be Bryan Robson

Tucking into football cake on his seventh birthday

Posing with Daley Thompson at Madame Tussauds

*Steve's couple of years as a Chicago Bears fan
was very much a phase*

*Radipole's star player had already developed an attitude problem and refused to remove
his wrist-watch for the team photo*

Steve shows signs of losing his marbles as he adjusts to life in Australia

Steve hones his batting technique in his back garden in Australia

Steve working on the Weymouth land train as a lad wearing a Washington Redskins cap and Manchester United away shorts

The intrepid Hampshire fan corners David Gower

Robin Smith looks at Steve's Weymouth shirt in disgust as the young autograph hunter pounces in Bournemouth

A teenage Steve dressed as Ruud Gullit for a New Year's Eve party

A young Steve is thrilled by Melinda Messenger's visit to Weymouth

Feeling the pain in the gymnasium torture chamber

Steve pretends to be Phil Taylor to take his mind off punting

home (about 80 hours later than originally scheduled, but home).

Fortunately I had a week off to recover and when I awoke I got straight back down to business, getting £104.09 on McDowell to win the Ballantine's Championship at 29-1.

Opening the poster was an enormous disappointment. It was merely a club crest. If I had known that, I would have thrown it straight in a Barcelona bin and had the use of another hand for two days. The news that British airspace was about to re-open was equally sickening.

CHAPTER 11

BATTLING THE BLUES

Neil Robertson

Tuesday, April 20

Feeling as weak as a kitten, I decided I needed to try some healthy food, so I had a pineapple ring on my gammon steak in the pub rather than a fried egg, and a top of lemonade on every pint of lager I bought. A slice of pineapple and some lemon – that's two of my five a year sorted!

Then I got more golf bets in place. Some reckless spending in Barcelona had eaten into my Masters winnings and I needed to land another coup soon.

For the Ballantine's, I got another £45.91 on the well-backed McDowell at 22-1, £90 on Willett at 39-1, £75 each-way on Hanson at 50-1 and £25 each-way on Colsaerts at 150-1. Then I had £200 each-way on Howell for the Zurich Classic at 28-1 and a £30 each-way double on McDowell (20-1) and Howell (28-1).

Wednesday, April 21

I remembered I had won the Masters raffle at my golf club, having picked Mickelson out of the hat, so had the first of my 20 free rounds, then I spent the evening supping ale in the local.

At about 10pm, it was just me, the landlord and the landlady left, watching Sky Sports News in virtual silence. I sometimes find it hard to work out whether I'm sitting in my lounge or the pub. What do you mean I've got to go? I live here!

Thursday, April 22

A night of Premier League arrers punting started with £200 on Baxter to beat Jenkins at 5-4 (oh dear), followed by £200 on Wade to beat Barneveld at 4-5 (oh yes), followed by £150 on Lewis to beat King at 6-4 (oh dear), culminating in £450 on Taylor to beat Whitlock at 1-2 (oh yes, big boy, that is exceptional!).

The Power's glorious 125 out-shot was one of those moments when you thank the Lord for having been blessed with eyes. Bull, 25, bull – watching that was a sexual experience.

Friday, April 23

Beers in the sun, followed by a lasagne. You don't need Delia Smith to tell you that's a recipe for pleasure.

Saturday, April 24

I had heard a few whispers that Rooney was not in the Man United squad to face Tottenham, so I had £200 each-way on Dimitar Berbatov to score first at 11-2, along with £100 on the draw at 7-2.

I was getting snooker frame-flashes while in the pub and Steve Davis was threatening to dump Higgins out of the World Championship.

Davis's ridiculous triumph put me £600 down for the day straight away, piling extra pressure on the football bets, and with Berbatov wasting chances before Spurs capitulated late doors, things quickly went from bad to worse.

I responded with a £200 double on Bolton to beat Portsmouth (4-7) and Sunderland to beat Hull (2-1) and then later (with Bolton 2-0 up and Sunderland 1-0 to the good) I threw £150 on Man City to beat Arsenal at 14-5, believing I was rapidly turning my day around.

What a disgraceful effort from Bolton. Call yourself the Trotters? Well, you certainly made a lot of punters pig sick.

When the teams came through at the Emirates, I realised I had overestimated City's ambition, with Patrick Vieira playing alongside Nigel de Jong and Gareth Barry in central midfield. "It's got nil-nil written all over it," I said to Trifleface before laying £300 of Arsenal at 11-10.

As the game wore on, I regretted my silly £150 on City even more, wishing I had stuck to the more sensible laying strategy. Trifleface was in ruthless form, asking as the minutes ticked down to full-time: "Why didn't you back nil-nil if you thought it had nil-nil written all over it?"

I couldn't provide a satisfactory answer to that one.

Sunday, April 25

It was time to reload my Crucible gun, so I got up early and assessed the situation, eventually having £175 on Neil Robertson at 6-1 and £125 on Mark Allen at 8-1.

Then I toyed with the idea of having a serious chunk on the Everton (to beat Fulham) and Chelsea (to beat Stoke) double, but it paid only about 4-7, so I decided to be more creative, having £200 on Everton to win to nil at evens and £100 on any unquoted scoreline at Stamford Bridge at 11-4.

Chelsea did the business for a small winner but Fulham's goal was a blow and I regretted missing the Toffeemen-Blues double.

Monday, April 26

For the Spanish Open golf I had £150 on Francesco Molinari at 17-1, £125 on Miguel Angel Jimenez at 21-1, £75 on Ignacio Garrido at 33-1, £30 on Bradley Dredge at 79-1 and £20 on Colsaerts at 179-1, and for the Quail Hollow Championship I had £100 on Adam Scott at 54-1,

£100 on Mahan at 45-1, £100 on Ogilvy at 64-1, £50 on Cink at 89-1 and £50 on DJ Trahan at 94-1.

Tuesday, April 27
Had a £50 each-way double on Molinari (16-1) and Scott (50-1).

Wednesday, April 28
Graeme Dott won the last three frames against Allen to triumph 13-12, so my dreams of a Robertson-Allen final died.

Thursday, April 29
Had £250 on Selby at 11-10, now anticipating a Robertson-Selby final. Then I turned my attention to the Premier League darts.

Whitlock's finishing has been nothing short of sublime and he had three arrers in his hand to hit double-six, beat Lewis 8-5 and secure me £1,000 profit on the night. A £100 lay of Wade at 1-2 against Baxter, followed by £500 on Taylor to beat King at 2-5 and £290 on Barneveld to beat Jenkins at 5-4 had put me in a position to go for the grand. But soon after the so-called Wizard took a 7-4 lead, I was calling him another word beginning with W when he spurned four darts to win the match. My £480 at 4-5 turned to dust when Lewis secured a 7-7 draw.

Friday, April 30
I was finding it hard to shake off the gut-wrenching disappointment of Jackpot's draw-clinching final arrer. A fair chunk has already been taken out of the Mickelson Augusta booty and a Whitlock victory would have stopped the bleeding.

Oh well, I'll just have to listen to the FC Barca club anthem on my megaphone for the rest of the day, then I'll probably feel a lot better.

Saturday, May 1
Faced with one of the dullest afternoons of Saturday sport in living memory, I branched out into the choppy punting waters of League

One, Super League and horseracing, first having a £200 double on Brighton to beat MK Dons at 6-5 with Everton to beat Stoke at 11-10.

I like watching Soccer Saturday – Messrs Stelling, Merson and Co always put on a good show – but it was hard to be gripped by the coverage of MK Dons nil Brighton nil and Stoke nil Everton nil.

The other bets I had placed before losing that £200 were faring much better. I had invested £100 at 4-5 with Ladbrokes on Harlequins plus eight on the handicap versus Hull.

I also had my first-ever horsey distances wager in an attempt to tackle the tedium, a distances addict having described over 46 lengths at Uttoxeter as "a knocking bet" at 13-8.

I invested only £40 – I'm yet to be convinced it is possible to predict which horsey is going to win a race, let alone predict how far the winning horsey is going to finish ahead of the runner-up horsey – but with 33 lengths in the tank at halfway it looked promising.

But then that pesky little fella they call Chocolate kept geeing up (is that the correct technical term?) the dirty grey beast that was chasing home the winner in the 4.25, so we were up to only 42.5 lengths with two races to go. Old Mustard, Aidan Coleman, then won cheekily in the penultimate race, meaning we needed at least a length and a quarter from the finale to bring home the bacon.

It inevitably turned out to be one of the closest horsey races I've ever seen. They put 'nk' down as the official winning distance on the results sheet. If that had stood for nine kittens we might just have scraped a winner, but unfortunately it stood for neck, so we definitely lost.

With Ogilvy stumbling from a promising overnight position at Quail Hollow, I placed £100 on Watney at 35-1 in the morning, but he too failed to get anything going. Francesco Molinari and Colsaerts, though, were bang in contention in the Spanish Open, so hope sprung eternal. Whatever that means.

Sunday, May 2

I walked into the local at lunchtime and did not leave until closing time. A recipe for disaster if ever there was one. I had not planned to stay so long, but there was so much entertainment all around me that I could not stop myself.

Everyone is so happy on bank holiday weekends. The human race would be so much more content if no-one had to work, wouldn't it? But if no-one worked, then society would collapse I suppose. There would be no pubs for starters. No, I haven't thought this one through. People have to work. No-one worked in caveman times and cavemen always looked extremely miserable. Case closed.

How could I leave the pub, though, with live bands on all day, a cider and cheese festival in full flow, two Premier League blockbusters to watch, the barmaid of my dreams serving the ale and various pals popping up out of nowhere bursting with bank holiday cheer?

A £600 wager on Chelsea to beat Liverpool at 10-11 made the day even more absorbing and watching the game while a professional Elton John impersonator hit top gear was nothing short of hilarious.

When Chelsea were controversially denied what looked a certain penalty just before half-time, myself and other Blues fans were going bananas, but the Elton wannabe just plugged on manfully over the shouting and hollering with his rendition of Sorry Seems To Be The Hardest Word.

Chelsea did the business in style, Colsaerts got close but no cigar in Spain, while Neil Robertson went 9-7 up in the snooker final.

By then, I was tired and emotional, I bought a painting (it's a long story), somehow managed to lose my jumper, then lost my marbles. It's a good job the Elton John act was on first and not last. If he had been blasting out Can You Feel The Love Tonight at 11pm, I would probably have been rolling around the floor crying like a baby.

Monday, May 3

Spent the morning watching a recording of the final round of the Quail Hollow Championship and was spellbound. McIlroy's 62 was literally breathtaking stuff.

While I wandered around my flat in San Miguel-induced agony, I then got a fillip in the form of an invitation to play 18 holes with

McIlroy himself in Dublin next week. The *Racing Post* has close ties with the 21-year-old genius and some of us are having a little get-together. Blimey O'Reilly.

Even with £1,225 on the line in the snooker, it was tough to stay awake to its conclusion, but thankfully Robbo got the job done by 1am.

Tuesday, May 4

Saw on the news that planes had been grounded in Ireland because of the Icelandic volcano!

If that ruddy volcano stops me getting to Dublin next week, I'm going to locate Hermann Hreidarsson, Eidur Gudjohnsen or Bjork and take them hostage until the Icelandic prime minister pays me £1m compensation to make up for my disappointment.

With a match alongside Rory on the horizon, I started to fret about not having much of a golf game anymore, so I went to a proper course to play 18 holes and try to shake off some of the rust. My golf went from the sublime to the ridiculous. I nearly killed a driver at the third hole. I don't mean I almost hit a perfect tee-shot with the Big Dog – I mean I hooked one that went careering into a neighbouring road and just missed a passing Volvo Estate. I might have to opt for a few smooth three-woods when in the company of a future world No. 1 next week.

Later I got my Players Championship bets in place (£215 on Els at 28-1, £195 on Westwood at 31-1 and £190 on Harrington at the same price), then for the Italian Open I had £190 on Edoardo Molinari at 16-1, £75 on Matteo Manassero at 40-1, £50 on Colsaerts at 59-1 and £35 on Clarke at 74-1. I had a £50 double on Els and Molinari (28-1 and 16-1) for added interest.

Wednesday, May 5

I was feeling as flat as a pancake. You know those days when you're just not right. They say that about horses a lot, don't they? He just wasn't right or whatever. I was having one of those days. I was dizzy and finding it hard to breathe. Maybe I had a dirty scope.

I decided to have a McDonald's to sort me out and was really looking forward to it until I got home and realised the cashier had forgotten to put my Dairy Milk McFlurry in the bag. My immediate reaction was to think: I'll drive back and weigh in with a mcflurry of punches to punish this gross negligence. But my chips were already getting cold so I just accepted I had to go without any dessert. God, life sucks sometimes, doesn't it?

Thursday, May 6

A day spent doing completely pointless things. Firstly, I voted, which as it turned out, was a wholly pointless act. Then I spent a few hours drinking stout in the local. There are hundreds of pubs in which I could have done that, but I always choose the local in the hope that the barmaid might suddenly throw her arms around me and whisper sweet nothings in my ear, so I sit in the corner like a pathetic love-sick puppy. Again, a wholly pointless act.

I don't know how my feeble brain justifies this behaviour. What does it think is going to happen? "Ooh, you drink that Guinness so impressively Stevie! I can't take it anymore, come here big boy!" I reckon unrequited love has to be one of, if not the, most painful suffering a human being can face. I personally would put it well above influenza, tonsillitis and starvation.

Friday, May 7

An "it's probably all fiction" accusation from a diary reader riled me. I often wish it was, pal.

CHAPTER 12

MEETING McILROY

Rory McIlroy and Steve Palmer

Saturday, May 8

"I hate it every time I come and feel physically sick almost immediately after walking through the entrance, but that's the idea, isn't it? No pain, no gain, eh?"

The woman in charge of my gym was struggling to come to terms with my reply when she casually asked me how I was getting on. I think the standard answer to her question is: "Oh yeah, I feel great, I feel energised, I feel healthier than a budding tulip."

But 20 minutes into half an hour of lung-busting, I was in no mood to pretend I was going through anything other than sheer hell, mind and body being tested to the limit in a man-made cesspit of sweaty flesh.

After 40 minutes in the bath afterwards (I try to make my enjoyable post-gym bath longer than my miserable workout to restore myself to some sort of functional happiness level), I settled down in bed to watch Colsaerts in the Italian Open because the resurgent Belgian boy was bang in contention.

Fredrik Andersson Hed somehow conjured a 63, though, my name becoming Bedsick Handon Head as the lanky Swede carded his tenth birdie of the round.

A few frames of snooker and a couple of pints revived me, and I was going to head home to watch the third round of the Players Championship, in which Westwood was looking like he might land me a £6,045 boost. But at 7pm, the golf suddenly appeared on the TV screen in my local, so I decided to have a few more sherbets while cheering on the tournament leader.

The landlord and landlady were celebrating their wedding anniversary by staging a 'back to school' party where everybody either dressed up as a schoolboy or a schoolgirl, so before long lots of Britney Spears lookalikes were turning up and I was telling the barmaid to hit me baby, one more lager.

I wasn't in fancy dress – I told anyone that asked that I was trying to achieve the look of a lad who had just been expelled from school – but stayed in the pub to watch Westwood maintain his position on top of the leaderboard.

Mickelson, on whom I had placed £45 at 59-1 in the morning, had also hauled himself into contention with a 66, so I was in reasonable spirits as the San Miguel flowed.

Sadly, my night soon took a turn for the worse, as I fired off some emotional alcohol-fuelled text messages. With eight pints of premium-strength lager inside me, I was convinced this was definitely a good idea. A little devil on my shoulder was whispering "send, Steve, send", but the devil always flees in the cold light of the following morning and leaves you to deal with the consequences. Never trust the devil, guys.

A lock-in ensued, meaning I was still in the pub eight hours after the departure time I had originally planned, and just as I was about to leave, a scrawny little weaselface started shouting his mouth off in my direction.

If I was a scrawny little weaselface, I would sit quietly in my burrow trying not to upset anyone. He resembled a Matchmaker – so feeble you could snap him in two – but some boys think they transform into David Haye after a few pints.

I staggered home in the early hours of the morning more bemused by the world than ever before, having unfortunately mislaid my house keys, ringing my dad at 3.30am to ask if he could bring my spare set round.

Gosh, he looked so proud when he found me slumped in my doorway like a tramp 20 minutes later. If I was 13, I could have said: "Sorry dad, I'm just going through a phase." Tragically, though, my digits are the other way around so I struggled for a decent excuse.

Sunday, May 9

Woke up full of regret and decided I would stop going in the local. I can't keep torturing myself by seeing Sophie the barmaid.

My liver will be pleased because I will probably not drink half as much as I have been doing. Falling for a barmaid is not good for your health.

Wouldn't it be great to fall head over heels for a girl who worked in somewhere like Holland & Barrett? You could pop in every day for a tub of vitamins and you would be glowing with wellbeing in no time.

I'm now on the lookout for a new pub, one which hopefully has a barmaid who used to be the Elephant Man's stunt double. In future, the only time I want my tongue to be hanging out in the boozer is when I'm about to wrap it around a pork scratching.

Westwood was my betting focus of the day. The Worksop Wonder's one-shot lead soon disappeared but he remained in the thick of things throughout, and another yard of carry on his second shot to the par-five 16th hole would probably have set up an eagle to tie Clark at the top.

That shot found sand, though, Westwood made par, and then, knowing nothing but birdie would do at the 17th, he tried to smash a wedge close, my hopes of a six-grand return finding a watery grave short of the island green.

I'm so used to seeing thousands of pounds quickly turn to dust on golfing Sundays that I get over the disappointment ridiculously quick nowadays. But the fact Clark emerged victorious – the man who cost me £40,000 when he laid up like a girl in January's Bob Hope Classic – was particularly galling.

Monday, May 10

My body finally collapsed under the strain of the constant mental and physical abuse. My throat was horrifically sore, my glands were up like cricket balls and my temperature was switching from Sahara-like to Alaska-like as quick as a flash.

Knowing I had a tee-time with McIlroy only 48 hours away, I was chain-eating Strepsils, downing flu-relief capsules and doing everything possible to get myself fit to fly to Dublin.

Tuesday, May 11

Still labouring badly, I got my golf bets in place. For the Majorca Open I had £160 on Canizares at 18-1, £144 on Hanson at 17-1, £143 on Chris Wood at 17-1 and £78 on Seung-yul Noh at 31-1, then for the Texas Open I had £135 on Scott at 26-1, £25 each-way on Ryan Palmer at 150-1, £25 each-way on Jimmy Walker at 150-1 and £20 each-way on Bobby Gates at 200-1.

I tried to go to sleep earlier than I have ever done before to give myself the best possible chance of being fit for my Irish adventure, but had no joy.

When you go to bed aware that you desperately need to get some sleep to prepare for the following day, it seems to make it much harder to drop off, doesn't it? God, this world is so full of pressure. Even going to bed can be a stressful experience.

I got about three hours' kip before setting off at 3.30am for Southampton airport.

Wednesday, May 12

I arrived wearily on the Emerald Isle just after 8am and Michael, my taxi driver to Royal Dublin Golf Club, was keen to chat. I wanted to prepare mentally for playing golf with the world No. 9, but Michael had a lot to get off his chest.

I thought he was going to cry at one point when he started explaining why he was a Manchester United supporter (he was a young lad at the time of the Munich air crash and Dublin-born attacking midfielder Billy Whelan was his favourite player) but then he suddenly switched to how enraged he was about the taxi drivers' canteen being closed down at the airport, so he quickly recovered his equilibrium.

I tucked into a hearty breakfast at the club with the *Racing Post* owners and some other successful businessmen, then the main man McIlroy joined the table, warmly shaking everyone by the hand.

I tried not to look too star-struck, even though every bone in my body wanted to leap up, ruffle his curly black locks and kiss his face.

I managed to resist and we soon got chatting about his Quail Hollow heroics, next week's BMW Championship and the forthcoming Majors. I told him I was planning to have the biggest bet of my life on him winning the Open at St Andrews in July and he certainly didn't put me off.

Hitting balls right next to Rory on the driving range proved inspirational. I was flushing my irons better than I had ever done before, feeding off his rhythm. Getting the right tempo is so important to a good swing.

The way the wind was blowing meant I kept getting flying debris in my face every time the boy wonder hit a shot, but I was so in awe I would probably have let him smack me round the chops with his driver if he fancied it, so I didn't complain about the troublesome divots.

There were more people attending this gathering than I had previously thought, which meant Rory would play only a few holes with each group, so I set off with my three playing partners knowing that the pride of Northern Ireland would be waiting for us on the eighth tee.

Alongside me was a chap called David, one of Ireland's top doctors, who looks very much like Chris Wood, and a couple of property tycoons, one of whom, Paul, looks like Anders Hansen, and the other, Gerry, who bears a passing resemblance to Billy Mayfair.

So Palmer, Wood, Hansen and Mayfair in a fourball, with McIlroy soon to be joining the fun – my dream of becoming a pro golfer was being realised. Well, sort of.

For competition purposes, I said my handicap was 25. Several years ago, I was off nine, but I'm not even a member of a club any more and play only a handful of times a year, so I thought 25 was fair.

Before long, though, in the groove after my range session with Rory, I was performing like Arnold Palmer and getting 'bandit' jibes raining in from all quarters. After a tap-in par at the first, I holed a long putt for birdie at the second to go under par and had visions of threatening the course record before a double-bogey at the fifth.

Wood was starting to play well, Hansen was grinding out the odd par and Mayfair's putter was coming to the boil, but we all felt the pressure crank up several levels with Master McIlroy and his entourage waiting for us on the eighth tee.

It was not just the great man himself and his caddie for the day, but dozens of Royal Dublin members had come out to watch Rory tackle their course, so we had to deal with a gallery that was larger than most competitors would face in the Open Championship.

It was the complete silence that I found most off-putting. Everyone was humbled in the presence of greatness and the army of onlookers made sure they kept noise down to an absolute minimum for their illustrious visitor.

Rory teed off first on the par-four, crushing a three-wood straight down the middle, then the four quivering amateurs attempted to follow suit. Inevitably, we all went to pieces.

It was a fascinating group dynamic to see a 21-year-old lad send the legs of four grown men to jelly. Our fourball had been playing some reasonably good golf up to that stage, but could not hack the sudden extra injection of pressure that came with partnering McIlroy.

We all hacked our way along the three holes we played with Rory. I hit a lob-wedge from a poor lie to the left of the par-three ninth that ballooned up in the air and headed towards him. Oh Christ, I'm going to kill the best young player in the world, I thought to myself.

Fortunately, Rory had his wits about him and jokingly got into a position to catch my ball like a cricketer before it fell just short of him into a bunker.

There was a photographer working his way around the course and he was crouched to my right as I wielded the Big Dog on the tenth.

After tugging my drive left, I did a Tiger Woods impression to try to break the tension, growling: "For God's sake, not on my back-swing, man".

The members seemed to think I had a really bad attitude problem and was genuinely raging, but fortunately Rory was quick to realise I was merely jesting.

I holed a couple of long putts in the company of the future world No. 1 – putting is the strongest aspect of my game – and I could tell he liked my stroke. I wouldn't be surprised if I get an offer to become McIlroy's short-game guru at some point soon.

I made par at 11 and 12 – as soon as we returned to a fourball we all started playing well again – then pars at 15 and 16 too. A round of 88 gave me 45 Stableford points and a chorus of condemnation for my handicap was awaiting me in the locker room.

Afterwards, it was time for drinks and dinner in central Dublin. I sat next to Rory while tucking into some duck and guzzling wine, and he cheerfully answered my questions on anything and everything.

I tried to convince him to skip the Scottish Open to rest up in the week prior to the Open, but he said at this stage of his career he does not want to concentrate his whole season on the Majors. He feels he needs to win more regulation events before he can justify such an approach.

Half an hour later, as the tarts were being brought out (this is not a sordid revelation – Rory is nothing like Tiger in a certain respect – I'm merely referring to the desserts), we were discussing which players were suited to which events and courses and I told my new pal that I fancied him to win four US Opens, five British Opens and two USPGAs reasonably swiftly, before finally nailing a previously elusive Masters in his mid-40s.

He had a chuckle at my predictions, but 12 Major wins by the age of 45 is a pretty modest target given his enormous potential.

After dinner, Rory presented my team-mates and I with leather Footjoy bags as prizes (my 45-point haul proved decisive) and it probably would have been a good idea to head back to the hotel for some sleep at that point. David the doctor fancied a casino visit, though, so off we popped.

I'm not a big fan of casinos – I like to have a proper influence on my bets rather than rely on Lady Luck – but I am now a member of the Sporting Emporium in South Anne Street. Membership director Albert Sharpe, a *Racing Post* reader, welcomed me in with open arms, providing ample sandwiches and Guinness, perhaps sensing it could be a lucrative night.

Fortunately, my lack of casino experience meant I was hesitant in the arena, spending most of the first hour watching David throwing 500-euro chips around on the blackjack table. I didn't have a clue what was going on, but the regular sighs coming from the 6ft 5in frame of my intrepid friend suggested he wasn't getting rich.

I headed for the roulette table (the only one I understand) to chance my luck, using my fail-safe casino system of 'it'll all even itself out over the course of a season' (if there have been a few blacks in a row, the next one will definitely be red, and if there have been a few odds in a row, the next one will definitely be even). Easy pickings, eh?

Well, it was easy to lose 300 euros in about ten minutes. The croupier shot me a sympathetic face and I headed back to watch David.

En route, a lad called Steve (solid name), another member of the Sporting Emporium team, grabbed me and told me how much he enjoys reading my stuff. Rory gets stopped everywhere he goes, while my fans reside only in betting shops and casinos.

Things seemed to be going from bad to worse for David, the portable cashcard machine a regular visitor to his table. I tried to calm him down and suggested calling it a night – a strange role reversal for me – but he was eager to mount a fightback.

I withdrew another 200 euros to try to salvage my lost 300 and achieved the feat in no time. A 50 on this, a 50 on that, a ton on this, a ton on that, bish, bosh, bash, arrivederci!

There was no way I was playing again after my lucky escape and it was with great relief that David finally waved the white flag of surrender at 3am.

Thursday, May 13

Got a couple of hours sleep (the casino shuts at 6am so maybe I won't bother with a hotel next time) then boarded the flight home, my brain almost exploding during landing in Southampton. My nephew was waiting to play 'guns and swords' on my arrival back in Weymouth. Just what the doctor didn't order.

By 7pm, I was showing signs of recovery and got drawn into some Premier League darts action, having a successful £150 on Barneveld to beat Baxter at evens and unsuccessfully playing up the winnings on King to beat Whitlock at 5-2. There was one more match left – Taylor versus Lewis – but my casino visit had given me a taste for ending the night level so I left it alone.

Friday, May 14

The wear and tear finally told and I awoke having lost my voice completely overnight. It was time to take stock. I made a vow to have fortunes on Rory for the Open this summer and being at the Old Course to watch him lift the Claret Jug may well be the highlight of my life.

CHAPTER 13
THE MISSED DOUBLE

Adam Scott

Saturday, May 15

I still didn't have a voice, due to over-egging the alcohol pudding, but I did have an FA Cup final ticket and, confident I wouldn't be the one selected to sing the national anthem on the Wembley pitch before the game, I set off for the capital to soak up the big-match atmosphere.

This was one of the most cheerful and menace-free cup finals I have been to, probably largely down to the fact Chelsea and Portsmouth fans could not distinguish between themselves and opposition supporters.

Everyone was wearing blue – Pompey supporters were covered in blue, Blues supporters were covered in blue – so if anyone did want to start trouble they had a devil's own job to identify a foe.

You either abused no-one or you abused everyone, and you've got to be pretty stupid to take on 88,334 people.

The sea of blue just merged into one giant friendly throng and I think the general feeling of inevitability about the result added to the air of calm. Portsmouth were just pleased to be in the final and a Chelsea victory was a formality, wasn't it? I certainly thought so and backed up my opinion with £400 at 5-2 that Chelsea would score four or more goals.

Chelsea could easily have scored ten and were connecting with the woodwork so often it was as if they thought that was the objective of association football. When Salomon, or Haventgotta as I like to call him, Kalou hit the crossbar from a couple of yards with an open goal in front of him, I knew it wasn't going to be my day.

After a remarkably goalless first half, I had given up on the bet, so reloaded the gun with £150 at 100-30 on Chelsea to win 2-0. I was in the company of the Soccer Boffin, Kevin Pullein, and he also thought it would be 2-0. I thought it would be 2-0, the walking laptop thought it would be 2-0 – it could not possibly end anything other than 2-0, eh? And when Frank Lampard was plopping the ball down on the penalty spot with a couple of minutes to go, the world and his wife thought it was going to be 2-0 too.

Nice one, Lamps. It was hard and low – a textbook penalty kick apart from the fact it went nowhere near the goal.

A few moments later, I was just in front of the Chelsea players as the celebrations were in full swing.

An ebullient Lampard was leading the orgy of fist-pumping and I should have been happily showing my appreciation for the double winners.

But I couldn't help thinking though – you just cost me a monkey, you careless muppet. At least have the decency to hang your head in shame.

I went out for a few pints on arrival back in Weymouth, but my lack of functioning vocal cords left a lot to be desired. Have you ever tried to socialise without being able to speak? There's not a lot of point really.

Sunday, May 16

I was in terrific shape going into the final round of the Majorca Open (well, betting-wise I was – I still haven't cracked the Peter Andre-style six-pack), with Canizares, Hanson and Wood all bang in contention, and I flopped around in bed with my phone switched off, basking in the inevitability of me winning at least a couple of grand.

Play-offs are usually very stressful for the golf punter, but a shootout between Canizares and Hanson, who both finished four shots clear of the man in third, was a joy to behold. I had a slight preference for Canizares (three grand return rather than two and a half) but was not really bothered who prevailed.

I felt quite guilty when I finally turned on my phone because while I had been focusing on financial matters, my dad had been suffering in hospital, having been rushed there early in the morning.

Before the final round of the Texas Open came on TV, for which I had two wagers going nicely (Scott and Walker were in the mix), I visited the old man in hospital, feeling rather queasy myself as soon as I went inside.

Hospitals are horrible places, aren't they? I suppose visiting a building full of ill people is never going to be as joyful as a trip to the circus, but I think I would rather spend a week in Wormwood Scrubs than in hospital.

At least most murderers don't spend the majority of their day coughing and spluttering. I hate being around people who are coughing and spluttering. Come to think of it, being around people who might fancy murdering you is probably not all sweetness and light either.

I felt so sorry for my dad when I had to leave him among Coughers United that I told him I would pay for him to switch to Bupa health care if Scott managed to get the job done in Texas.

On arrival back home, I found the musclebound Aussie was atop the leaderboard and cruising. Straight on the back of the Majorca Open success, another three-and-a-half bags were coming my way if Scott could hold on, while Walker was looking good for a £962.50 place return.

I should have been full of beans – it is not every day you get seven grand being thrown in your direction – but I could not shake off the feelings of regret that I had failed to place a Hanson-Scott double.

I have a double on the golf every week but did not bother this time because I could not really distinguish between Canizares, Hanson and Wood as my No. 1 choice. I fancied them all strongly.

But given that Scott was by far my No. 1 choice in America – the only player under 150-1 who I backed – I could have just done three doubles (Scott-Canizares, Scott-Hanson and Scott-Wood) without staking too much. So, tragically, while Scott was being handed the trophy and Walker claimed third place, I was ruing a missed 493-1 double.

Monday, May 17

I woke up with what Harry Enfield would call loadsamoney, but was in no position to celebrate with a spot of disco dancing. I was still speaking like Darth Vader and offering 5-6 your-choice whether I would last the week. The Beatles ironically made a fortune out of their smash hit Money Can't Buy You Love and I'm currently in the process of penning a song called Wealth Can't Buy You Health.

I sat down on my sofa for about an hour to try to think of things to spend my money on – coupled with my Mickelson Masters coup I've got plenty to play with – but as long as you've got enough for a pint and a pie that is all you need isn't it? What do rich people spend their money on? I reckon going on holiday to a sunshine isle with a beautiful girl for company is about the only thing other than pints and pies that is worth bothering with.

Trouble is, if you go up to a beautiful girl in the street waving two tickets to Barbados in her face, she is more likely to call the police than accept the offer. The 'rules of society' are such a hindrance to generous lunatics like me.

I decided that I would use a fair chunk of my money to try to win some more money, hoping that by the time I had won some more money it would have dawned on me what to do with my money.

I steamed in with £500 at 14-1 about McIlroy winning the BMW PGA Championship, then had £40 each-way on Anders Hansen at 100-1.

Flicking through the TV channels in the evening, I stumbled across Danny Wilson saying he was going to instruct his Swindon side to attack in the live match against Charlton, so I compulsively had £100 on three or more goals in the game at 6-5.

Reckless, thoughtless, spur-of-the-moment wagers get a bad press, but my goals bet turned what was going to be a dull evening pottering around my flat into one that was quite entertaining. I was singing: "Goals, goals, goals – looking for a good time" when Swindon notched the decisive third late in the second half.

Tuesday, May 18

I had £150 on Francesco Molinari at 35-1 for the BMW, £115 on Justin Rose at 47-1 and £113 on Hanson at the same price. For the Byron Nelson Championship, I had £159 on Mahan at 21-1, £100 on O'Hair at 33-1, £75 on Sabbatini at 45-1, £62 on Campbell at 54-1 and £46 on Senden at 74-1. I also threw in a £100 double on McIlroy (13-1) and Mahan (21-1).

I felt obliged to do a spot of shopping in the afternoon so that I was spending a few quid on something other than just bets. I upgraded to a more powerful laptop, bought a bucket of fried chicken, then purchased an identical set of darts to the ones that Barneveld uses.

I gave up throwing the darts that Taylor uses because I couldn't throw them anything like Phil, and after ten minutes practice I gave up throwing the darts that Barneveld uses because I couldn't throw them anything like Raymond.

Next week, I'm going to buy the darts that Wade uses and see if that does the trick. Maybe I'm a left-handed darts player but won't know it until I've got some of Wadey's tungsten in my fingers.

Wednesday, May 19

Bursting with betting ammunition, I would have welcomed a Champions League final to get stuck into, but Uefa bigwigs have decided to stage it on a Saturday. How very dare they.

Thursday, May 20

My Wentworth quintet made a disappointing start. Maybe I should have bought some more chicken rather than placed such big bets.

Friday, May 21

Hmmm, chicken.

Saturday, May 22

I staggered around the back streets in bright Weymouth sunshine at 7am, trying to find my house with enough vodka to sink a Russian battleship inside me, an all-day-all-night imbibing session that culminated in 30 minutes under the covers with Sophie the barmaid having taken its toll.

I knew I was ill prior to going out for a drink – I had spent several days coughing up blood and was getting regular bouts of nausea and fever – but I thought a few lagers and some sharp spirits might blast all the poison out of me.

My father always taught me that a pint had supreme healing properties. Feeling ill? Have a pint, son. Down in the dumps? Have a pint, son. Broken your arm? Have a pint, son.

I remember being in Tenerife once with the old man, rolling around in agony with a severe case of gastroenteritis, wondering if I would ever see England's green and pleasant lands again. Frantic with worry, dad rushed out to find a shop selling San Miguel.

So my natural instinct is always to try to solve ailments with a revitalising tincture, but when feeling even worse after a short Saturday morning nap, I was starting to question the method. The trouble was, my mate's birthday meant I was obliged to be back on the sauce by 2pm (it was his 32nd and you can't miss someone's 32nd can you?), so I tried a few ciders to see if they would provide a cure.

They did afford some short-term relief and then, before long, a Champions League final was on hand to distract me further from my dismal condition. I rang a colleague for team news and got it in my head that we were in for a European finale short of goalmouth action, instructing my assistant to place £500 on under 1.5 goals at 9-4.

The pub we were in did not have a TV, so the plan was to uproot to a more suitable venue for the Bayern-Inter showpiece, but it just became impossible to get everyone to finish their pint at the same time.

"Oh, I'll get another one if you're still finishing up that one," became something of a communal catchphrase and the revolving table of pints was never empty. It would probably have been about a 66-1 chance (maybe Kevin 'The Soccer Boffin' Pullein can work it out for me) to get all the glasses empty simultaneously.

Maybe it was just a deep-down lack of desire to watch the game – I couldn't have given a monkey's who won without a bet so maybe the non-punters were equally disinterested – but for whatever reason we missed the entire 90 minutes and I was reliant on my mate Sam getting a phone call from his girlfriend Sophie (common name) every time a goal went in.

Needless to say, I failed to welcome Sophie's two phone calls with much glee, the second one informing me that I had lost £500. "Oh, f*** off, Sophie," was my completely illogical reaction to the second goal, as if she was to blame for Jose Mourinho's side killing the game. Losing half-a-grand without even getting any viewing pleasure out of watching the sporting drama unfold was particularly sickening.

Why did I bother with that bet? I was so cidered-up when I was analysing the team news, I could hardly claim to have had a complete handle on the tactical strategies of Mourinho and Louis van Gaal, so it certainly wasn't a rock-solid money-making exercise. I guess I did it because I had not had a bet all day and really wanted to have one. Gosh, I hope I'm not addicted to betting.

Several ciders later, it was 4am, and I was starting to feel okay. Maybe dad was right after all, I thought to myself.

Sunday, May 23

No, he is definitely wrong. I felt shocking and did not even have any decent golf bets running to cheer me up. At dinner time, it dawned on me that I hadn't eaten anything for 48 hours, which probably wasn't helping my cause, but I was physically unable to move so I had to stay hungry.

Monday, May 24

It was time to see a doctor. I never go to the doctor unless absolutely necessary, but I had to concede I couldn't shift this problem on my own. Unfortunately, I could not get an appointment until 4pm the following day, so another 30-odd hours of infirmity lay in store.

I mulled over a chunky double on England to beat Mexico and Taylor to win the Premier League – Ladbrokes were top price about both at 1-2 and 3-10 so it was there for the taking – but having shipped so much at the weekend on golf and football I did not have the stomach for the fight.

I was too ill to bet like a man, so had a token £75 on Wade at 13-1, believing he was the only one capable of humbling The Power. I also had £125 on under 2.5 goals in the England game at evens, anticipating a drab, training-style match on the notoriously dodgy pitch.

I badly misjudged the football, but at least I could ignore it from half-time onwards and focus on the arrers, which turned into the greatest match in history. Wade at 13-1 was a good bet – Taylor needed to produce unbelievable tungsten to defeat him – but it was a losing bet.

I went to bed shivering despite having two jumpers on. My body is a temple. Indiana Jones did a film about my body – the Temple of Doom.

Tuesday, May 25

Got my Madrid Masters wagers in place before heading to the surgery – £200 on Francesco Molinari at 21-1, £200 on Kaymer at 17-1, £50 on Richard Green at 79-1, £30 on Oliver Fisher at 89-1 and £20 on Sam Hutsby at 129-1.

I arrived a little early, so popped into a betting shop and had £10 on Trap Five in the 2.47 at Crayford, a hound that was described as 'gutsy' in the formguide. I'm guessing they must have been referring to a weight problem – it ran slower than a sack of spuds.

The doctor made me wait until 4.30pm and was such a serious character. I tried to have some banter to lighten the mood as he typed symptoms into the computer, saying: "It's probably not an official medical term but I've felt like utter s***e for about a fortnight. I suppose you can't type that in there, eh?" There was not a flicker on Doctor Serious's face as he slowly replied: "No, I won't type that in."

He reassured me that I was not in any peril and just had bronchitis, which could be treated with antibiotics, so I arrived home popping pills and placing Colonial golf wagers. I had £310 on Mickelson at 8-1, £90 on Gay at 43-1, then a £50 each-way double on Molinari (21-1) and Gay (40-1).

I dug deep to attend a scheduled hair appointment in the evening, renewing acquaintances with my canine friend Poppy. This diary can get me into plenty of trouble – I'm not really able to have any secrets – and I had a lot of making up to do (both to dog and owner) having described my hairdresser's beloved pet as a 'rancid mongrel' in a previous diary entry.

It, oh sorry, Poppy, was staring at me the whole time I was being trimmed. It was as if she knew I had called her a nasty name in a national newspaper and it made me feel quite uneasy. Let's be honest, we don't know for sure whether dogs or other animals understand what we're saying or not.

They might not be able to speak words (either that or they're very shy), but they could easily be able to understand words. Who is to say dogs can't read? You may think I'm being silly, but how do you actually know for sure that dogs can't read? You don't. And on the evidence of the hour-long evil-eye session I was getting from Poppy, I'm not taking anything for granted.

Wednesday, May 26

The magic pills were slowly kicking in. I'm sure they were doing me good, but they were also making me incredibly tired. I had invited Sophie on a date to the Sealife Centre for the day and it was a good job she couldn't make it or I may have fallen asleep in the shark pool.

Unfortunately, my nephew popped round to visit me with the sort of energy levels that I can't reach unless I've necked 20 cans of Red Bull, so I had to raise my game for an hour. I've taught him a catchphrase which he repeats as soon as I give him the signal – "Super Daniel can do anything!"

I've explained to family members that it is an attitude which will make him one of life's champions, but his mother is rather concerned he will soon attempt to stop an oncoming vehicle with his little finger.

Thursday, May 27

How on Earth would I keep myself entertained without golf?

Friday, May 28

Mused that I would probably be a millionaire if I had avoided the last ten years of football betting. Still, it's not like there is any decent football on the box in the next month or two, so I should be able to wean myself off it, eh?

CHAPTER 14

WORLD CUP FEVER

Landon Donovan

Saturday, May 29

Maybe it's just me, but do you have really weird dreams whenever you're on antibiotics? I tend to go on some strange adventures during my slumber at the best of times, but when popping pills the middle-of-the-night brain-twitching sessions seem to get even more intense.

It took me a few Saturday-morning minutes under the duvet to shake off the bewilderment of the previous night's mental gymnastics. The dream was still so vivid in my mind, I struggled to convince myself it hadn't actually happened.

There was a girl I know who was playing the lead character in a stage production of Snow White and the Seven Dwarfs. I just went along to watch her in action, but then one of the dwarfs failed to turn up, so she asked me if I would step into the breach.

Happy to help, I adopted the role of the dwarf called Bashful, but then while I learned my lines I ended up having a fight with Dopey over artistic differences. As a result, we both got chucked out of the show and Snow White had to perform with just five dwarfs for company.

Christ only knows what the dream says about my fragile state of mind – a shrink would have an absolute field day with me – but I was feeling tender between the ears as I assessed the afternoon ahead.

I was also short of motivation for betting. When I won £7,000 in a day three weeks ago, I realised I had nothing to spend it on apart from bigger bets. The only time money is going to have any really positive impact on my life is when I get enough to retire and can do entirely as I please every day.

With an adequate retirement fund still a long way from sitting in my bank account, there has been a lazy, carefree, what-the-heck air to my betting of late, a feeling that it doesn't matter a great deal whether I win or lose.

The only decent wager I have struck in the last fortnight was my £200 on Molinari to win the Madrid Masters at 21-1 and I watched the third round with interest as the little Italian strengthened his position near the top of the leaderboard.

Safe in the knowledge that Molinari would be in contention going into Sunday, I made for the snooker hall, but after only five frames my playing partner, Trifleface, and I were both too physically exhausted to continue. I'm not sure I can blame the antibiotics for this one, but neither of us had enough puff for frame six.

You know you're short of fitness when even playing snooker becomes too much of a physical challenge. It got to the stage where we were both willing the other to successfully compile a break so that a nice sit-down could be taken in the table-side chair.

Getting the chance for a nice sit-down proved problematic throughout the afternoon, an outrageous situation developing in McDonald's when we went to park ourselves at our favourite table. I'm not sure I've ever been so horrified in all my life – an opened condom was lying on the seat in front of me as I was about to plonk myself down.

We were so appalled, we immediately left the building. Maybe if the dirty urchins responsible for this misdemeanour employed contraceptives properly rather than throwing them around fast-food restaurants willy-nilly, taxpayers' money would not have to be wasted on benefits for so many illegitimate children. To use the words of Graham Taylor, Rotterdam, 1993: Absolutely disgraceful.

Sunday, May 30

The sun was shining outside and the rest of the world was no doubt doing something wonderful, but I was inside watching Molinari finish third in Madrid. He got into a share of the lead after an eagle at the 16th hole, then Luke ruddy Donald nailed an eagle of his own to end my hopes of a £4,400 return.

After the golf, I went to watch my sister's guitar-playing boyfriend perform a gig in front of a large crowd by the harbourside, and yet again I was awash with regret about my career choice. I should definitely have been in a band. If you've got a young son and you want him to be happy, tell him to be in a band. If he says he wants to do a journalism degree, call him a square and do everything possible to put him off.

Monday, May 31

It was time to get my game-face back on. I had spent too long foolishly being distracted from my punting by a dangerous vixen and had been placing haphazard wagers with my priorities lying elsewhere. Betting, and golf betting in particular, requires a great deal of devotion and only those with a steely focus are likely to succeed.

Concentrating on the Memorial, I had £145 on Els at 24-1, £123 on Choi at 29-1, £120 on Scott at 29-1, £115 on Ogilvy at 31-1 and £52 on Jeff Overton at 69-1.

Tuesday, June 1

I turned my mind to the Wales Open, having £125 on Rhys Davies at 25-1, £115 on Wood at 28-1, £55 on Louis Oosthuizen at 59-1 and £30 on Oliver Fisher at 109-1. I also had a £70 double on Davies (25-1) and Els (22-1), seeking a £41,790 boost.

Later in the day, I got some terrific news when Warnock was named in the England World Cup squad. Just before the Bridge-Terry scandal broke, I had £150 on Warnock to make the squad at 9-4, so was delighted to see Leighton Baines omitted.

I had been delaying my World Cup bets until as late as possible to make sure I knew all the runners and riders. If Rooney got injured, for example, England would instantly have no chance of success. But the surprise monkey from the Warnock bet got my juices flowing and I spent six hours researching the forthcoming tournament, my first World Cup wager being £50 on the USA for outright glory at 94-1.

Wednesday, June 2

I was still in the grip of World Cup fever and soon found bets pouring out of my body. Bet365's cashback concession on outright bets if your selection is knocked out on penalties is an absolute cracker and I had £400 on Holland at their 11-1. I'm expecting Holland to beat England in the first semi-final, Spain to beat the USA in the second, then Spain to beat Holland in the final.

Later, I had £175 on the USA to be eliminated at the semi-final stage at 20-1 and a £50 cover-shot on the USA to be World Cup runners-up at 50-1. Then I had £125 on England to be eliminated at the semi-final stage at 4-1, along with £75 on England to finish as runners-up at 7-1 just in case they sneak past the Dutch.

Thursday, June 3

Had £1,100 on Spain to win the Cup at 4-1 with Bet365, then £25 on a Holland-Spain final at 22-1. The Spanish, and David Villa in particular, won me fortunes at Euro 2008 and I see no reason to desert them.

Friday, June 4

Mulled over whether I needed to buy a new Spain shirt or stick with the very similar Euro 2008 version.

Saturday, June 5

A traditional full English breakfast can often provide an instant cure to the worst of hangovers, but if you eat a poor-quality traditional full English breakfast then you will find it merely adds to your woes.

My friend Lee and I took the gamble at a town-centre cafe and it all started off so promisingly – I was in good form chatting up the waitress and she was giving us her undivided attention – but when the food emerged we knew we were in trouble.

I suspect it may have been deliberate sabotage – it looked like a family-run business and I don't think the old man (the cook) liked our over-enthusiastic banter with his probable daughter – but the breakfast was revolting.

The egg whites tasted like wet marshmallow and the sausages tasted like human fingers (I've never actually eaten a human finger before but I'm taking an educated guess as to what it would be like).

I couldn't get more than half of it down my tender gullet but still left a tip – that girl needs all the help she can get with such a spiteful dad in tow – and it was a disappointing start to the day.

We had a pint to settle our stomachs afterwards and there was a wedding just getting under way in the church across the road. A young Thai girl was marrying an old white guy. I wonder how they met? I'm sure it was your classic romance – eyes locked across a crowded room, etc.

Or maybe not. God, I felt physically sick as I watched these two characters about to join together in holy matrimony, and it was only partially down to the previous night's lager and the dodgy breakfast. Some people are absolutely shameless, aren't they?

Imbibing in the evening, a new barmaid called Megan caught my eye in a different pub. What is it about barmaids that gets me going so much? Maybe it is the way they happily provide ale for me. I suppose if you end up marrying a barmaid and ask them for a pint while you're both sitting on the sofa at home watching Britain's Got Talent, they may not be quite so forthcoming with the goods.

I guess I need to imagine these girls serving me a cup of tea and work out whether I would still like them then.

Sunday, June 6

I had £40 on Edoardo Molinari to win the Wales Open at 43-1, but I shouldn't have given up on my original No. 1 selection (Davies) so quickly. He charged through the field to take the lead and suddenly a £3,250 return looked on the cards.

Davies shot a 62, which on any other day would have been enough for victory, but tragically McDowell also woke up full of beans and produced a 63 to leave my man as runner-up.

I got over the disappointment by accepting an invitation to go on a ramble with my pal Keith, who guided me to an ancient castle 20 minutes' walk from my house which I had no idea even existed.

Looking out to sea from the castle provided some spectacular views and there was a little cafe on hand from which I purchased a strawberry milkshake.

If you spend most of your life watching golf, you don't half miss out on a few things. You can devote seven hours a day, four days a week to golf, grimacing at every twitch of a Titleist, or you can wander around castles in the sunshine, supping on milkshakes and feasting on the magnificent Dorset coastline. Maybe I've taken the wrong path in life.

But then I wouldn't have known Davies was the most likely winner of the Wales Open if most of my time involved castle capers, would I? I suppose balance is the key. A little bit of golf, a little bit of castle, a little bit of fruit, a little bit of veg, a little bit of Monica in my life, a little bit of Erica by my side, a little bit of Rita is all I need, a little bit of Tina is what I see, a little bit of Sandra in the sun, a little bit of Mary all night long, a little bit of Jessica here I am, a little bit of you makes me your man.

Sorry, I don't know what came over me there. I was deep in thought and then suddenly turned into one-hit wonder Lou Bega. I hate it when that happens.

The US Tour golf ended on a much happier note. Overton was floating about on the leaderboard, but I added another string to my bow, placing £125 on Rose at 8-1 going into the final round. Rose soon caught Fowler and cruised to a three-shot success. I won £1,000, meaning I made £10 from the golfing week. Nothing ventured, nothing gained, eh?

Monday, June 7

For the Portugal Open, I had £203 on Wood at 12-1, £82 on Garrido at 29-1, £67 on Dredge at 35-1, £30 on Alastair Forsyth at 84-1 and £23 on Tano Goya at 109-1, and for the St Jude Classic I had £110 on Crane at 25-1, £99 on Toms at 29-1 and £85 on Gay at 33-1.

Watching Dunkirk: The Soldiers' Story in the evening was a truly humbling experience. I've been feeling rather frazzled between the ears lately, but programmes like this one immediately sort me out.

Those boys at Dunkirk had to go through such horrific traumas. Whatever challenges we may face a few years on, we are so lucky to have been born in relatively peaceful times, and should be permanently dripping with glee.

Tuesday, June 8

Had a spot of lunch at the local and, as usual, opted for the paté. You can't beat a good paté, can you? I think you could put a chunk of paté on anything and it would taste good. You could eat a bar of soap if it was smeared in paté.

Lost a ton in the evening on some televised greyhound racing to quell my boredom.

Wednesday, June 9

Having already invested £2,000 on World Cup bets, I was reluctant to add anything to my portfolio, but the more I looked at Group E and Group G, I just could not get away from what stonking-value bankers Holland and Brazil were to win their sections, so I had a £500 double at 6-4.

Thursday, June 10

Had £250 on Mexico to beat South Africa at 15-8 on the eve of the great World Cup adventure.

Friday, June 11

Had £150 on McIlroy at 22-1 for the St Jude. Go on my son (he's not actually my son – I jolly wish he was though).

CHAPTER 15

DOPEY DUSTIN

Dustin Johnson

Saturday, June 12

I left it up to The Lord to decide. If he had made the weather in Weymouth too cold for me to wear nothing but a short-sleeved shirt outside, then I would have left my USA colours in the wardrobe and gone quietly about my business. If he made the temperature sufficiently high, though, I would ease into my USA shirt and begin my quest to convince the people of England that we are all God's children and must learn to get along with each other regardless of where we were born.

I opened my curtains and got the green light from Him Upstairs – he was beaming his torch in my face and clearly wanted me to spread the message of world unity – so I made myself look like Landon Donovan and prepared to head out on to the streets of England.

I got a few wagers in place beforehand. Having lost £250 on Mexico the previous night, I aimed to get it straight back with £125 on South Korea to beat Greece at 2-1, I laid £500 of England to beat the USA at 1-2 and I had another £150 on McIlroy to win the St Jude Classic at 15-2.

Taking in the Korea game in the local, I was pleased to find only a handful of people in there, but one burly chap who was watching rugby on another TV swiftly gave me my first "you're going to die" glare of the day as he clocked my shirt.

Fortunately, I was with my mate Sam, who is unquestionably the hardest bloke in Weymouth, a psychopath who relishes physical confrontations. With him by my side I knew I could safely antagonise approximately 25 people in the same pub and I was still as safe as houses.

Buoyed by Korea's success, I moved into the town centre, where levels of hostility towards me started to increase. At times I had to take evasive action. The USA home shirt is all white so when I threw my jacket over my left shoulder it covered up the badge and to casual observers I looked like just one of the many in England colours.

I still found a disappointing amount of abuse coming my way, though, and I was struggling to get across my message of peace to all men. Anyone not prepared to offer unwavering affiliation to England's World Cup campaign is fiercely vilified on these shores.

Some people looked at me as if I was wearing a ruddy Ku Klux Klan gown. I've only been to the States once but I loved the characters I met over there – Americans are a tremendous bunch if you ask me – so why can't I support their football team if they are going to win me some money?

I retreated to a barbecue where I knew everyone in attendance and thought it would be a tension-free zone, but once the game started, the atmosphere became strained. From minutes four to 39, I was being mocked. From minutes 40 to 90 I was being hated.

I didn't care, though. I played keepy-uppy in the garden with a beach ball for 15 minutes after the game, content with my £750 profit from the day, while everyone else calmed down in the lounge.

We went into town later for a few beers. I'm usually Mr Generous anyway and like to buy the drinks, but friends typically step in and insist on getting a round or two themselves. On this occasion, though, the fact I had profited from opposing England seemed to make me some kind of evil thief and it was clear I had to buy every single drink all night. I was made to feel like a criminal who had stolen £500 off the nation.

I felt further vindicated by my unpatriotic position as the night wore on and the inevitable carnage ensued. As is always the case when England fail to get the desired result in a big game, grown men were fighting each other and smashing up anything that stood in their path.

Again, there is a supreme logic to this, isn't there? I love England so much and England haven't won a football match, so before I go to sleep I'm going to beat up as many Englishmen as possible and demolish as much of England as I can. Yep, that makes perfect sense lads.

Sunday, June 13

A £200 wager on Slovenia to beat Algeria at 6-5 got my day off to a solid start, but the Portugal Open golf was not bringing home any bacon. Garrido, Goya, Wood and Dredge were all just on the fringes of contention but not threatening Thomas Bjorn.

I successfully laid £200 of Serbia to beat Ghana at 11-10 and was getting a real taste for laying. You can't beat a good lay, can you? Laying £200 of Germany to beat Australia at 8-13, though, was a lay too far and left me feeling rather sore.

Gay was in the mix in the St Jude before dropping away and, feeling the effects of Friday and Saturday night excess, I was struggling to stay awake. To keep me interested, I had £300 on Westwood at 8-11, feeling the opposition was so weak that even with his recent problems in closing out tournaments the world No. 3 should find this one a piece of cake.

Well, it was cake that needed a lot of chewing. Robert Garrigus finally capitulated with a triple-bogey on the 18th hole and Westwood got into a play-off (before which I had another £100 at 6-4), winning despite two other players trading at 1-100 for the title.

Monday, June 14

Had £150 on Cameroon to beat Japan at 11-8, then £20 on the draw at 15-2 with Japan 1-0 up and five minutes to go. The Africans had a gilt-edged (whatever that means) chance to equalise late on, but the game yielded a £170 loss. I immediately laid £170 of Italy to beat Paraguay at 11-8 in response, then focused on the US Open golf, having £700 on Mickelson at 8-1.

I went for dinner at McDonald's and was almost knocked down by a young girl when I walked through the door. Her fuming father shouted at her: "Stop running around like a headless chicken." Her reply, which she screamed at the top of her voice, was a classic. "I'm not a chicken," she angrily barked back at her even angrier dad.

Paraguay heroically got my £170 back, then I had my other US Open investments, £188 on Els at 33-1, £150 on Dustin Johnson at 41-1, £97 on Choi at 64-1, £85 on Bo Van Pelt at 74-1 and £25 on David Duval at 249-1.

Tuesday, June 15

This was a day that would have been wonderful if football matches lasted only 88 minutes, but unfortunately they last for a little while longer than that. I had £400 on Slovakia to beat New Zealand at 1-2 and a sickening 93rd-minute equaliser for the All Whites ripped £600 from my clutches.

I won about £700 on the Ascot horseys in the afternoon, so decided to go all guns blazing on the Brazil-North Korea correct-score market, having £300 on any unquoted score at 9-4, £150 on 3-0 Brazil at 5-1 and a £100 saver on 2-0 Brazil at 9-2.

The 89th-minute Korea goal, which made it 2-1, was greeted with much glee by the commentators, who clearly don't give a monkey's about the punting community.

I turned to the Saint-Omer Open golf to take my mind off the late anguish – there was £1,150 swing on the New Zealand and Korea goals – and had £145 on Raphael Jacquelin at 14-1. I also had a £110 double on Mickelson (8-1) and Jacquelin (14-1) with the same firm.

Wednesday, June 16

Inspired by McIlroy, who told me when I played with him in Dublin a few weeks ago that I had the potential to be a very good golfer if I practised more, I had booked my first-ever lesson. The timing of it turned out to be disastrous, though, with Spain losing 1-0 to Switzerland and 15 minutes to go.

With my £1,100 outright wager on Spain getting off to a horror start, I had no interest in improving my golf swing, being virtually frog-marched from the TV in the club shop to the driving range by resident professional Jon Bevan.

With four Open appearances under his belt, Bevan knows what swinging a golf club is all about and this no-nonsense character told me I had the ball about a mile too far back in my stance, the biggest problem in an action bursting with technical faults.

I nonchalantly dropped into conversation that my mate Rory – the world No. 10 – said I was actually quite good. But Jon just smiled, clearly believing I was a deluded fool with an imaginary friend.

Stressed by Spain's defeat and the issues with my swing, I needed a fillip, and it came in the shape of having £200 on Uruguay to beat South Africa at 6-4.

"Stick your vuvuzelas up your arse," I chanted enthusiastically to myself in my flat during the Diego Forlan masterclass.

Thursday, June 17

I could not believe Els had drifted to 43-1, so felt compelled to have a further £25. My only football wager of the day was £200 on Mexico to beat France at 11-4. Bosh.

Friday, June 18

Had £250 on Germany to beat Serbia at 8-11. Hmmm, let me try to think of the best word to describe the referee in that match. Oh, I think I've got it. Dick.

Saturday, June 19

There was misery in the air as dejected Englishmen came to terms with their football team's drab draw with Algeria the previous night, while I was still feeling as flat as the proverbial pancake because of the USA's disgracefully disallowed late winner against Slovenia. Different priorities, but the same emotions.

I had not intended to commit suicide on the strength of the disallowed USA goal – that would have been a slight overreaction – but I nearly slit my wrists accidentally while trying to make myself beans on toast. Having broken my tin-opener a few months ago, the only way I could gain access to the can of beans I found in my cupboard was by stabbing it through the heart with a sharp blade, then attempting to create a hole large enough to release some beans.

Trouble is, when bean juice starts oozing from a tin, it becomes a slippery little blighter and it is very easy for the knife to misbehave. If anyone finds me lying on my kitchen floor covered in a pool of blood and bean juice in the near future, don't presume I've done a Kurt Cobain (smells like bean spirit). I was probably just trying to make myself some breakfast.

Fortunately, the US Open golf was providing a sharp ray of light behind the football and beans-related problems – I had four players in contention going into the weekend and had a great chance of a significant return.

Mickelson, Els, Dustin Johnson and Choi were all in the mix, and when Jacquelin moved to within a shot of the lead after three rounds of the Saint-Omer Open, I was full of beans (well, I did manage to get seven or eight out of the can before drawing blood).

At that stage, Mickelson and Jacquelin were both short-price favourites to win their respective tournaments and I was looking like having a £23,325 cash injection to enjoy on Monday morning.

Wearing my Holland shirt, I popped over to my mate's new cafe at the Wessex Stadium to treat myself to some proper food (he possesses one of the finest tin-openers in the land), knowing that I could afford to purchase 13,720 rounds of beans on toast (£1.70 a pop) if Mickelson and Jacquelin did the business.

As I was eating, a strange man came up to me and shouted: "Wolves, wolves" while staring intensely in my eyes. I was quite alarmed – wolves are extremely feared creatures – and I looked around to see if I was under attack.

But he just started pointing at my chest, repeating the same word again and again. It turned out the confused old card thought I was wearing the colours of Wolverhampton Wanderers, so I had to explain I was actually showing my appreciation for the Netherlands.

"Have you got some Dutch in you then?" he asked. "No, I've just got some money on them to win the World Cup," I replied. Then, quick as a flash, he was back with: "What are the burgers like here then?"

It was an amazingly swift change of subject matter. Is that what happens when you get super-old? Maybe you forget conversation topics almost instantly, so you have to start afresh every few seconds. I guess it happens to us all eventually. I'm not looking forward to becoming a human goldfish.

After the third round of the US Open, Johnson had kicked three shots clear of the field and become an 11-10 chance, leaving me in a wonderful position going into Sunday.

Sunday, June 20

I woke up expecting a £6,300 cash boost courtesy of big Dustin – he had played so nicely from tee to green for three rounds – and it was a huge comfort to know I had two of his biggest challengers (Mickelson and Els) also winning me fortunes.

Confident of imminent riches, I had a real lust for punting and the moral of the following story is to never count your chickens before they hatch. Or, more accurately, never assume you are going to win a bet until the bet has actually won. As Dave Brent once put it: never assume – it makes an ass out of u and me.

I don't entirely regret my first punt of the day – I maintain Bet365's 4-5 about Italy beating New Zealand to nil was probably the best price I have seen on anything in this World Cup – but there is no way I would have staked £1,000 if it were not for wrongly assuming I had the US Open by the short and curlies.

The same bet with Coral was a 1-4 chance – surely the wily old Italian foxes would secure three points off this rabble with the minimum of fuss – but I forgot it was a game of football (a sport with too many variables for any sane man to bet on it with complete confidence).

I failed to factor in the possibility of poor officiating (with a Guatemalan referee, and linesmen from the footballing hotbeds of Honduras and Costa Rica, what could possibly go wrong?) and my bag of sand turned to dust when New Zealand scored a blatantly offside goal after just seven minutes.

I was at the family home at the time and had to pretend all was well. My nephew was having a go at me because I had drawn the elephant he had requested with "only four legs" (he is convinced elephants have six legs) and I had to take this wholly unfair criticism on the chin while still smarting at the other injustice of the New Zealand goal.

I drew a six-legged elephant to keep the peace, then sneaked off to have a couple of bets, placing £265 on Andy Roddick to win Wimbledon at 19-1 (this is definitely his year) and £350 on Brazil to win to nil against Ivory Coast at 8-5.

Did you enjoy Didier Drogba's late consolation for the Ivorians? I didn't. It left me £1,350 down for the day when the final round of the golf started, but with Johnson, Mickelson and Els batting for me, I felt that was only a temporary deficit.

Johnson then capitulated in spectacular fashion, Mickelson birdied the first hole before faltering, and before long my hopes rested squarely on the shoulders of Els, who had assumed a share of the lead with McDowell. I got £7,492 if the Big Easy won, so I wanted him to triumph more than anyone, but suddenly I was prepared to accept there was a possibility of someone I had not backed winning the tournament.

McDowell refused to go away and I decided I would back him if he made it through the tricky 14th hole without seriously hurting his scorecard. Once G-Mac got through the 14th relatively unscathed with a bogey, I had £800 at 8-11, looking to limit my losses, and when Els missed a tiddler for birdie on the 16th hole, I knew my hopes of making any decent money were dashed.

I reacted in typically moronic fashion to the setback, eating 48 pieces of Toffifee in quick succession. God, they're so ruddy moreish.

Monday, June 21

It was time to throw myself back into golf betting. The previous night was a massive disappointment, but if you fall off your bike, you get back on and try not to fall off again, don't you? Or do you leave your bike where it is and walk to the chemist to buy some plasters? I'm not sure – I haven't ridden a bike for years.

Anyway, I had £171 on Schwartzel to win the International Open at 22-1, £100 on Quiros at 35-1, £69 on Willett at 49-1, £55 on Jacquelin at 64-1, £50 on Colsaerts at 74-1 and £40 on Noren at 99-1.

Tuesday, June 22

Had £150 on Mahan at 23-1 for the Travelers Championship, £135 on Van Pelt at 26-1 and a £130 double on Mahan and Schwartzel (22-1), then later threw £55 on Molder at 66-1 and £45 on Boo Weekley at 80-1.

Wednesday, June 23

Had £100 on England to win 1-0 against Slovenia at 9-2 and the same stake on 2-0 at 5-1, pocketing £350 profit with a fair degree of comfort.

Thursday, June 24

Had £250 on Denmark to beat Japan at 11-8. I'm not sure I've ever placed a bet from which I got less enjoyment than this one.

Friday, June 25

My £500 Holland-Brazil group-win double copped to provide a timely fillip. Shall I have it all on our brave warriors to defeat The Hun on Sunday? Have you noticed how good our potential penalty-taking quintet could be (Lampard, Gerrard, Defoe, Barry and Rooney)? I'm off to get my face painted – this is our year!

CHAPTER 16

GUARANTEED RICHES

Wesley Sneijder (centre)

Saturday, June 26

Well, I'll never be 31 again. Yep, another birthday struck, leaving me sighing at how old I have become. It may be the easiest checkout on a dartboard, but 32 is a figure that disturbs me when it comes to my age. Double 32 and I'm as old as my mother. I don't want to be as old as my mother.

Still, my wisdom levels are now enormous. Even in the last week, I have learned new life lessons which will help me in future. It is just such a shame that the shell in that all this wisdom is stored is showing so many signs of wear and tear.

If I only I could have possessed this amount of wisdom in the days when I was my school's Iron Man champion in Perth and arguably the most beautiful young man alive. Ooh, I could have done some damage. Young men look at old men and think they are fools, old men look at young men and know they are fools.

One thing I have learned in my time is that during the trauma of a birthday (they are not celebrations anymore – they are wakes to mourn the passing of another valuable year), it is essential to seek solace in a public house as soon as possible, so after watching Schwartzel and Quiros play a few holes in the International Open (they were close to the lead but frustratingly faltering in the third round) I headed up the local.

A few pals started to appear to offer nice birthday wishes. I was having a reasonable time, enjoying a few refreshing lagers, but then these so-called friends decided to up the ante by bringing other more sinister concoctions to the table.

This is one of the latest lessons I've learned – you do not have to accept gifts that will harm you. Fiery sambucas were being thrown my way in supposed acts of kindness, but there is nothing kind about encouraging someone to drink himself to oblivion. The spirits quickly turned a cheerful, sociable, 32-year-old man with a twinkle in his eye, into an angry, morose, 32-year-old nutcase with a tear in his eye, who was inconsolable when Kevin-Prince Boateng gave Ghana the lead after just five minutes of their quarter-final against USA.

In fact, I don't remember anything much after that goal. Apparently I was as joyous as I have ever been when the USA equalised, before again collapsing in a heap of despair after extra time, and I was last seen singing Kumbaya outside a town-centre church in the early hours.

I'll never accept 'birthday drinks' anymore. They taste disgusting and make you act even more disgusting. I'm quite happy with my pint, so just sod off.

Sunday, June 27

Schwartzel got close but no cigar in the International Open and my attentions quickly turned to the £600 I had invested on England to qualify from their tie against Germany at 10-11.

Feeling as rough as the proverbial old boots, I returned to the local to watch the game, having a few ciders to sharpen myself up. As the game unfolded, I wished I had stayed in bed.

I suffered the horrible sensation of being uncontrollably close to tears throughout the first half. My body and mind had been so battered by the previous day, I was an emotional wreck, and Frank Lampard's disallowed goal absolutely tormented me.

Fortunately, the landlady brought round some free half-time hot dogs to cheer up the anguished throng. Eating, something I often forget to do at weekends, was just what the doctor ordered to stem the tidal wave of negativity that was building up in my skull. I must be more patriotic than I thought I was, or maybe shipping £600 had more to do with this mental breakdown.

A fillip came after the game when Trifleface informed me that his wife had given birth to their baby late the previous evening (so it has the same birthday as me). "You've got to call it Steve now – we've got the same ruddy birthday!" I demanded.

"No, sorry mate, we're calling her Emily."

Monday, June 28

Flat as a pancake, I needed a morale-booster, and Roddick's defeat to a little Chinese fella was certainly not it. This is not his year after all.

I fired a few arrers on the French Open golf – £79 on Francesco Molinari at 47-1, £68 on Hanson at 54-1, £57 on Bjorn at 69-1, £48 on Gregory Havret at 79-1 and £48 on Maybin at 109-1 – knowing it was looking like only a Spain or Holland World Cup triumph could halt my losing run.

Tuesday, June 29

I was getting a bit twitchy about the Spain game and finding myself easily irritated. Is there anything more annoying than drivers who don't acknowledge you when you stop your car to let them pass by on a street where parked vehicles are blocking half the road? It is so easy to do – just raise a few fingers off the steering wheel if you haven't got the energy for a full-blown wave – but so many rude idiots just charge by without so much as a glance at the kind soul whose time they have wasted.

These scumbags probably think they are never again going to see the driver who has let them pass, so can't be bothered to be civil to them. Well, the next person who does it to me, I'm going to immediately do a U-turn, follow them to their destination and demand an explanation for their ignorance while wielding a baseball bat. I expect I'll get some courtesy then.

A power cut hit my house just after 6pm, so I had to go up the local to watch the Spain game, and unfortunately I bumped into the type of person I despise even more than rude drivers. People who wear caps in pubs.

Ooh, it's very sunny in here, isn't it? Is that why you're wearing your cap? Or are you using it to shield your face from the wind? It can get very windy inside buildings, can't it? Can I use the word tosser? The cap certainly fits. He is probably the stupidest person I have ever met and went even lower in my estimation when he had a pop at me for wearing a Spain shirt. He told me because I was born in England, I should have thought England were going to win the World Cup, and that I was wrong to think anything else.

My jaw literally dropped at how staggeringly dumb this man was. I was wrong to think England would not win the World Cup? What was he watching on Sunday? Had he been living in a cave? Actually, by the look of him, there is a strong chance he does live in a cave.

Wednesday, June 30

Very little was going right, but an incident on my walk up the pub had me chuckling. I'm so relieved to be single sometimes, particularly during a World Cup, but also when I see warring couples. Anything and everything can be a source of tension between supposed lovers and I witnessed a classic showdown between a pair in my road which culminated in the WOG (wife or girlfriend) screaming: "Why are you being so funny about someone commenting on your fishing rod? For God's sake."

It seems the HOB (husband or boyfriend) had taken offence about someone criticising his fishing rod and caused a scene. I couldn't resist offering them both a cheery smile as I sauntered by, with hurt fishing rod pride surely being the most ridiculous reason in history for human conflict.

It was the first day without any football for ages and I was a lost lamb in the evening, incredibly stumbling into an episode of Big Brother. After the fishing rod saga, I thought I had seen it all, but then a 'character' called Shabby started wildly screaming, crying like a baby and kicking cushions around because Big Brother had asked her to remove her 'lucky hat'.

Yep, perfectly understandable behaviour, Shabby. Small children are quietly dying of starvation on the same planet where you shout and bawl about not being able to wear a hat.

Thursday, July 1

Had a golf lesson with Bevan, two days after he failed to qualify for the Open at final local qualifying, shooting nine over par in a threeball featuring 2005 US Open winner Michael Campbell. I expected him to be in a bad mood but he was in reasonable spirits and quickly got my back-swing sorted.

By the end of the session, I was hitting the ball ridiculously pure, and beaming like a Cheshire cat. But then I thought to myself: If I'd had this lesson 15 years ago I would probably now be world No. 1. So many talents are wasted through lack of opportunity.

Friday, July 2

I love you, Wesley. Let's make babies together, Wesley.

I spent the night dancing in my Holland shirt, making merry around my new favourite bench. I know it is only tramps who are supposed to have favourite benches (there but for the grace of God, go I) but I have discovered a wonderful spot that is tucked behind a church and affords a spectacular view of Weymouth harbour.

No-one dares to go near this bench in the dark of night – it is a location too spooky even for drug addicts, villains or badgers to consider – but as someone who has never been afraid to take a gamble I have been making regular visits in the wee small hours to contemplate my navel.

With my £400 at 11-1 on Holland to win the World Cup going gloriously after their victory over Brazil, my navel was looking more impressive than it usually does (you could eat your dinner off that beautiful navel) and I tucked into a couple of meaty baguettes with an air of contentment.

Saturday, July 3

A few weeks earlier, I had committed to attending my mate's wife's 30th birthday bash, so was devastated that it clashed with Spain's quarter-final against Paraguay.

I watched the first half in a pub nearby, but then had to uproot to a fancy Italian restaurant. As you would expect, the Italians were not that interested in the World Cup, so there was not a TV in sight or any other means of following the action. I was completely reliant on text messages.

Trifleface has just had his first kid, so I suppose I was asking a lot by hoping he could provide thorough Spain updates in my hour of need, but I thought the midwife must have stolen his marbles when the texts started coming through.

Missed Paraguay penalty, Spain scored penalty but disallowed, missed Spain penalty, Spain should have had another penalty...

What the hell is going on, I cried? Is this a game of rugby ruddy union? What's coming next – a penalty try? I was going out of my mind and the waiter was not helping by serving me silly little bottles of lager that can be drunk in two sips. In the style of Margaret Thatcher, I demanded: "Four more beers!" You think this gentleman is for turning? This gentleman is not for turning.

Finally, while chomping on my lasagne (you can't go wrong with lasagne, can you?), I got the text I had been waiting for. It was not the most lavish of messages – maybe old Trifles was busy getting a crash course in nappy-changing – but it was like fine poetry to me. Spain 1-0. Villa. 83.

Sunday, July 4

I didn't hold out much hope of Molinari landing a blow in the French Open once he had double-bogeyed his first hole of the final round, but he suddenly hit top form and charged to the top of the leaderboard on the back nine.

Then after almost six excruciating hours watching from my sofa, Molinari lost in a three-man play-off.

With a £3,792 Molinari injection slipping from my clutches after I had devoted the entire day to following his progress, I slumped into a massive depression. Morrissey knew what he was talking about when he wrote Every Day Is Like Sunday. Every day is like Sunday, but I find Sundays are particularly like Sunday.

Monday, July 5

One's bed is typically a safe haven in a dangerous world. What can possibly go wrong in bed? Well, mine is not entirely safe. On this occasion, I almost broke my right hand in bed, punching a wall in my sleep.

I blame the light on my TV for my sleep problems. When it is on stand-by, a blue light shines brightly in my direction. In a half-asleep state, this blue light can be rather distressing. It is easy to believe you're under attack from a UFO and come out fighting. I often find pillows have mysteriously made their way several yards across the room during the night, and there is no harm in that, but a misdirected punch meant for aliens which actually lands on the wall can be extremely harmful.

I could turn the TV off at the mains, so the light goes off, but that would involve getting out of bed. The walk to and from the plug would stir my body too much, so I would then struggle to drop off to sleep. If I use the remote to turn the TV off, I can slip straight into sleep, but then the stand-by light will eventually wake me up with its piercing blue strobe. It's your classic Catch 22 situation. Whatever that means.

In the morning, while I tried to nurse my badly bruised hand, a small fillip came in the shape of finding out McIlroy was not playing in the

Scottish Open. Loch Lomond is always poor preparation for the Open and I must have successfully talked Rory out of playing there when we met in Dublin a couple of months ago. I'm sure he will thank me in his winner's speech at St Andrews next Sunday.

Of those who were jetting to the Loch, I fancied some more focused outsiders, having £100 on Schwartzel at 33-1, £95 on Ross Fisher at 35-1, £50 on Willett at 69-1, £45 on Edoardo Molinari at 79-1, £40 on Havret at 84-1 and £20 on Colsaerts at 239-1.

For the John Deere Classic, I had £235 on Stricker at 16-1 and £115 on Fowler at at 33-1. I also had a £50 each-way double on Fowler and Willett (33-1 and 66-1), so when the former world No. 1 amateurs both triumph, I'll be receiving £121,993.75 from my friends at the Magic Sign.

I might let them keep the 75 pence as a gesture of goodwill.

Tuesday, July 6

This was the first of two massive days in my punting year and watching Holland step up a gear after 70 minutes against Uruguay in the first World Cup semi-final, while Carling Black Label was starting to work its way through my veins, was a satisfying sensation.

Again Wesley was my hero. The Wesser may have turned me gay. I call him Wesley Sniper. White men can punt.

Wednesday, July 7

With two of the three teams remaining in the World Cup winning me bundles, I had to have a token bet on Germany, so I invested £550 at 5-2 as a little cover shot and marched back to the local in my Spain shirt.

Bosh. That is what you call a header. With £575 coming back from my name-the-finalists wager, £5,500 if Spain win the final and £4,800 if Holland do, I was rich again and treated myself to a few extra chicken drumsticks to consume on the special bench.

Thursday, July 8

Edoardo Molinari was leading the Scottish Open when I switched on my TV and I was starting to feel invincible.

Friday, July 9

A massive week lies ahead. The World Cup riches have given me a war chest for St Andrews, so I can bet like a man. If Graham Taylor was giving me a team-talk now, he would probably say: "Go f***ing take the opportunity, Steve – it's there for you – and wring every little bit out of it, okay?"

I'm not going to let you down, Graham. I'm not going to let you down.

CHAPTER 17
OPEN WARFARE

Rory McIlroy

Saturday, July 10

I was packing my bags for St Andrews with an increasing sense that Open week was going to prove a pivotal one in my life. With so many wagers ticking along wonderfully, I had a strong feeling that after 32 years of struggle, my time had come.

Edoardo Molinari was jostling with Darren Clarke at the top of the Scottish Open leaderboard, Stricker was controlling the John Deere Classic and guaranteed fortunes were coming from the World Cup final, so my financial situation was improving rapidly at the perfect moment.

With £575 already in the bank from having £25 on a Holland versus Spain World Cup final at 22-1 and certain riches forthcoming from my other ante-post bets (£400 on Holland at 11-1 and £1,100 on Spain at 4-1), a serious Open war chest was developing. I was getting myself into the position I had hoped to be in prior to the Masters (when I wanted to go for a Mickelson 'facespitter' but could not raise enough ammunition).

Sunday, July 11

I commenced my epic journey from Weymouth to St Andrews (basically from the bottom of Great Britain to the top) and had to follow Molinari's progress on Radio 5 Live.

The British Grand Prix was outrageously dominating their coverage. I presumed they would just mention who was leading that dull procession at the end of their regular travel bulletins (the M25 is not great clockwise into roadworks, slow from Heathrow, the M42 is blocked northbound at junction four and an Australian has been spotted driving a Renault irresponsibly fast in the Silverstone area), but they couldn't get enough of their Lewis Hamiltons and their Jenson ruddy Buttons.

I greeted confirmation of Molinari's triumph with a double-handed fist-pump (it probably wasn't a sensible celebration given I was on a motorway at the wheel of a power-packed Volkswagen, but you're only young once, eh?) even though he had beaten one of my favourite players (Dazzler Clarke). Love can't buy you money, as the old saying doesn't go.

After the £3,600 cash injection, I pulled into a Travelodge beside the M6 in Carlisle to take stock and watch the World Cup final. Because I placed my World Cup wagers with Bet365 (with their cashback concession if your selection was defeated in a penalty shootout), my only desire for the match was that it went to penalties (which would yield me a £5,900 return regardless of who triumphed).

The match remained goalless when the full-time whistle blew and, as extra-time began, I received textual confirmation that Stricker had converted his six-shot final-round lead into victory in the John Deere Classic (a £3,995 return).

With only a few minutes left in South Africa, penalties looked likely to put the cherry on the cake of a perfect betting day, but then Spain finally broke the Dutch resistance.

I was gutted – that goal had cost me £400 – but then I quickly slapped my face and told myself not be so ridiculously greedy. I had banked £13,095 in one day and was heading into Open week with more firepower than ever before. It was time to polish my weaponry with gusto – there was a serious battle ahead.

Monday, July 12
Completed journey to the Old Course.

Tuesday, July 13
Calm before the storm.

Wednesday, July 14
As usual I turned up for Open week full of enthusiasm for the biggest golf tournament of the year – even more so this time after a wonderfully profitable Sunday set me up to have some man-sized bets at St Andrews – but the dismal weather quickly sucked plenty of that zest from my system.

It all started off so well when I arrived on Monday night. A St Andrews Open is special – there is a unique buzz at the Home of Golf – and everyone who has made the pilgrimage this year was busy getting their picture taken on the famous Swilcan Bridge at the 18th hole in the early-week sunshine.

First up were an American party who asked me to snap them, then my dad got involved, then a pair of Italians requested I act as official photographer again, then we moved aside to allow Fowler and Bubba Watson to pose for personal pictures with their girlfriends and mates. A St Andrews Open is the only golf tournament where you will see the competitors running around like kids on Christmas Day, actively seeking visual mementoes of their visit.

The players adore St Andrews. Plenty of professionals who are not even in the championship come along anyway to be a part of things.

I walked past six-time European Tour winner Per-Ulrik Johansson while he was soaking up the atmosphere by the clubhouse on Tuesday night. Per-Ulrik has got three houses – one in his native Sweden, one in West Palm Beach, Florida, and one in Marbella, Spain – so he could be getting a massage from a pert blonde in his homeland, tanning himself in the Sunshine State or messing about with some other wealthy playboys in Marbella. But he has chosen to spend the week in Fife, worshipping at the altar of golf.

Mickelson has said he would love the Open to be played at St Andrews every year, but the fact it is staged on this masterpiece only every five years is probably the reason for such fervour. Roast beef with Yorkshire puddings is my favourite meal, but if I had roast beef with Yorkshire puddings every day, I would probably quickly get tired of roast beef with Yorkshire puddings. Absence makes the heart grow fonder.

Yesterday's dramatic weather deterioration was all the more disappointing then, given so many people have patiently waited half a decade for another trip to the Home of Golf. This tournament deserves better than to be drenched from on high.

In the merchandise stall 'double-canopy Open umbrellas' were going like hot cakes for £36 a go. Actual hot cakes would probably have gone like hot cakes too – I could have murdered a hot cake to take my mind off the chill in the air – but they weren't selling them.

The umbrellas were pushed out to the front of the stall by the wily shop manager, but he was hedging his bets because Open caps (£16 each) were also in prominent position in case the sun reappeared. I wonder what sells well when it is overcast but not raining? Open teddy bears, I expect (£15 each). There is nothing quite like stroking a nice teddy bear, whatever the weather, eh?

It may have been grim but the Open staff were all being commendably cheerful. I overheard one youngster saying to an American chap: "Sorry about the weather."

I thought about chipping in. It's not your fault mate – if anyone should be apologising for this fiasco it is The Lord. Then again, maybe this lad was The Lord. I'll go back and check tomorrow. He didn't look like The Lord, but then how do I know what The Lord looks like? I've never seen him before.

A few yards further along the links, a bonny Scottish lass who was selling grub greeted me with a hearty "Hello!" as I walked past her pantry. Wow, I thought to myself, maybe I've suddenly developed an animal magnetism that makes me irresistible to women. Either that or she's been told to be nice to people who look like they have a penchant for Mars bars.

She should have been targeting the Americans, not me. The Yanks are the biggest eaters in the world, as one couple illustrated so well yesterday. I witnessed a wife ask her husband: "Have you had any ice cream today?" to which he sternly replied: "No, not yet." Fair enough, you might say, but it was only nine o'clock in the ruddy morning!

I think alcoholics get such a bad press when compared to gluttons. Have you had any Special Brew today? No, not yet, darling. A couple would be vilified if they had that conversation at nine o'clock in the morning, but no-one bats an eyelid when ice-cream fiends bow to their cravings.

I moved on to find Quiros making his way to the driving range and, as usual, the swarthy Spaniard was flashing a broad smile. I wish I was like Alvaro and always smiling. How is it possible to be always smiling? Oh yeah, you get an amazing life. I must get cracking on that one soon.

Not much was happening as I trudged the fairways and the poor weather had kept most spectators away from the final day of practice. The marshal in charge of the empty stand by the fourth fairway was holding a 'Quiet' sign, which was a statement of fact rather than anything else. He will probably have a sign that reads 'Noisy' when the championship gets going.

The biggest gathering of spectators I could find was beside the tenth green, where about 50 people were waiting resolutely for the twoball of Glen Day and Van Pelt to appear. I had to chuckle at the madness of the situation. I know Van Pelt has been hitting the ball quite nicely this year but, come on, let's not pretend we're enjoying this. What a ridiculous species we are.

My legs had become soaked to the bone as I went to take relief in the gents, which is a challenging task at a weather-ravaged Open. When you are cold, wet, shaking and have several layers to negotiate through, you really do have a devil's own job to unearth Wee Willy Winky. This event can be a humbling experience in more ways than one.

By the time I had returned to the sanctuary of the media centre, I removed my jacket and was horrified to find a saturated mobile phone in my pocket, complete with blank screen. Disaster had struck.

I borrowed a tea towel from a pretty girl who was serving in the canteen and we both set about furiously rubbing the stricken tool in an attempt to bring it bounding back to life. Then we put Wee Willy Winky away and got to work on the phone, phwar, phwar!

No, in all seriousness, it looks like I need to buy a new phone and I'll do so when one of the six players I've backed for Open glory gets the job done. I added a couple of mudlarks to my four original fancies when the weather forecast worsened.

I was in a position to have some serious Open wagers and invested £4,000. After two days of betting, I had £2,670 on McIlroy at 17-1, £540 on Harrington at 25-1, £380 on Poulter at 36-1, £280 on Donald at 50-1, £75 on Shane Lowry at 260-1 and £55 on Paul Lawrie at 631-1.

Thursday, July 15

I felt the need to do a sun dance before opening my curtains in St Andrews at 6.30am – I was desperate to see pleasant morning conditions ahead of McIlroy's tee-time – but then I realised I didn't know what a sun dance was (there isn't really an opposite of a rain dance, is there?) so instead I briefly prayed to Him Upstairs for clear skies and then drew the blighters back.

That action prompted the first of many grunts of approval that emerged from my mouth – the weather was hardly Barbados-like but there was only a light spit in the air and barely any wind – and I eased my pants on with a quiet confidence that this could be a satisfying day.

Rory was chilling out on the practice putting green by the time I arrived at the course and just before he headed on to the first tee we shook each other by the hand and shared some banter about how promising the weather was looking.

I tried not to appear too pumped up because I didn't want to transfer any tension from me to him – I think I might want him to win this tournament more than he wants himself to win this tournament given that I'll get £45,000 if he does – and I cheerily wished him all the best before setting off on my mission to watch every stroke he played.

The boy wonder was as cool as a cucumber marching up the opening hole, setting up an immediate birdie chance with two rock-solid shots, but I quickly lost some composure when a passing seagull started screaming while Rory was preparing to putt. If I had been in possession of a gun, that seagull would have been in serious strife.

I've got a press pass that allows me to follow play from inside the ropes but I didn't want to throw the pride of Northern Ireland off kilter with any of my often anguished facial expressions, so I kept a respectful distance at all times, leaving him at peace to tear up the links.

I tried to position myself at the distance his drives would be landing on the early par-fours, so I could act as a buffer for any errant tee shots. I would never consider any skulduggery – the champion must win fair and square – but if Master McIlroy's golf ball happened to smash me on the head and deflect back into the fairway then I would happily accept the bruising.

I need not have bothered with this tactic because he was producing a tee-to-green masterclass – striking the ball with a seemingly effortless purity that had amateur observers shaking their head in disbelief – and every hole was being made to look ridiculously easy.

I found myself in a poor viewing position for his drive on the fourth hole and following a small white sphere in grey skies is not easy, so I instinctively turned to the chap to my right and asked: "Any ideas?"

In a thick Scottish accent, he replied: "A wee bit right." Then our brief dialogue concluded with me saying: "Really? Oh shit." You can't beat a good nine-word conversation.

I should not have listened to him, though. I charged on to discover the ball in perfect position and the Scotsman had clearly not allowed for the trademark McIlroy draw. I think the locals are all still obsessed with the Colin Montgomerie fade. Well, there's a new kid on the block now boys who hits it the other way, so you had better get used to it.

Shot two on the fourth drifted a little further right than Rory had hoped and I lay the blame squarely upon the shoulders of the moustached marshal who failed to get the gallery under control. It was such a lacklustre effort. With noise then coming from a neighbouring green as Marcel Siem converted a putt (why get so ruddy excited? – he's got no chance), I was starting to get rather hot under the collar, deciding it was time to assume the role of marshal myself. Enough was enough.

At the sixth hole, I was giving my death stare to anyone who was not behaving as if they were browsing books at a library. You could be opening a packet of crisps 300 yards away and you would get the death stare.

There was nothing I could do about the fighter jet that screeched overhead as Rory was putting for birdie from ten feet. Honestly, the seagull was putting him off on the first, an ignorant pilot distracted him on the sixth – we could all be writing about a 61 but for outside interferences.

After a par at the eighth hole, my man was only one under par, despite creating countless chances with his majestic approach play. We needed the putter to come to life, and on the ninth hole everything suddenly started going wonderfully well. Macca hit a monstrous drive and nonchalently rolled in a 15-foot eagle putt.

This sparked my first huge release of the day – sometimes you've just got to release, haven't you – and I greeted the giant eagle in orgasmic fashion. Big birds don't usually bring me to orgasm but this bountiful beauty left me quivering with a warm after glow for several minutes.

By now Rory had clicked into top gear and his ball was dancing over every flagstick he targeted. I was buzzing and created a new song by revising the Status Quo classic 'Rockin' All Over The World'. Let me introduce 'Dancing All Over The Flag', a collaboration between Rory McIlroy and Steve Palmer.

Altogether now: 'Oh here we are and here we are and here we go, all aboard and we're hitting the road, here we go oh, dancing all over the flag . . .

'Well giddy up and giddy up and get away, we're going birdie crazy and we're going today, here we go oh, dancing all over the flag . . .

'And I like it, I like it, I like it, I like it, I li-li-li-like it, li-li-li-li, here we go, oh, dancing all over the flag.'

Eagle, birdie, birdie, birdie, par, birdie, birdie, par, par, birdie! I've stopped singing now – that is just a quick summary of Rory's final ten holes. And that was with a missed three-foot putt at the 17th!

He hit the front after 14 holes and I turned to the chap next to me and said: "I expect the bookies have already started an Open without McIlroy market!" He is obviously not a betting man, though, because he looked at me as if I was a moron. I resumed singing 'Dancing All Over The Flag' to further bolster his initial impression.

The whole McIlroy family were watching Rory make merry at the Home of Golf. His mum looked more stressed than most (like mums usually do) but his dad occasionally fired up a soothing cigarette as his son threatened to complete the lowest round in Major history. His gorgeous girlfriend was by far the most relaxed, merrily tucking into Mars bars and following the action with less intensity than the others, but over the closing holes even she seemed to realise the magnitude of what her man was achieving.

I had arranged to meet a few characters in the famous Jigger Inn beside the 17th green after the round and was eager to toast Rory's 63 with a couple of pints, but the security guard wouldn't let me pass and because my phone is still out of action thanks to Wednesday's downpours, I couldn't contact anyone inside.

I went back to the media centre instead, where Rory was doing a press conference, and my 'comrades' were winding me up no end. So many pointless questions came raining in from all directions. One bloke even asked him to detail every score he has ever recorded as a professional at St Andrews. Bloody hell, pal, have you never heard of the internet? The lad probably wants to go back to his hotel for a lie down and you're getting him to do your research for you. Rory being Rory provided the information while I shot my final death stare of the day.

There is a long way to go and I must not get carried away, but what a superb start. I'm praying for decent weather tomorrow afternoon and then the new king of St Andrews can get back to work. Tiger who? The status quo is changing.

Friday, July 16

Your correspondent was rather despondent, having managed about two hours sleep the night before, the squeakiest bed in the St Andrews University Halls making rest extremely hard to come by.

If you move, you wake yourself up, so any inadvertent muscle twitch acts as an alarm call. Maybe a shag-happy Prince William destroyed this bed when he was a St Andrews student. Someone has clearly given it a pasting.

The usual battle to avoid having an eye gouged out by an umbrella at the course added to my woe. I like being tall most of the time – you can reach up to high cupboards, put the angel on top of the Christmas tree, etc – but being tall at an Open puts your precious eyes at the same level as umbrella spokes. I might walk on all fours for the rest of the week just to be on the safe side.

I decided to leave the confines of the track in a bid to raise my morale. As the old saying goes, if you can't stand the heat, get out of the kitchen. If you can't stand the umbrellas, get out of the Open.

Fortunately, I came across some rabbits, some seagulls and some dogs on my way into the town centre, which soothed me no end. When you need a fillip, immersing yourself in the natural world is often the way to go.

St Andrews must boast the largest population of rabbits in the world. Walk through any one of the little parks and, I kid you not, you will see about 30 rabbits frolicking on the grass. If Chas and Dave did a concert up here and blasted out their famous hit 'Rabbit' with all these little floppy-eared cuties hopping around in the background, I reckon it would almost certainly prove the most spectacular piece of entertainment mankind has ever conjured.

After leaving the rabbits, I spent a few minutes watching seagulls go about their business on the beach. They were splashing around in various gullies, gliding in the wind from one puddle to the next, clearly at complete peace with the world. The seagulls had quite a serious impact on me. It is easy to think it is all about survival for other creatures – us humans are supposedly the only ones intelligent enough to desire fun – but that is clearly not the case. Life is all about having fun, whether you be a seagull, a human or a mongoose.

Humans think they know everything, don't they? We are the best, eh? Well, why did I then walk past a policeman pulling a sniffer dog around? Why wasn't the policeman pulling another human around? Because dogs are better sniffers than humans. And seagulls are better fliers than humans. And rabbits are better, urm, hearers than humans. So let's stop being so ruddy arrogant, eh? We're nothing special.

After I got a new phone, a girl standing in the street handed me a free £1 bet voucher to use in the local betting shop. They (whoever they are) say never look a gift horse in the mouth (whatever that means), so I had my £1 on McIlroy to win the Open at 3-1.

I wrote down 'Rory McIlroy to claim the Jug' on my slip and striking blonde Agnieszka (obviously a local lass) looked very confused, so I explained that I meant 'win the tournament' and she gave me 3-1. Every little helps.

The buzz of the betting shop hit me like an anvil – I always feel at ease around punters – and I elected to stay a while longer to have some dog bets. I had £6 on Trap Three at 5-2 in the 12.27 at Hove, which won by half the track, then £5 on Trap Two at 9-4 in the 12.32 at Oxford, which also led his rivals a merry dance.

I felt quite smug. That has backfired on you, hasn't it Mr Ladbroke? You gave me a free £1 bet to lure me into your shop and tempt me into punting on bad-value greyhounds. Well, ha, ha, ha – I had the last laugh – and when Rory wins I'll have taken £29.25 off you because I bumped into your employee. How does that make you feel?

Back in the kitchen, chilled out from my little break, I walked past something you don't see every day. An attractive police officer. She was even carrying handcuffs – the kinky bitch.

I was less impressed by a bloke who was wearing a Chicago Bears baseball cap, which is definitely the most inappropriate piece of clothing I have seen this week. Was he expecting to see William 'The Refrigerator' Perry on the first tee? What a douchebag.

With Rory's 1.31pm tee-time fast approaching, I was getting concerned about how strong the wind was becoming, with the roof on the media centre threatening to come off. I was pretty demoralised by the prospect of 35mph winds blowing the McIlroy Open challenge off course, so I found a quiet corner to come to terms with the tragedy, knowing the trading community would definitely be choosing this moment to lay off if they were in my position.

I didn't lay off a bean, though. Life is too short to dilly-dally. I want some fun – like the rabbits munching on leafy weeds, like the seagulls flapping their wings in the sky, like the dogs sniffing out semtex – and winning £45,000 would be fun.

The Open organisers might be doing all they can to scupper this bet – suspending play for more than an hour and then sending the players back out in identical conditions was not the R&A's finest moment – but despite McIlroy's 80 I certainly haven't given up on it yet.

There is much golf to be played this weekend. Much ruddy golf. As The Carpenters would put it: We've only just begun.

Saturday, July 17

My head was thick (even thicker than normal) because I had spent the previous night imbibing quite heavily to get over the trauma of watching gale-force winds ruin McIlroy's second round.

I felt sad when walking beside the 18th fairway on his final hole of round two, but sadness was replaced by raw anger when a trio of rowdy Australians (are there any other type of Australian?) shouted all sorts of nonsense up at the green when Rory and his playing partners were putting.

The problem with late weather-delayed Open finishes is not just that it ruins the flow of the tournament, but that morons who have been drinking all day suddenly become a serious nuisance.

When one of the Australians (I will never again use the more affectionate term of Aussies) sarcastically called out "Good luck" while Rory was about to putt for par, a serious rage built up inside my body that left me with the decision to either murder the offender and face a stretch behind bars or get to a public house and drink several pints of calming ale.

Mortified by the way the afternoon had unfolded, I propped up the bar in a little pub called The Raisin, where Friday-night revellers were going about their business without a care in the world and I stood out like the sorest of sore thumbs.

Walking around a golf course all day without taking on board any fluids can leave you prune-like by the end of the day, so I was a prune standing in The Raisin, swiftly drinking three pints of Carling Black Label without having the slightest urge to visit what posh folk like to call the lavatory.

People who felt sorry for the tragic loner at the bar started talking to me when they ordered drinks. I told one bloke I still felt McIlroy had a chance to get back into the tournament over the next couple of days and in the most patronising tone I have ever heard anyone say anything he replied: "You can't shoot 80 and win a Major, son."

Oh right, thanks for that pearl of wisdom, pal. I love the way he included the word Major. If he had said you can't shoot 80 and win a golf tournament, I wouldn't have been so riled, but he nonchalently threw in Major like he was some kind of sage. According to him, you can shoot 80 in an event like the John Deere Classic, where a par score is about 59, but not in a Major, where scores are always much higher. He deserved to be murdered too.

I ended the night with a pizza from the takeaway round the corner, then found a nice bench to eat it on, and the incident that followed just about sums up what a day to forget it was. A young man called Hamish parked himself down next to me for a chat and, unless I'm very much mistaken, made a romantic play for me.

I knew it was time to run for the hills when he weighed in with the line: "Do you want a lift home?" How unlucky can I get? When I was in St Andrews in 2005, I met and enjoyed a brief dalliance with a beautiful Texan girl, but this time I spent the week alone until the only gay in the village decided he wanted to cosy up to me. Infuriating.

Back at the course for third-round day, the sun was out for the first time since Monday night and optimism abounded once again that McIlroy could haul his way back into contention. I pressed up with £50 at 45-1 and had £250 on Kaymer at the same price.

Spectators were loving the improved weather and a Spanish couple were playing with their toddler daughter beside the second fairway. The beaming father had his arms outstretched to catch her as she ran towards him, but to everyone's horror she fell over on a mound and started crying. The humps and bumps of St Andrews have made many people burst into tears down the years.

I don't think she was badly hurt – more a blow to her pride than anything else (can two-year-olds feel pride?) – but the Open first-aid unit was only a few hundred yards away. I thought about popping in there to ask if they had anything to fix hearts broken by second-round 80s, but I had to rush to the first tee instead to see McIlroy commence round three.

I had planned to give Rory a Graham Taylor-style pep-talk to pick his chin up off the floor (what we've got to do is go to St Andrews and, if at all possible, win that tournament), but when I started chatting to him he knew he still had a good chance and was just praying not to have another 18 holes being bashed about by the wind.

A short, sharp blast of rain suddenly burst from the sky while he was about to putt from short range for birdie on the first – and I was once again cursing the weather gods (or the weather sods as I now call them) – and as I followed McIlroy over a frustrating first four holes the continual cries of "Come on Rory" were also started to grate.

It reminded me of when I used to play five-a-side football every Sunday night and had people 'encouraging' me from the sidelines. I had the touch of an angel but an unreliable engine, so in the closing stages the "Come on Steve" shouts would exasperate me. Come on Steve? I couldn't move, let alone come on anything.

Rory knows he wants to 'come on' so leave him to it. Or use your imagination if you want to lend vocal support. "Come on Rory" is too basic – how about "Light up the links you little bundle of brilliance". If someone shouted that, I would give them a round of applause.

Following the rest of the round in the media centre, the most depressing words I've heard in a long while were "He's up against the wall" from a *News Of The World* character who was listening to a radio feed. I quickly laid £50 at 47-1 to extinguish the press-up and the double-bogey at the Road Hole was like having a dagger shoved through my underpants.

What a stupid place to put a road.

Sunday, July 18

After a Saturday evening spent drinking in the company of some superstars – Els was enjoying himself in the Jigger Inn while Duval and Allenby kicked back in the Old Course Hotel bar – I didn't expect Sunday to reach the same dizzy heights.

My morale was already on the way back down when I walked past DJ Spoony en route to my lodgings and he was getting all sorts of acclaim from various people. All he does is put one record on, then swap it for another one. Does that really deserve any acclaim?

My hopes of winning money from the Open were slim – McIlroy had an 11-shot deficit to overcome while Kaymer was seven adrift – so a relaxed final day on the links was in store. I pressed up on McIlroy and Kaymer on Betfair (£40 at 169-1 on the former, £160 at 16-1 on the latter) and had £500 on Rory to win his twoball against Ricky Barnes at 8-11 to give me some sort of betting interest, but it was essentially a Louis Oosthuizen-ruined tournament.

With plenty of blisters on my feet from a week of walking, I decided to position myself by the practice putting green for several hours to take stock, watching dozens of players fine-tune their flat-stick technique. And to entertain myself, I got stuck into the 'would I rather be him than me?' game, a past time I hadn't played in a long while.

My first subject matter was Tom Lehman, which was a tricky starter. He is 51, so I might have a few more years to live than him, but then he can look back on a very successful golfing career, including his Open victory of 1996. It must be nice to sit by the log-fire as Tom Lehman, watching a video of that Lytham triumph while sucking on a packet of Werther's Original. So, yes, I would rather be Tom Lehman than me.

Beside him on the putting green was Fredrik Andersson Hed, and again, it took me a little while to reach a judgement on him. He is a healthy 38-year-old, he won the Italian Open this year and is enjoying a very lucrative season on the European Tour. But he has got a very silly name, hasn't he?

Hmmm, could I put up with the "You've got a silly name" jibes? Yes, I would rather be him than me.

Cink was next to appear at the putting green. He's got no hair and is five years older than me, but he has drunk from the Claret Jug and constantly has peace of mind because he completely believes in The Lord, so I would rather be him than me.

Now then, who's this angry-looking chap? He's got lovely teeth. Oh, it's that Tiger Woods character. Hmmm. Probably the greatest golfer of all time and had arguably the greatest life of all time up until a few months ago, but now everyone thinks he is evil.

I wouldn't like to go to bed at night with everyone thinking I was evil. But yes – no matter how difficult it is for him to sleep at night – I would definitely rather be Tiger Woods than me.

After a couple of hours by the green, I noticed how sore my lips had become, with the week's sharp breezes having sapped all the moisture from my face. I would have given someone £20 for a tube of lip balm. You should never leave home without your lip balm. How did cavemen survive in the dark ages before lip balm had been invented? Did all caveman have chapped lips? I'll guess we'll never know.

Back to the game. Overton? Yes, him. Mickelson? Such a joker – always buzzing – yep, definitely him.

Donald? Him. Stephen Gallacher was blowing his nose a lot and might have a cold, so in the short term, me (sore lips are easier to handle than a cold), but long term, him. He has won almost 500,000 euros on the European Tour this year and can probably afford the finest hankerchiefs money can buy.

I got chatting to a couple of the 'spotters' who go around with each group to track the balls and they were having trouble identifying the players they had been assigned to help.

"What does Kevin Na look like?" one of them asked me. I pointed out Na and he said: "Oh, that Chinese fella?" I replied: "Born in South Korea but has lived in California most of his life." He couldn't get his head around that.

"What about Marino?" said the other chap. "Look for a beard," I told him. After asking me who I worked for, he weighed in with: "It always amuses me the amount of people that bet." I didn't really know how to respond to that. Hang around with me mate and you'll be laughing your cotton socks off.

Montgomerie was coming up the 18th fairway as we chatted. A big groan went up when his ball pitched just short of pin-high and rolled back into the Valley of Sin. Monty and groans never seem to be far apart. "He's a nightmare to spot for," said one of my new spotting friends. "They say he's very charming off the course, but on it he is rather fidgety."

There is a section for specially invited disabled golf fans to watch the action from just to the right of the first tee and one late arrival was driving her mobility scooter to a prime spot just a few yards from where Mickelson was passing by. I don't know why I found this funny, but it was the most I laughed all day. A mobility scooter provided a peculiar backdrop for a man known as Phil The Thrill.

Jimenez (him) was practising putting with a thick cigar hanging from his mouth. Tiger was still working away too and they greeted each other like long-lost pals. Miguel affectionately stroked Tiger's arm in a rather fatherly fashion.

Someone certainly needs to give Master Woods a few words of fatherly advice. Amid an abysmal display of putting on the green, he suddenly holed a 50-foot snake, which was greeted with whoops, hollers and a cry of "Good luck, Tiger" from a lad who was standing two yards away from him. But there was not a flicker on the chops of Woods, who remained stony-faced throughout his session, seemingly determined to ignore all those around him. Would a little smile have been that hard?

Seagulls were squawking up above at this point and Tiger looked slightly concerned. Would I have been the only one who would have found it amusing if a gull had deposited all over his blood-red shirt? One of his minders would probably have fired a missile to intercept any falling turd anyway.

Garcia was next up, wearing a star on his shirt to symbolise the Spanish World Cup success. I would rather be Sergio than me, but he would probably rather be Xabi Alonso than him. There is a chain of desire that leads to the most content man on the planet, whoever that may be.

I ended my game and left the green when Retief Goosen started chipping on the edge of it. You may have won a couple of US Opens, buster, but you would get chucked out of my local course if you started chipping on the putting green there, let alone at the Home of Golf. I can't believe the marshals didn't intervene.

Well, there it is. Another dismal Open with another champion hardly anyone backed, and yet another tournament where my chronic inability to place each-way bets has savaged my bank balance. I had £2,670 win-only on McIlroy when £1,335 each-way at 17-1 (which Paddy Power were when I laid down my initial chunks) would have returned £7,008.75.

I'm now so full of self-loathing, I'd rather be Bruce Forsyth.

CHAPTER 18

DRY AS A BONE

Nicolas Colsaerts

Monday, July 19

A long drive south from St Andrews. Departed at nine, arrived at nine. I'm sure in the future it will be possible to cover 525 miles instantly in some kind of Tardis-like machine, but this journey took 12 hours.

On the way home, it dawned on me that my No. 1 choices for the first three Majors of the season have all finished in the places (Mickelson in the Masters, Mickelson in the US Open and McIlroy in the Open) and before next year's Masters I am definitely going to place a potentially life-changing each-way treble. That's something to look forward to.

At least I've got something to look forward to. Halfway through my drive back, I saw a lorry-load of lambs parked at a service station. They were clearly on their way to an abattoir and it was heartbreaking to see them crammed together, baaing away in distress. For these poor little blighters, it was all over bar the baaing.

When the truck driver popped inside the service station for a pee, leaving the lambs unattended, I thought about attempting to unlock the back door of the truck to release my doomed woolly friends. But my dad said I would be arrested for a breach of the peace and that the lambs would probably wander on to the nearby motorway.

A stun gun to the head or mowed down by a Vauxhall Zafira? Either way the lambs would be silenced. I shouted "murderer" at the driver when he returned to make myself feel a bit better, but I couldn't look the lambs in the eye as the truck wheeled away.

Tuesday, July 20

Suffering from Volkswagen-lag, I assembled my Scandinavian Masters wagers, having £182 on Hanson at 19-1, £170 on Fowler at 20-1, £116 on Willett at 31-1, £43 on Oliver Fisher at 84-1 and £29 on Colsaerts at 129-1. For the Canadian Open, I had £170 on O'Hair at 19-1 and the same stake at the same price on Donald. I also had £20 on Chris DiMarco at 159-1 as well as a £100 double on Fowler (20-1) and O'Hair (18-1).

Wednesday, July 21

Well, Clarice, have the lambs stopped screaming?

Thursday, July 22

Hanson double-bogeyed his final hole to leave me screaming like a butchered lamb.

Friday, July 23

Unconvinced by the leaders in Canada, I pressed up on O'Hair (£82 at 41-1), Donald (£85 at 39-1) and DiMarco (£33 at 249-1), then had a £500 Matchplay arrers accumulator on Wade to beat Wayne Jones (1-7), Whitlock to beat Jelle Klaasen (1-3), Barneveld to beat Stompe (2-7) and Taylor to beat Kevin Painter (1-40).

Saturday, July 24

My arrers accumulator had nailed me a monkey once Taylor had demolished Painter and, as a result, I awoke with an unhealthy lust for punting.

I try not to stake more than a grand on a regulation week of ante-post golf bets and a bag of sand is usually enough to generate sufficient interest in the four days of action, but even with a couple of pre-tournament fancies in contention in the early stages of the Scandinavian Masters third round, I did not feel an adequate twitching of the adrenal glands. I was like Oliver Twist – I wanted more.

Maybe it was because I had a £50,000 green figure next to McIlroy's name on my Betfair interface during the final round of the Open, but bets on Hanson (who was in position to reel in the leaders from the fifth-to-last group out) and Colsaerts (who had made two early birdies to put himself in the mix) did not get my juices flowing at all.

I was as dry as a bone. A juice-free zone. I'm usually one of the juiciest men on the planet – they call me Mr Moist in places and I have the ability to impregnate women from ten yards away – but my body wasn't secreting any juice at the prospect of a potential three-and-a-half bag return. My adrenal glands were defunct.

During the first round of the Open, when McIlroy was making merry, adrenalin was bursting from my every pore. The adrenal glands were twitching like Bill Oddie on steroids. But unfortunately when you've been test-driving a Ferrari for a week, slipping back into your Mini Metro is a huge comedown, so I had to quickly up the stakes on Hanson and Colsaerts to get some sap into my parched skin.

I had £200 on Hanson at 15-1 and £100 on Colsaerts at 60-1 just as he was putting the finishing touches to a three-under-par front nine. I then had a further £50 on Colsaerts at 64-1 after he had birdied the tenth hole.

Hanson got off to a horror start and never recovered, but Colsaerts compiled a 68 that only one player could better in the third round. With Choi five shots ahead of Colsaerts, though, my man was again dismissed as an also-ran going into round four, Betfair punters happily laying enormous prices about the big-hitting Belgian boy.

I couldn't understand why he was being shown such a lack of respect, so I had another £20 at an average of 132-1, meaning he would win me more than £15,000 if he could overcome the five-shot deficit on the final day.

I had a few beers in the evening to add a little more fluid to my arid carcass, inadvertently sending new father Trifleface to the doghouse when we didn't conclude our drinking session until very late. He has quickly discovered that new-born babies don't do anything positive – they are either crying or pooing (or both simultaneously) – and the lure of peaceful beers, baguettes and benches proved too much for him.

When he was close himself to crying and pooing in the early hours, he eventually returned home. If you can't beat 'em, join 'em, eh?

Sunday, July 25

Colsaerts got off to another fast start and was soon stalking the leaders. By the time he birdied the ninth hole, he was clear at the top and trading at 7-4 for victory.

Colsaerts' great strength is his natural power and with three par-fives on the back nine, I was loath to lay off at that point (well, even more so than normal), and I held my position. The 12th and 13th holes were back-to-back par-fives, so my plan was to see him through those two (expecting him to pick up at least a shot), then strongly consider the possibility of doing some trading.

A par at 12 and another one at 13 were not what the doctor ordered. He was still tied for the lead, but on the drift. This was the point I had pinpointed to start laying – several bags could have been 'locked in' (as the traders love to say) – but I dilly-dallied.

The 14th was a relatively straightforward par-four and the 15th was the final par-five. Right, I'll wait until he is through the 15th and then lay like a rampant rabbit before Colsaerts hits the difficult final three holes.

The best-laid lay plans of mice and men often go awry, eh? If par-par through 12 and 13 was slightly disappointing, bogey-bogey through 14 and 15 was like having a hungry Alsatian let loose at your lunchbox (very disappointing).

I had blown it. I had missed my opportunity. The fun was over. After Colsaerts had hit his tee shot into the water off the 15th tee, I managed to lay £4 at 69-1. Not quite the trade I had been mulling over two holes previously.

It was a sunny day outside and had I had no golfers in contention for the Scandinavian Masters title, I probably would have enjoyed a wonderful time frolicking in God's garden, but instead I endured a dark, miserable time in my lounge, a fly-by-night Belgian teasing me rotten before turning frigid at the business end.

I did not have to wait long before the leaders went out in the Canadian Open. I was still hoping Donald could shoot a super-low final round to bring home the bacon, but I also added Clark (£200 at 11-2) to my staking plan.

A frustrating night followed. Donald and Clark were tied for second at one point, hot on the heels of long-time leader Dean Wilson, and when Wilson wobbled I fancied my chances of ending the day on a high. My men failed to take advantage, though, and Pettersson clicked up a gear to sweep past everyone for victory.

Oh, Sunday. Bloody Sunday.

Monday, July 26

Having frittered money away so recklessly during the previous week's golf – not being sufficiently excited by ante-post investments and quickly leaping into in-running press-ups – I decided to have a proper pre-tournament punt that would retain my interest throughout. I was planning another chunk on Rory.

And the time had come to bet each-way. Many a pal has suggested I would be a millionaire by now if I had always done my golf bets each-way – so many win-only selections seem to fall just shy – and I am now looking to slightly revise my tactics. I just hope the horse hasn't bolted.

First up I had £250 on Ross Fisher to win the Irish Open at 22-1, £135 on Clarke at 39-1 and £115 on Lowry at 47-1. Then I had £100 each-way on Trevor Immelman for the Greenbrier Classic at 50-1, then £50 each-way tickles on DiMarco (90-1) and Gay (70-1).

Tuesday, July 27

I had my fourth-ever golf lesson in the evening, which comprised a three-hole match against club professional Bevan, and much to everyone's surprise I romped to a convincing victory.

I chipped in for birdie at the first, holed a 20-foot left-to-right snake for bogey at the second and then speared a five-wood straight at the flag on the final hole that was inches away from resulting in an ace.

"You do realise that had nothing to do with you," chuckled the bewildered pro, revelling in his successful tutelage.

I'm planning 28 years of intensive practice, then will be making a serious assault on the seniors circuit when I turn 60. If the Champions Tour schedule remains the same, my debut event will be the Dick's Sporting Goods Open in New York at the end of June 2038. See you there, Dick.

Wednesday, July 28

Had £1,000 each-way on McIlroy at 7-1.

Thursday, July 29

An Irish horse-loving pal of mine told me Aattash was a tremendous bet in the 2.10 at Goodwood, so I had a tickle (£35 win at 18-1, £15 place at 11-4). I should have tickled something else.

Friday, July 30

Punting frustration is setting in and the evidence of last weekend indicates that four-figure winners do not set my pulse racing any more – only five-figure ones get me going now.

I guess punters who start getting five-figure winners on a regular basis then start getting bored of them and need to chase six-figure winners. I'll settle for successfully following in their footsteps, but there is obviously much more chance of me losing everything in the process.

Patience has never been my strong point, but when the likes of Alex Higgins are dying at the age of 61, there doesn't seem a lot of point to tip-toeing towards a happy retirement. Official retirement age is 65, so after 33 years of toil I can retire a weary man, or I can blow like a Hurricane and try to hit the punting jackpot as soon as possible.

CHAPTER 19

STALKER ALERT

Trifleface, Simon, Teri, Steve, Keith, Ali and Carl

Saturday, July 31

The worst thing that can happen is the worst thing that can happen, as a wise man once told me.

I foolishly believed sixth place was the worst possible position McIlroy could finish in an Irish Open short of strength in depth, so invested a grand each-way ante-post with gay abandon, but the little master stumbled into the pack as the tournament wore on in Killarney to put me under severe punting pressure.

With the three outsiders I had backed in the US Tour event having failed to make an impression, my £2,900 outlay on the golf was looking a tad reckless, but fortunately one wager (my £250 on Fisher to triumph in Ireland at 22-1) was still going extremely strong.

I threw a speculative £50 at Aaron Baddeley for the Greenbrier Classic at 28-1 but this weekend had become all about the Fisherman. I was floundering stricken in a dark swamp, with thieving octopuses pinching £20 notes from my pockets at regular intervals, but the

Fisherman was dangling his rod tantalisingly close to my grasp in an attempt to rescue me and his tackle-box contained a £5,750 'welcome back to dry land' gift-voucher with my name on it.

Fisher went into the third round with a three-shot lead and soon forged further clear with four birdies in his first seven holes. Feeling the tension lift from my shoulders, I decided to break free from the golf-watching shackles for a little while, heading off to see Weymouth FC in their latest pre-season friendly.

The manager lives in the same block of flats as me, so I feel almost obliged to show my neighbourly support for his team, despite the fact my home-town club are now virtually a lost cause. I used to watch the Terras home and away, but the days of 'living the dream' under Steve Claridge have long since passed and the prospect of starting this season in the Zamaretto League with a ten-point deduction for financial irregularities doesn't exactly set the pulse racing.

"League football in our lifetime!" used to be the motto of me and my pals, with promotion to what is now League Two a genuine ambition, but that has been revised to "League football in our grandchildren's grandchildren's lifetime!" in recent years as the wheels have fallen off spectacularly.

As much as I tried to forget about golf and concentrate on the football, with the teenagers entrusted to represent my town doing well enough to take a 4-0 advantage into half-time against the might of Longwell Green, I simply could not muster the enthusiasm to stay for another 45 minutes.

Before games in the distant past, my mates and I used to text each other 'Meet you behind the goal we're attacking. NEM'. NEM stood for Nothing Else Matters (we were utterly devoted followers), but plenty of things seem to matter more these days because I hardly knew anyone in attendance. It was time to get back to the sofa.

I was hoping to be greeted by a Fisher price of 1-10 or shorter, but his lead had eroded and he finished the day only one shot to the good. I was facing another Sunday being molested by octopuses in that metaphorical swamp, staring up wantonly at Ross's resplendent rod.

Sunday, August 1

Fisher-mania was all I could think about – the golfing week was either going to end in a hefty win or an equally considerable loss – but having spent so much time stressing about this silly sport of late I decided I owed it to The Lord to get out of the house for a bit on the traditional day of praise.

I had been invited to a gathering where a few new mothers were showing off, quite literally, the fruits of their labour. Various pals have become fathers in recent months and all the proud parents were getting together to spend an afternoon in a coffee shop inspecting each other's off spring.

As strong favourite to become godfather to Trifleface's daughter (she couldn't want for a better guide through the potential pitfalls of modern life), I felt obliged to attend this baby convention, even though the last coffee shop I had visited was in a rather insalubrious district of Amsterdam.

It felt strange to be behaving like a normal human being for a change. I supped on a hot chocolate (I don't like coffee) and we all chatted about the babies (while I received regular text updates from Killarney). Ooh, look at me, I thought to myself. Mr Coffee Shop – acting like an adult. Maybe I'm not such a freak after all.

My focus soon waned, though. I flirted with a few WAGS, made some typically inappropriate comments, then headed back to follow Fisher's progress on the old gogglebox.

I had intended to go straight home, but could not turn down the chance to take in a spot of professional beach volleyball en route, which is probably the best-value free entertainment on the planet. Fighting-fit fillies wearing hardly any clothes were leaping all over the place in their quest to become volleyball champions. And, during any breaks in play, dancing girls in hotpants strutted into the arena to keep the crowd entranced. It all felt so wrong, yet at the same time, so ruddy right.

Men who visit lap-dancing clubs are looked down upon by society as lecherous perverts, but throw some sand into the equation and a little bouncy ball, and suddenly this pursuit turns into a family fun day!

I returned to the torture chamber of my lounge just in time to see Padraig Harrington putting the willies up Fisher, but my man steadied himself to get the job done, meaning I was loaded once again.

The day was going swimmingly but unfortunately the Greenbrier Classic stepped in to end my feeling of euphoria. Because I had such a chunk on McIlroy for the Irish Open, I tried to trim my Greenbrier Classic shortlist to as small as possible, and the last two names to face the axe (cutting the list from five to three) were Sergio Garcia at 40-1 and Stuart Appleby at 75-1.

Appleby's final-round 59, which saw him cut through the field like a hot knife through hot butter for victory, was a savage late dig to the bread-basket.

Monday, August 2
I was dripping in ammunition thanks to Fisher and lined up some each-way hand grenades, having £175 each-way on Donald for the Bridgestone Invitational at 35-1, £125 each-way on O'Hair at 50-1, £75 each-way on Cink at 80-1 and £50 each-way on Scott at 100-1.

Then I turned my mind to the Turning Stone Resort Championship, having £150 each-way on Howell at 25-1, £120 each-way on Sabbatini at 33-1, £60 each-way on Sim at 66-1, £60 each-way on JJ Henry at 66-1 and the same stake at the same price on Andres Romero. I also threw in a £50 each-way double on Donald and Howell (33-1 and 25-1) for added interest.

Tuesday, August 3
I set off on a two-day trip to London for some business at *Racing Post* headquarters. I can't believe inspectors on the train still use the ludicrous line "Any unchecked tickets please?" to identify fare evaders. No wonder the honest mugs like me who buy a valid ticket before boarding have to pay so ruddy much for them.

Wednesday, August 4
Returning south in the evening, I foolishly forgot to press the lock

button on the electronic train toilet when popping for a tinkle. It is such a complicated procedure – you have got to press open, walk in, then press close, then press lock. They must have been designed by such a mischievous character. Why can't the door just lock automatically after closing?

Well, the door opened while I was in the process of doing up my strides, a horrified woman getting all a fluster as she baulked on entry.

Had she arrived five seconds earlier, given the pan is directly behind the door, that incident would definitely have entered the top five most awkward moments of my life. "That could have been a lot worse," I joked to the red-faced woman as I eased sheepishly past her.

Thursday, August 5

I don't usually get involved in threeball or twoball betting because the odds are never sufficiently big to excite me, but eager for more punting action I slipped a £250 Bridgestone first-round accumulator on which comprised Appleby to beat James Kingston (4-7), Ben Curtis to beat Ross McGowan (4-6), Van Pelt to beat Martin Laird (8-11) and Watney to beat Mike Weir (4-6).

Friday, August 6

The twoball four-fold, which took five minutes to devise, won me £1,635. That works out as a £327-a-minute wage. And some people still like to call betting 'a mugs' game'?

Mugs.

Saturday, August 7

There was no day time golf to enjoy and the top-flight football season was yet to start, so I again got tempted into spending an afternoon watching Weymouth continue their preparations for the impending Zamaretto League campaign.

This was no ordinary pre-season friendly – it was a clash with deadly rivals Dorchester – and I got my face painted terracotta, filled my holdall with a vast array of weaponry and braced myself for

90 minutes defending my town's honour in the civil war of Dorset.

I do, of course, jest. In the past, this fixture would attract a bumper crowd and really matter to me (being one of 3,734 who witnessed an 8-0 home win on Boxing Day 2003 was one of the highlights of my life), but this time it was just a way of killing a couple of hours before the third round of the Bridgestone Invitational golf resumed.

I had to chuckle when the plucky PA played rock classic 'The Final Countdown' at 2.55pm, trying to whip the 560 spectators into a frenzy. I saw an old fella standing along from me react by stirring his cup of tea, but I think the PA was hoping to create a little more fervour than that.

I had a few pints afterwards to perk me up (even though it was essentially meaningless, the 3-1 defeat still irked a little), then I dropped into my favourite bookies to meet the shop manager for a swift ale during his dinner break.

While I was waiting for him, I thought I would have a quick dog bet, so I got to work on the formguide, but then a burly bloke I didn't know bowled over with some intensity in his eyes and growled: "I've been looking for you all day."

My immediate reaction was: Oh Christ – this must be the husband, boyfriend or father of a woman I've made unwelcome sexual advances to at some point recently.

The instinctive animalistic fight-or-flight response suddenly kicked through my nervous system. Shall I fight him? Hmmmm, he is much bigger than me, I'm wearing a rather flimsy pair of trainers (I find feet are always crucial in fight situations) and I don't really want to get banned from my favourite betting shop.

Or shall I take flight? Hmmmm, this is surely the best option. I was like a grazing zebra who had spotted a lion approaching. The fact I was smaller and wearing light shoes became advantages in this scenario, and I couldn't get banned from the shop for running, could I? The whole shop is based around people betting on galloping zebras (well, sort of), so it would be extremely hypocritical if they objected to me acting like one.

Just as I was about to take off, though, my pursuer explained why he had devoted his day to trying to find me and I was able to graze calmly on the dog form once again.

He was a keen punter and *Racing Post* reader who had come all the way from Torquay, setting off just after 7am, to spend the weekend in Weymouth with the aim of meeting me. He had trawled the betting shops of the town from 11am asking after me and then, eight hours into his mission, I strolled through the doors of the Corals on the seafront and into his clutches.

He was waxing lyrical about the Sunday column, detailing his passion for punting and asking if he could buy me a drink or two, while I went flush with embarrassment (I've always struggled with taking compliments).

I was relieved I did not have to fight or flight, but my thoughts turned to the episode of Alan Partridge where he bumps into his 'biggest fan' and is held hostage in a Partridge shrine as the fan pulls up his shirt to reveal a life-size tattoo of the radio presenter on his chest.

This chap didn't seem to be what Partridge would describe as 'a mentalist', though, so I accepted his drink offer, and the prospect of briefly imbibing with him became more alluring when he mentioned he had come down with his "24-year-old blonde barmaid girlfriend". This guy clearly knew my areas of weakness.

And so the ale flowed. I introduced Simon, who is a hotel singer/ comedian in Torquay, and his girlfriend Teri to some of my usual drinking partners, my pals completely bewildered by the fact I had 'a fan', and getting home for the start of the Bridgestone Invitational coverage became impossible.

Simon later said his dad had rung to ask "have you found him yet?", so I had to speak to him, and fortunately he was at home watching the golf. He informed me O'Hair was leading in the clubhouse on nine under par and that Scott also had some hope of success.

Simon was eager to get his photo taken with people he had read about in the betting diary. Trifleface was greeted like a king and could not believe the level of acclaim he was getting. A humble postman who is used to anonymously dropping letters through front doors, with angry dogs usually the only ones looking to get a piece of him, was enjoying some hero-worship for the first time in his life.

I was equally bemused by the whole situation but fortunately too inebriated to worry and, according to reports, I gave Teri a very affectionate kiss on the cheek as they departed in the early hours. I don't think Simon minded, though. There is a bit of a grey area when it comes to your heroes and your partner. My friend Keith is a massive New Order fan and he has always said he would let lead singer Bernard Sumner make love to his wife if it meant he got to meet him. But I don't know what Keith's wife, Laura, would make of it all if Bernard suddenly turned up at their house expecting to seal the deal. These transactions surely need three consenting parties to run smoothly.

Sunday, August 8

I woke up fully clothed on my sofa and in poor condition. Before going to bed I checked the golf scores and saw that Sabbatini still had a good chance of getting in the places in the Turning Stone Resort Championship and O'Hair had held on to his lead in Ohio.

A strawberry milkshake and a sea swim, the best hangover cure I know, set me up nicely for the night's golf and, although O'Hair's poor putting touch cost him victory, he brought home the each-way bacon with fifth place.

At Turning Stone, Henry fired a final-round 63 to claim second place and Sim tied for third, so I had well over three grand coming back from place money. I've come to the conclusion that each-way is certainly not gay. It can make you gay (as in happy), but even masculine men bursting with heterosexuality should never be ashamed to grab some each-way value.

Sabbatini finished eighth and Scott finished ninth. If they had contributed to the place-money too, I would have been rolling in it, and I went to bed with an outrageous thought. Is it possible to conjure an each-way facespitter?

CHAPTER 20

PREMIER AMBITIONS

Joe Hart

Monday, August 9

Spent the evening devising my plan of attack on the USPGA
Championship and found little in the way of value at the top of the

market. With many firms offering each-way terms of a quarter the odds the first six places, five outsiders who were being underrated tickled my fancy, and I had £400 each-way on Scott at 66-1, £125 each-way on Garcia at 90-1, £100 each-way on Ogilvy at 100-1, £75 each-way on Cink at 125-1 and £50 each-way on Immelman at 200-1.

Sadly, I stumbled across a programme called 'The World At War: Genocide' after going to bed, which told the horrific story of war-time concentration camps, the gas chambers, and the millions who were murdered by the Nazis.

I was sickened to my very core by what I saw and also with the poor quality of the history lessons at my school. I could tell you everything about General Custer and the Battle of Little Bighorn (basically cowboys and Indians nonsense from the late 1800s), but my lessons hardly touched at all on the World Wars.

I never knew the full extent of what happened in those concentration camps until watching this programme. Seriously heartbreaking stuff.

Tuesday, August 10

Had £10 on King Of Reason at Ffos Las at evens and then £20 on Trap Two at Newcastle at evens, turning £10 into £40 in ten minutes. You can't beat a good even-money chance, can you?

Wednesday, August 11

Was handed a set of photographs from Simon and Teri of the Saturday-night action, which they had posted to the betting shop from Torquay. In the grip of lager, I don't remember them being taken. I think Wayne Rooney was caught out in similar fashion when he was pictured urinating up against a wheelie bin a couple of weeks ago.

With Henrik Stenson labouring badly with illness, it seemed madness that he was sharing favouritism with Hanson for top Scandinavian honours in the USPGA, so I had £300 each-way on the fighting-fit and in-form Swede at 4-1 (a quarter the odds the first three).

Had another illuminating episode of World At War been on in the evening, I would not have watched England's friendly against Hungary, but I got sucked in and ended up having £100 on 2-0 at 9-2 after the goalless first half. As it turned out, it would have been a successful wager but for an over-zealous French linesman. Instead, I ended up losing £150 (had £50 on 1-1 at 2-1 after Hungary had taken the lead).

Thursday, August 12

Fog delayed the start of the USPGA. How very inconsiderate of The Lord, eh? Actually, I can't pretend any longer. After watching World At War on Monday, I simply can't believe in The Lord anymore. Are you going to tell me he let that 'happen for a reason'?

Friday, August 13

I need to treat the impending Premier League football season with extreme caution. That England game provided further compelling evidence that it is impossible to have a strong opinion on the correct score of a football match.

Just think about it for a bit. You see? It is impossible.

Saturday, August 14

With my system full of ale and feeling typically sluggish, the USPGA leaderboard made for disturbing reading, with none of my ante-post wagers landing a blow. A £1,500 loss was long odds-on and my winning streak appeared to be coming to an abrupt end.

I decided to have £100 on Els at 49-1 to give me another string to my feeble bow, but I certainly wasn't resembling the Robin Hood of Whistling Straits, my new each-way policy threatening to cost me dear.

Still, it was the first day of the Premier League football season, so who cared? Tottenham were about to play Man City on the box and suddenly weekends had a bit of structure to them once again.

Married men usually wake up at weekends and have a hectic schedule of events mapped out for them by their wife – the weekly shop, a trip to the garden centre, change that nappy, change this nappy, build a fence there, knock that fence down, etc – but the single man lacks such direction.

It is a positive to not have to push a trolley around Asda, fake admiration for a pot plant, get a face full of baby turd or perform unpaid manual labour, but without a set of football fixtures to work from, a blank canvas can take plenty of filling.

Not anymore. City's line-up was ludicrously defensive – Roberto Mancini opted for the sort of park-the-bus selection that a team like Chievo (well, a rich man's Chievo) would employ away at Inter – and I thought the White Hart Lane clash had bore draw written all over it.

But avoiding correct-score betting is one of my two main rules of the new campaign (along with not punting until I know the team line-ups), so I had a conservative £500 on under 2.5 goals at a fraction bigger than even-money.

City cat Joe Hart was magnificent and almost single-handedly (actually he used both hands for some saves) won me £510, but I couldn't help taking a little peek at the correct-score market on Betfair as the minutes ticked by to full-time just to see at what price 0-0 had traded. It had been matched at 16-1 and I was already starting to question my new strategy.

For the 3pm kick-offs I had two draw-no-bet wagers – £600 on Everton to beat Blackburn at 8-11 and £400 on Stoke to beat Wolves at 6-5 – as I was convinced defeats for the Toffeemen and the Potters were out of the question.

Unfortunately, defeats for the Toffeemen and the Potters were very much in the question, meaning I swiftly went from £510 up for the day to £490 down. But recent punting successes left me in no mood to quit, so £600 on Chelsea to win to nil against West Brom at 5-6 pumped me back into profit. I made £10 on the day, having staked £2,100. You have got to speculate to accumulate, haven't you?

I celebrated my £10 triumph with a few sherbets, ending my evening with a mission to go up to every person in a nightclub and talk to them. It is what people go to nightclubs to do, isn't it? To socialise.

Well, clearly there is something peculiar about trying to socialise in a nightclub, because pals say I did nothing but frighten the vast majority of those I approached and most conversations concluded swiftly.

I'm not sure I'm ever going to get to grips with the rules of society. If you don't want to socialise, stay at home, yeah?

Sunday, August 15

I believed the shape of the USPGA leaderboard gave Kaymer an excellent opportunity of landing a first Major title, so had £300 on the efficient German at 11-1, before betting attention turned to Liverpool's meeting with Arsenal.

I had £200 on Liverpool to win to nil at 11-4 with Ladbrokes, the type of bet that is tougher to strike than any other over the telephone. The telephonist automatically tries to get you on your team to win 2-0, which is obviously a much more common wager, and explaining you want to nil rather than 2-0 is almost impossible if you get a dozy operator on the other end of the line.

The exasperated Magic Sign telephonist who took this bet actually cried "What does that even mean?" as I tried to guide him through the technicalities of a to-nil wager. I would advise bookmakers to re-name this market 'to win without conceding' to avoid further confusion.

Having battled so manfully to get the bet in place, the last-minute Arsenal equaliser that snatched £750 from my grasp was particularly galling. Welcome back to the world of last-gasp horrors, I said to myself. Do you think I'll have any more of them in the next nine months?

My mood was not aided by having to give a dog-loving mate a lift in my car. He assured me the dog would cause no problems and was "an excellent traveller", but by the time the mutt alighted at their destination, the back seat of my GTI was covered in pungent grey hair.

Apart from being the master of a very fast racing greyhound that can win you lots of money, I'm yet to see the value in owning a dog. Man's best friend, eh? Can't I just have another man as my best friend?

Men don't moult quite as much as dogs.

The early stages of the USPGA final round went well – Hanson scraped the top-Scandinavian place return (£600) – and Kaymer soon eased his way to the top of the leaderboard.

Even though he needed to hole a considerable putt at the final hole of regulation play to qualify for the play-off, I was confident at all times that Kaymer would emerge triumphant and did not have any further wagers.

In fact, I was disgusted with myself for not pressing up prior to the play-off because I have always rated Bubba Watson something of a joke golfer who must always be opposed. Anyway, it was another profitable week of golf punting and I walked to bed with the relaxed strut of a financially secure Cancerian.

Monday, August 16

It was ruddy marvellous to have Monday night football back on Sky and I hosted a low-key party (bought some breadsticks and invited a few pals round) to mark the occasion of Man United versus Newcastle. I had £600 on Man United to win to nil at 4-5 (online to avoid any telephone travails), along with £200 on any unquoted scoreline at 3-1, so I managed to sneak £280 to pay for the breadsticks.

Oozing confidence and momentum, I got my Wyndham Championship wagers in play, having £250 on Snedeker at 33-1, £200 on Henry at 49-1, £190 on Jonathan Byrd at 47-1, £170 on Sim at 49-1 and £140 on Marc Leishman at 65.

Tuesday, August 17

My betting-shop manager pal alerted me by text that two new characters had approached him at the counter to ask after me. It seems some *Racing Post* readers are adopting copycat tactics, following in the footsteps of the now legendary Simon, with whom I shared a few beers a couple of weeks ago.

I'm deeply flattered that there is such interest in the diary and will always be courteous to readers, but I urge others to avoid such

The spectacular view from the 'special bench'

Coming to terms with life's challenges on the 'special bench'

Locking horns with the enemy in a betting shop

Beavering away in his Weymouth office

A look of love as Gemma the hairdresser works her magic

Taking stock at the local

Relaxing among the wildlife of his punting lair

Steve and Trifleface enjoy a light snack at their favourite restaurant

Trying to solve another greyhound puzzle

Steve snaps Nick Faldo on his phone as he flies with Team Europe to the 2008 Ryder Cup

Steve smuggles a dart board from a busy pub during some booze-fuelled mayhem

Steve and his pal Henry have a cuddle with Phil Taylor at the World Grand Prix Darts

Steve and Rory McIlroy pose for pictures in Dublin

Steve banters with Terry Venables after again being named the Sports Journalists' Association Betting Writer of the Year

A frazzled Steve ends up on a winning team at Wentworth and is congratulated by Ernie Els

Steve unleashes a three-iron during a golf day at the Grove,
wishing he could play sport for a living

pilgrimages. To be completely honest, I'm a loner at heart, who does not really enjoy adulation. I like adulation from attractive females who are about to smother my body in adulation, but not anyone else.

In the afternoon, I gathered my Czech Open tanks on the lawn, having £320 on Jimenez at 20-1, £250 on Canizares at 28-1, £100 each-way on Garrido at 40-1, £65 each-way on Richie Ramsay at 66-1 and £40 each-way on Zanotti at 100-1. I threw in a £70 win double on Jimenez and Snedeker (20-1 and 33-1) for good measure.

The irrepressible Hamann then texted to inform me that 'Dynamo Kiev is as good an even-money shot as you will ever see'. Having shunned his advice to back MK Dons to beat Walsall on the opening day of the League One season, I felt obliged to follow The Kaiser in this time, so invested £200.

Final score – Dynamo Kiev 1-1 Ajax Amsterdam. If that is the best even-money shot I'm ever going to see, I'll have to make sure I avoid all even-money shots in future, eh Didi?

Wednesday, August 18

It was Carnival Day in Weymouth, allowing me to bowl around saying to everyone: "Ooh, there's a carnival atmosphere, isn't there?"

I think that is my second favourite wisecrack behind sitting in a sauna and saying: "Ooh, it's like a sauna in here, isn't it?"

The highlight of Carnival Day is always the Red Arrows display, although I was demoralised to discover that one of the pilots was only 30 years of age. This lad is two years younger than me yet part of the world's leading aerobatic team. I'm so jealous. He must have had better parents than me.

I was watching the action with Trifleface and he got a little over-excited when the Red Arrows were using their vapour trails to create a giant love heart in the sky. As they started doing it from the top down, the commentator asked in Rolf Harris style: "Can you guess what it is yet?"

"It's the Golden Arches!" shouted Trifles – he thought the pilots were in the process of making a colourful McDonald's logo – but big boy's prediction was well wide of the mark.

I later tried to win a stuffed cow. I like to adorn my lounge with animals – I've got tigers, crocodiles, cats, chickens, snakes, spiders, etc, livening up the room – and the prospect of claiming a prize cow, complete with a mooing button, proved too much.

Trouble is, it seemed virtually (and was possibly completely) impossible to win (by getting a baseball into the tiny entrance of a large milk jug from three yards) and at £3 for five attempts I was fast damaging the wallet, so I gave up and asked if I could just buy one, being quoted £24.99.

This raised my suspicions further – that is not the sort of figure you would just pluck from the air – but my strong desire for the cow meant I handed over the wedge anyway.

As you can imagine, carrying a cow from the busy town centre to my house made me the centre of attention, with comments ranging from the tragically simplistic ("Hey, cow!") to the more imaginative ("Oi, oi – Farmer Palmer's pulled for once!").

Thursday, August 19
Was struck down with Zamaretto fever and enjoyed my team's gripping 0-0 draw.

Friday, August 20
Onwards and upwards. Whatever that means.

CHAPTER 21

SEEING THE FUTURE

Matteo Manassero

Saturday, August 21

I was in reasonably high spirits, with Snedeker leading the Wyndham and other players tucked in just off the pace, so the weekend had a promising feel about it.

Well, that was until I made one of my poorest decisons for several years. I agreed to the challenge of a younger pal to face him in a three-set match of tennis, a sport from which I had long since retired.

Oh, what harm can it do? That was my attitude prior to the match and, with the benefit of hindsight, I now realise what a ridiculously carefree position it was to take. The answer was a lot of harm. A full week's worth of harm, in fact.

I got a football wager in place first – a £1,000 double on Arsenal to beat Blackpool at 2-11 and Everton to beat Wolves at 1-2 – then set about transforming into Roger Federer.

It all started off so well (I think the captain of RMS Titanic used those very same words just as that pesky iceberg began spoiling his party in 1912) and I cruised to a 6-3 first-set success. But a huge turning point came when I trailed 3-2 in the second set.

Having chased down a measured lob from my opponent, handy Andy, I did not have time to position my body correctly to send the ball back up court and a desperate swoosh of my racquet resulted in me missing the ball completely and smashing the left side of my temple.

I crashed to the ground as if nailed by a sniper, losing consciousness for a few seconds, reeling in agony as a bump the size of one of our tennis balls began emerging on my forehead.

We called for a trainer, but unfortunately there were no passing trainers available, so I just had to sit down quietly for five minutes and assess whether I could continue. I was clearly delirious because I asked a nearby couple who were heading for the beach if they had any witch-hazel I could borrow. It was a question which, not surprisingly, drew a negative response (right, we're off to the beach – sun cream, check, sunglasses, check, towels, check, bucket, check, spade, check, witch-hazel . . .).

I so dearly wish I had called it a day at that point, retiring hurt and awarding Andy victory, but my competitive instincts overwhelmed me and after consuming a Kit-Kat I pressed on in search of glory.

Dizzy and struggling for vision, I quickly lost the second set 6-3, and a gruelling decider was in store. Fitness was always going to be a massive handicap for me. Bjorn Borg retired at the age of 26 – tennis is a young man's game – and my 28-year-old opponent (a regular footballer with a six-pack and sharp hair) was always going to have the edge over 32-year-old me (a regular drinker with a one-pack and rubbish hair).

I again considered retirement prior to set three – I knew I was wilting fast and about a 50-1 chance to triumph – but he got his fancy phone out and updated me on the afternoon's sport. Arsenal and Everton were both winning and Jimenez had charged into second place in the Czech Open, so I got a timely injection of enthusiasm for life and bounded back on court like Mats ruddy Wilander.

Tragically, after about a million deuces, I finally surrendered my serve to go 1-0 down. No matter how many betting fillips came my way at that point – even if Jimenez had gone ten shots clear and Snedeker had suddenly been awarded the Wyndham title on grounds of having the prettiest little nose – I would not have been able to compete in the remainder of the set.

My head was throbbing, my back was seizing up, blisters were fast appearing on my feet and I had Bruce Grobbelaar jelly legs. There was nothing left in the tank. Andy skipped to a 4-0 advantage and my new target was just to avoid being bageled. There is nothing more embarrassing in the tennis world than being on the wrong end of a bagel.

In due course, though, a fat bagel was shoved down my throat as I crashed to a 6-3 3-6 0-6 defeat.

I trudged wearily to Corals to get the final football scores and a hot chocolate, and I knew from the look on the shop manager's face that my day was going to quickly go from bad to worse. He was glumly sipping tea from his Everton mug and a four-word conversation ("They still winning?" followed by "No") was enough to see me slump over the shop counter in despair.

Still flush from the tennis, my flushometer reading was off the scale after the news of Wolves' equaliser. My name was Ian Flush from Flushing Meadows and by all accounts my face resembled a beetroot farm as I was guided through Sylvan Ebanks-Blake's leveller.

I sat down and had a quiet moment of contemplation before ringing my colleague Mark to get the teams for the Wigan-Chelsea 5.15pm game. I also asked him where I could access the best price about Chelsea winning to nil and he told me even-money with Ladbrokes, so with 15 minutes until kick-off, I rang the Magic Sign with view to a £500 investment.

I expected it to be a challenging call – win-to-nil bets over the phone are notoriously tricky to place – but I ran in to an incredibly unhelpful telephonist. I explained the bet I wanted as clearly as possible ("Chelsea to win without conceding a goal, which will be on your screen as Chelsea to win to nil"), but he quickly told me they weren't offering prices on that market.

Knowing full well that they were, and that they do so for all live Premier League games, I gently urged him to keep looking, but after another token effort, he again reasserted his claim that there were no prices and then told me he would put me through to customer services.

As the hold music played in my ear, I started to fret about not getting my bet on in time, with kick-off fast approaching. After about four minutes on hold, my already battered morale sinking to dangerous depths, a voice came on the line at last. But it was not customer services – it was the telephonist again – who was clearly flabbergasted that I was still waiting patiently on the other end of the line. "Oh, I've been through to customer services and they say there is no market on that," he said.

Never mind the beetroot look – by now I was turning into the Incredible Hulk. I appreciate how hard it must be to find each market on a football match for which so many are on offer – being a telephonist is not easy – but some are so lazy that they will just try anything to get you to hang up.

"You're lying to me now, aren't you? I know you're lying to me," I said while taking a disturbing glance at my watch. "Why didn't you put me through to customer services like you said you would?"

"Ok, I'll put you through," was the last I heard of Mr Unhelpful. The incessant music began playing again and I realised I had no hope of getting my bet on unless I sprinted to the nearest Ladbrokes shop.

Having to do a Roger Black impression was not what I needed after the tennis ordeal. I battled through the pain barrier as the clock ticked to 5.14pm, still clutching the phone to my ear in case the telephonist miraculously redeemed himself, and I was short of puff when I reached the shop counter with about 30 seconds to kick-off at the DW Stadium.

Thankfully, a chap called Robin was the complete opposite of his colleague. He was awesomely efficient, even finding time to nonchalantly ask me if I wanted any cash back on my card transaction, processing my bet comfortably inside the 30-second window and sending me home with some hope in my heart.

Robin's heroic effort meant I salvaged something from the day, as Chelsea dominated, but suffering from tennis elbow, shoulder, leg, arse and head, I was in no mood to celebrate at a discotheque.

Snedeker threw in a couple of late bogeys to jeopardise his chances of Wyndham success and I was about to surrender for the betting day, but then I found out Rooney was ailing almost as much as me and would miss Man United's game at Fulham, so I had £250 each-way on Dimitar Berbatov to score first at 5-1.

Sunday, August 22

I could hardly move. The tennis injuries had worsened overnight and I was literally bedridden. I managed to get £400 on Lucas Glover for the Wyndham at 6-1, then battened down the hatches to watch Jimenez in the Czech Open.

The Spaniard was in contention until finding water at the 15th hole, then Berbatov had a volley saved from close range. The Bulgarian failed to notch, I lost a further £216.31 backing Peter Lawrie at 2-1 to win the Czech Open play-off, and I rolled around in bed bored out of my tiny mind.

Snedeker struggled in the Wyndham, but Glover soon went atop the leaderboard, with Sim and Leishman not far behind, so I was anticipating a late golf boost. Glover fell to pieces on the back nine, though, and Arjun Atwal went one shot clear of clubhouse leader

Toms with two holes to play. I still didn't fancy the Indian, so had £500 on Toms at 4-1, losing a disturbing amount on the tournament when Atwal holed a seven-footer for victory.

Monday, August 23
Had some Johnnie Walker Championship investments – £75 on Colsaerts at 49-1, £75 on Havret at 49-1, £65 on Lowry at 54-1, £35 on Bjorn at 110 and £25 on Lee at 159-1.

I was stunned by the negativity of the Man City line-up for their fixture with Liverpool, so had £500 on under 1.5 goals at 2-1. I take it all back Roberto – Yaya Toure is clearly an excellent support striker – you are a genius.

Fast haemorrhaging money, I got my Barclays bets in place, having £175 on Casey at 33-1, £125 on Mahan at 41-1, £75 on Scott at 74-1, £50 on Fowler at 109-1 and £50 on Cink at the same price.

Tuesday, August 24
Still crippled by tennis injuries.

Wednesday, August 25
Had £250 each-way on Fisher for the Johnnie Walker at 16-1 and a £125 each-way double on Fisher and Casey (16-1 and 30-1).

Thursday, August 26
Tiger took the lead in the Barclays. You can't beat a good divorce, eh?

Friday, August 27
Left my house nervously, still mindful of my bagel shame. What are you looking at? Never seen a bagel victim before?

Saturday, August 28
A dismal fortnight of punting meant I had rapidly gone from a position of great financial strength to one where I could not even afford to buy a new Ford Fiesta (not that I wanted to buy a new Ford

Fiesta). I forked out a sizeable amount on a fancy Yonex driver (as used by Colin Montgomerie) as a present for my old man's birthday so that I (or at least he) had something to show from my money if the losing streak continued to a devastating extent (are there any rules as to how many brackets a writer can use in one paragraph?). I'm a maverick (I don't play by the rules), so stick your rulebook where the sun (bright thing in the sky) don't shine (your back passage).

The lavish gift went down well, allowing me to leave the birthday bash at regular intervals to check on the progress of Fisher in the Johnnie Walker, a little tinker who had taken the lead the previous morning before swiftly clicking into reverse gear.

With Fisher faltering further, the golf was not looking good, so I sneaked another 15 minutes away from the sausage rolls and the family niceties to get £350 on Newcastle to beat Wolves at 6-5 on the draw-no-bet market and £250 on Fulham to beat Blackpool at 6-4.

I could have cosily brushed the football betting day under the carpet had I done both wagers using the draw-no-bet option – Fulham were 4-6 in that market – but I had been too ambitious. I rate ambition as one of the eight deadly sins (wrath, greed, sloth, pride, lust, envy, gluttony and ambition).

So, instead of possessing a slightly raised carpet with two draw-no-bet wagers festering among the dust mites underneath, I was in chasing mode and targeting retribution in the Man United-West Ham evening kick-off.

I thought the Hammers might hold out for a while, so had £100 on draw half-time, Man United full-time at 9-2, and as I headed for a sea swim after a goalless half-hour I was optimistic.

But as I returned from my ever-invigorating salty bath, I discovered Rooney had notched after 33 minutes, further eroding my fast-dwindling finances. I ended the night munching on a lamb doner kebab with the feeling that my hopes of securing a £30,000 bank balance any time soon had been skewered in a similar fashion to the poor baby sheep I was consuming.

Sunday, August 29

I had a couple of desperate late pokes at the Johnnie Walker – £50 on Soren Hansen at 109-1 and £50 on Marc Warren at 54-1 – but I was just hoping Edoardo Molinari (who I had so nearly backed ante-post at 22-1) would fail to triumph.

For the football, I had £150 on one goal or fewer in the Sunderland-Man City game at 3-1 as soon as I saw Mancini had picked another ludicrously cautious line-up, then £150 each-way on an advanced Steven Gerrard to score first in the Liverpool-West Brom game at 5-1.

One solid wager then, and one sloppy one, but my biggest bet of the day was always going to be on Everton to beat Villa on the draw-no-bet market. As is my new policy, I waited for the teams, and even though I was disturbed to see Jermaine Beckford had replaced Louis Saha, I still weighed in with £400 at 10-11.

Everton's defeat made for a disgusting afternoon, made all the more repulsive by Molinari's victory in Scotland. With three holes to play, the Italian was two shots behind and it looked like I was going to get away with leaving him out of my staking plan, but the swarthy rascal birdied all three.

Scott was contending in the Barclays, but a double-bogey at the eighth hole was his death knell, meaning my losing streak continued.

Monday, August 30

I was like a lost lamb (better than being like a dead lamb on a skewer I suppose), concerned about my punting woes, wandering around Weymouth town centre short of enthusiasm for the world. I messed about in the bookies, then decided I would pay a long-overdue visit to the fortune-telling gypsy who sits in a little caravan on the seafront during the summer.

It was getting on for 5pm and I mulled over whether she would still be open for business. I reasoned that, if she was that good at seeing into the future, she would know I was about to come over and be ready for some valuable overtime.

And she was. I entered the caravan with much trepidation – you don't expect palm-reading, crystal-ball-gazing clairvoyant types to be easy characters to get along with – but 'Zara' was nothing like the scary old witch I was expecting to find.

I had been working on potential ice-breakers en route to the caravan (my name is Palmer, you're a palmist, etc) but Zara was a friendly sort in her late 30s and we immediately got on like the proverbial caravan on fire.

In fact, the session turned into a bit of a shambles because she couldn't stop laughing. She described me as the funniest customer she had ever had and said that just looking at me made her laugh (I didn't take that as a compliment).

When she finally pulled herself together, some startling revelations began spilling from my palms and her crystal ball, leaving me completely bewildered about the future.

According to Zara, who said she can identify a homosexual within seconds of looking at their palms (the teenage boy who had been in front of me in the queue certainly didn't want to be told that he would soon be getting hitched to a big-breasted blonde), I am going to marry a girl who has a surname starting with M and father five kids with her.

Zara said I had been walked all over by girlfriends in the past and that there was a new girl on the scene at the moment who could be about to repeat the dose if I succumb to her physical charms. But she said there was another girl waiting in the wings who will treat me well, and that is the one I will marry. She regularly hit me with the line "Love is blind, but marriage is an eye opener" (suggesting that it is very easy to fall in love with a pretty little princess and be blind to their faults but that marrying one of them is disastrous and quickly opens your eyes to reality).

This is a subject close to my heart and I was starting to believe Zara's crystal ball could indeed contain images of me blindly drooling in front of another nubile vixen, but my confidence in her future-reading abilities waned with other predictions.

Apparently I'm not going to be living in England much longer, I'm soon going to be self-employed and have lots of people working for me and, most alarmingly, I'm heading for serious back problems unless I start paying more attention to what is set to prove a very troublesome spine.

I suppose it is possible my vast team of foot soldiers and I could soon be providing a golf tipping-line service while I lie down on a waterbed in Sweden resting my vulnerable vertebrae.

But it is also possible Zara is talking complete and utter bollocks.

When she asked if I had any questions after she had delivered her various verdicts, I said: "Are you from London?" She said elf when she meant to say health, so I knew she was from the capital, and further investigations revealed she lives in Weymouth during the summer doing her fortune-telling work and then goes back to Staines to do her fortune-counting work (£20 a pop and with a seemingly regular flow of customers).

I suppose I should have got my money's worth and asked her who was going to win the Deutsche Bank Championship, but I felt I was more qualified to make that prediction, and later I had £320 on Stricker at 14-1. I also had £100 each-way on Casey at 40-1, £100 each-way on Brett Rumford for the European Masters at 40-1, £30 each-way on Goya at 150-1, along with a £100 each-way double on Stricker (14-1) and Schwartzel for the European Masters (18-1).

Tuesday, August 31

Had £115 each-way on Scott at 35-1 for the Deutsche Bank and some European Masters investments, £250 on Schwartzel at 18-1, £65 each-way on Manassero at 60-1 and £60 each-way on David Horsey at 66-1.

Wednesday, September 1

Attended a golf day at the Buckinghamshire, where meeting Jeremy Kyle was the highlight. I told him I was a massive fan of his show and watched it avidly every morning. He responded with the wisecrack:

"Really? Get a job!"

I wanted to cajole him into saying his other catchphrase – "put something on the end of it" – but I could not work out a way of getting our conversation on to prophylactics.

My late-night drive back south was made hugely enjoyable by the magnificence of Oasis, a band I'm only fully appreciating now they are gone. There is nothing quite like singing along to Live Forever playing at full blast while you are launching a GTI round some country lanes at high speed.

Even if I had the option, though, I wouldn't want to live forever. Would you? Imagine the pressure if you had a really abominable life and you knew it was going to go on forever. It's comforting to know that nothing goes on forever, isn't it?

Thursday, September 2

A crucial betting weekend lay ahead. I needed to stop the rot. But then again, I could get run over by a bus any second now (nothing lasts forever), so it might not matter at all.

CHAPTER 22

ALL THE FUN OF THE FAIR

Fabio Capello

Friday, September 3

A thoroughly unprofessional approach to punting cost me a £550 cash injection. I had planned to stay at home and watch England's fixture against Bulgaria – I liked the look of the 11-10 about the Three Lions winning to nil and was considering a £500 investment – but then some pals asked me if I wanted to join them on a trip to the Great Dorset Steam Fair.

A professional would have placed the bet anyway before heading off to the village of Tarrant Hinton for the fair fun, but a plonker would think to himself: Ooh, I'm not going to get to watch the match now, so there's no point having a bet, is there?

What a numbskull. It is obviously more enjoyable to watch a bet emerge into a winning one than be blind to its successful development, but you still get paid the same amount whether you have viewed your little egg hatching or not. My revised schedule should have had zero impact on whether I placed the bet.

I failed to make any money then, but I still don't regret putting the fair ahead of Fabio Capello's team. It was top-drawer entertainment, which started with a tongue-orgasm at the hands of some Isle of Purbeck Fossil Fuel. That is one real real ale.

Steam engines may not be everybody's cup of tea, but for my pal Keith the sight of some heavy haulage road locomotives pulling vast loads of granite and machinery on huge trailers clearly provided a succession of eye-orgasms. It is a good job Keith was not born in the 1890s – he would not have been able to contain himself.

All sorts of traditional country capers were taking place around the steam engine orgy – ploughing, threshing, woodsawing, etc – but our party got lured into more modern thrills and spills that could be claimed for a few sovereigns.

The 'Ghost Train', as I've found is typical at such events, was a massive disappointment. The look of shame on the face of the woman in charge said it all as we alighted her ride completely unflustered. "Was that scary?" she asked sheepishly. "About as scary as my alarm clock," replied Keith.

Things soon took a turn for the better, though, at the 'Wall Of Death', where daredevils were driving motorbikes at high speed inside a small cylinder. I felt in grave danger just as a spectator popping my head over the top of the chamber and I was not surprised to hear the bikers announce afterwards that insurance companies refuse to do any deals with them because the risks are too great. They asked for donations to help, but we were feeling aggrieved at the time ("they promised us a wall of death and I didn't see any death"), so their negotiations with Aviva will have to continue.

I felt like I was stepping back into medieval times in the next tent that took our fancy. It housed a boxing ring where two scruffy country boys in jeans and a T-shirt were bashing each other's lights out for the amusement of the assembled throng.

The master of ceremonies, a black version of arrers legend Russ Bray, claimed they just plucked the toughest-looking lads out of their clan and threw them in the ring. "We don't even know these boys," he shouted as two meatheads slugged it out. "They are just ordinary folk who live and work among us. Come on lads – open yourself up now ."

The Fossil Fuel was obviously going to my head because I barked "I wanna see more blood!" as the tiring fighters struggled to stand up, so it was clearly time to sober up at the hog roast stall.

As the night wore on, I managed to add a bloodhound to my collection of living-room animals, slipping the cuddly-toy stallmaster a tenner rather than attempting to unearth a winning ticket. He scandalously made a big song and dance about presenting me the supposed prize, bleating "We have another winner, another winner", trying to prove to the crowd that it was possible to succeed legitimately. But I quietly whispered in the ears of the people around me to put them straight because I didn't want to be part of a potential swindle.

With a taste for real ale, we stopped in a Dorchester pub on the way home, purchasing a round of a local brew called Sheep Dip. It was absolutely disgusting, but the fact it tasted like actual sheep dip meant we had no easy grounds for complaint. The judge would throw that case out of court immediately, wouldn't he?

"The drink tasted terrible your honour – much like sheep dip."

"Well, what is the drink called?"

"Sheep Dip."

"Not guilty. Next."

Saturday, September 4

A Saturday without Premier League football is like a pork chop without apple sauce. Ok, but could be a lot better.

Sunday, September 5

Fairs are like buses – you wait ages, etc – and I bowled into the Dorset County Show in Dorchester eager for more action.

First I saw the 'Adams Axemen', who chopped up some wood. It was not the most absorbing 15 minutes of my life, but the chief axeman redeemed himself when wrapping up the display with the line: "And, above all, be nice to each other, eh?" Lovely touch.

The 'Dancing Diggers' were a bit of a flop. 'Dancing' JCBs. Sound rubbish? You're right, it was. Animals are what this show is really all about and I got up close to some wonderful creatures.

From the crack of dawn, the animals were on display. It said in the official programme that at 6.30am in the 'Goat Ring' a typical 'Full Udder Inspection' took place. I bet you're glad you're not a goat, eh? Imagine getting woken up at 6.30am every morning to have your udders given a full inspection. I would have a good mind to unload the contents of my udders all over the inspector's face.

I marvelled at the size of the bulls' testicles, tickled a pig, stroked a giant rabbit and then discovered there was a type of chicken named after five-times world darts champion Raymond van Barneveld (the Barnevelder chicken).

I watched some sheep shearing (according to the commentator, the top shearers shear 500 sheep a day, using up as much energy as they would by running two marathons), some ferret racing, a hound parade (disappointingly there was no sign of Westmead Hawk), then found another hog roast stall.

While eating my latest chunk of hog, I saw a wasp fly into my can of Diet Coke, leaving me shaking my head at how dangerous the world can be. Had I not spotted the wasp's entrance, I would have no doubt swallowed him with my next gulp, leaving me in all sorts of strife. There is such a fine line between happiness and misery, isn't there? There you are, cheerfully tucking into some hog without a care in the world, then suddenly a wasp is stinging every inch of your gullet, making you more distressed than you have ever been before. Madness.

While monitoring wasp movements, I was also following the progress of my two golfers in the European Masters by phone, with Manassero and Schwartzel battling for places in Switzerland.

Manassero finished third and Schwartzel tied for fifth, so it was comforting to know some bacon was being brought home while I devoured the remains of my hog sandwich.

Monday, September 6

Started an exciting Monday night by again battling the elements in the ocean. My three-man party had masses of washed-up weed to overcome this time, as well as waves, rain and the ever-troublesome pebbles.

Sea swimming can be a serious test of mettle and pushing back the boundaries of mandom is my new passion. There are too many men who bowl around believing they are 'hardmen' just because they are in possession of big arms or have the same hairstyle as the lead singer of Guns N' Roses, but the ultimate examination of a man's toughness can be found in the English Channel.

The final round of the Deutsche Bank added to my fervour. I was hoping Stricker could complete the place part of my double with Schwartzel, but he finished ninth, although Scott scrambled into fifth place to bring me some reward, meaning I came through the golfing week unscathed.

Tuesday, September 7

Had £300 on Francesco Molinari to win the KLM Open at 14-1, £40 each-way on Horsey at 100-1, £100 each-way on Gregory Bourdy at 50-1, £100 each-way on Wood at 40-1 and £50 each-way on Joost Luiten at 80-1.

For the BMW Championship, I had £210 on Scott at 25-1, £75 each-way on Cink at 55-1, £40 each-way on Leishman at 110-1 and £50 each-way on Van Pelt at 80-1. Then I tried to avail myself of Blue Square's stand-out 125-1 about Haas, but their website was down. Half an hour later the site came back to life but Haas had been cut to 100-1 (add an expletive of your choice).

I decided to punish Blue Square by having my double with them (£100 each-way on Molinari and Scott at 13-1 and 25-1). I suppose being given £200 will not be much of a punishment if one of these two finishes outside of the first five, but having to give me £39,481.25 if they both win will be a rather chastening slap round the chops.

Later I threw the remainder of my Betfair balance (£337.65) on England to beat Switzerland at 11-10 and then went out to discover that passion for the Three Lions is still very much alive despite the World Cup woe. Either that or I live in a town full of alcoholics because every pub was rammed and my gang could not find a seat in the first boozer we tried.

On the walk to the second option, I had a peek through the open curtains of one house to see the score had changed to 1-0 England. Looking through a stranger's window is not really the done thing at any other time, but when the national side is involved in football combat you can just about get away without police involvement. I gave a soothing thumbs-up to the slightly scared-looking mother who spotted us gawping at her television.

England were in full control by the time we found a suitable venue and the team have now won three matches in a row. We all know what that means, don't we? World domination is obviously imminent, eh?

Wednesday, September 8

Caught up in Three Lions fever, I wrote down my preferred England team. I'm very much in the 'build for the future' camp and would go with: Joe Hart, Glen Johnson, Steven Taylor, Ryan Shawcross, Kieran Gibbs; Jack Rodwell; Adam Johnson, Steve Gerrard (captain), Joe Cole, Ashley Young; Wayne Rooney.

Now if I can just get a massive head, some thick-rimmed spectacles and an appalling grasp of the English language, I might get the manager's gig.

Thursday, September 9

Isn't it about time for some Premier League football?

Friday, September 10

Departed north for three days of leisure in Liverpool, the centrepiece of which is a seat at Goodison Park for Everton versus Manchester United. Come on you ruddy Toffeemen.

CHAPTER 23

MERSEYSIDE MAYHEM

Mikel Arteta

Saturday, September 11

I knew I was going to like Liverpool when on Friday night, having just stepped into the city centre, I found a place called Williamson Square that had a Betfred, Hills, Ladbrokes and Paddy Power shop within a few yards of each other.

It is a ridiculous spot. If you had four butchers in such close proximity, three of them would soon close down, with only the one selling the best-value pork chops surviving. Four bakers, four candlestick makers, four anything would find the laws of supply and demand too much to stay afloat with so many rivals nearby, but bookmaking is clearly a thriving business that can profit regardless.

I found this a rather sobering thought, trying to console myself that it was probably the FOBT players who were lining the pockets of the betting-shop bosses, not super-shrewd greyhound judges like me. After having a hound loser in every single shop, though, I was not so sure.

Still, I shrugged aside any negative thoughts because I was in Liverpool for fun, principally to watch Everton versus Man United, and left the square to go on what can only be described as a great adventure, arriving back at my hotel at 4.30am thoroughly loosened up for the 12.45pm Goodison Park fixture.

By 9.30am, I was in a city-centre shopping mall internet cafe studying football prices, knowing that being among the hurly-burly of a top-flight humdinger would mean I would have no choice but to abandon my usual policy of not having a bet until the teams are announced.

Before long, I had £400 on Everton to beat Man United on the draw-no-bet market at 9-4, £500 on Tottenham to beat West Brom at 23-20, £500 on Sunderland to beat Wigan on the draw-no-bet market at 6-5 and had laid £500 of Arsenal to beat Bolton at 1-4 on the exchanges.

Then off we rocked for Goodison, arriving at a pub round the corner called The Elm Tree in perfect time, 11am sharp. The boozer was immediately full to bursting and Rooney was the hottest topic of conversation.

My Everton-supporting pal Carl, who was a season-ticket holder for several years and the architect of my trip north, started getting all misty-eyed about 'that' goal against Arsenal, which put Wazza on the footballing map. Blues fans can't help but speak fondly about the day when a 16-year-old local wonderboy ended Arsenal's 30-match unbeaten run with a curling 25-yard rocket.

I knew I needed to take drastic action. I was already pumped to the eyeballs about Everton claiming three points – I did not want to hear about the past achievements of an opposition player – so I weighed in with a few verbal haymakers.

"Shut up now – you shouldn't be talking like this – he's no friend of yours. He kissed the Man United badge at Goodison in 2008. He's a philandering judas."

I nicked some lines off Graham Taylor to complete my sermon, closing with: "Come on, rise yourself, we're here for business. Eaaa . . . ver . . . ton, Everton, Everton . . ."

With full focus regained we made for a pub called The Winslow, which neighbours Goodison, and it was buzzing with pre-match anticipation. The playing of several Oasis songs confused me at first, but then I remembered the Gallagher brothers are Man City fans who would be cheering for Everton in this match, so I think it was a deliberate ploy to build a 'World against United' atmosphere.

On getting through the stadium turnstiles, we tried to nail a quick pint of Chang lager, but sensationally none was available and we were forced to drink Foster's. Mr Chang will no doubt be furious when he reads this – Tim Cahill obviously has far too much influence at Goodison and should be transfer listed immediately.

The combination of lots of alcohol and no food usually makes me feel very unstable. Throw in a high-octane Premier League blockbuster and I'm ready to burst into tears at any moment, and on arrival to my seat in the Gwladys Street end, I was arguably the most emotional Everton supporter in the ground.

I spent much of the first half bemoaning David Moyes's negative formation – "you can't win football matches with no strikers on the pitch" – but after 39 ding-dong minutes Steven Pienaar opened the scoring and I found myself high-fiving the stranger in front of me.

Four minutes of elation was followed by pancake impressions all round after United equalised, making for a long, deflating half-time period. In the gents, I tried to rouse the gloomy troops by quipping, "If it was still nil-nil we'd all have a smile on our face!", but the rapid surrender of a lead had savaged morale.

United soon drove further daggers into the broken Toffeemens' hearts. The visitors' third goal was such a distressing sight I had to cover my eyes with my hands for a full five minutes so that I could come to terms with the tragedy in private.

By now, my fury at the formation had reached fever pitch and I was vociferously demanding the introduction of Yakubu, beating my chest like King Kong while shouting: "My name is Yakubu – release me."

With 20 minutes to go, I got my wish and Yakubu added much-needed muscle to the home forward line. The pressure was building at the Gwladys Street end and Cahill popped up with what looked like a consolation just into injury time.

"That just makes it all the harder to swallow," mumbled a defeated Carl to my left, and no-one bothered to rejoice the goal.

But hello, here they ruddy well come again! Surely not, surely not . . . ARTETA!!!!!!

What followed was an explosion of joy that will live with me forever. Everyone was hugging everyone. Tears were streaming down my face as I embraced the lad to my right. Carl virtually had full intercourse with me during the melee, while I dived into arms of the two women behind me before giving the chap in front another enthusiastic high-five.

The celebrations were still continuing as the Toffeemen incredibly surged towards us chasing an outrageous winner and Phil Jagielka found himself through on goal. If a ruddy elephant had blown the full-time whistle at that stage, no-one would have heard it, so Jagielka was oblivious to the fact his shot at Edwin van der Sar counted for nothing. Thank Christ he failed to convert.

"In all my years, Steven, in all my years," spluttered an emotional Carl as we sat stunned at the finish. This was the unbridled joy that only sport can bring. I was relieved to be getting my £400 back from Skybet but this moment transcended betting. I was patting everyone on the back as we headed for the exits, shaking hands with more strangers, a people united by Mikel Arteta's half-volley.

We were both unable to stop smiling as we walked up Gwladys Street in a beautiful daze – it was worth travelling from the moon for that match let alone the south coast of England – but our progress was delayed by the unbelievable sight of a car trying to force its way through the masses.

Quite how the police allowed this to happen, I'll never know, but it sparked a huge commotion.

Initially I could not understand why there was so much menace being shown towards the car – he had taken a wrong turn but we all make mistakes – but when we got closer I could see the driver was wearing a Liverpool shirt.

What a shocking error of judgement. Either that or it was a suicide attempt. Driving a small car through 37,000 Toffeemen wearing the colours of their rivals? Carl and I just chuckled at the madness of the situation as outraged Evertonians kicked and screamed at the stricken vehicle, ripping the registration plate off, the wing mirrors, and anything else that could be easily removed.

I felt sorry for the poor lad in the passenger seat who was probably the driver's son – he looked about 11 and was cowering inside his hoodie shaking like the proverbial leaf – but I had no sympathy for the braindead Red who was desperately trying to inch his car forwards. If he had taken his shirt off, put it under the seat, and driven bare-chested he might have been shown some mercy. But he defiantly clutched his steering wheel and we headed back to The Winslow fearing the worst for him.

The Winslow was full of atmosphere and I loved the way the packed pub fell silent when Moyes was being interviewed on Sky. "Shhhhhhh" was the cry as their hero came on TV.

We continued to imbibe in other pubs near Goodison, finding one showing Soccer Saturday so we could follow the 3pm kick-offs, and Tottenham's draw meant for a bad betting day. Nothing to lessen my spirits, though, as I was still on a glorious natural high from the Everton comeback.

We drifted into a few betting shops while trying to find a taxi to take us to the city centre and my assertion that at least 25 per cent of Liverpudlian women look like Abbey Clancy was given further credibility by a girl called Gemma who was serving in a Hills branch. She was a spectacle-wearing Clancy lookalike who I immediately fell in love with and I had a few virtual greyhound wagers to give me more scope for banter.

Disaster struck, though, when her boyfriend parked outside to pick her up in her dinner break. "Ooh, he seems very controlling," I told her. "He's a control freak – it'll never last!"

I found myself in conversation with some local punters after Gemma's departure, with the subject inevitably moving on to football, and one man was determined I wouldn't leave the shop without knowing everything there was to know about a former player called Alex Young.

"Alex Young – The Golden Vision – the greatest footballer that ever lived," the rabid Scouser repeated over and over, before writing down more Young information on a betting slip and putting it in my pocket.

I saw plenty more golden visions in the evening (of the Clancy variety rather than former Everton centre-forwards), then finally had some breakfast around midnight. Up the Toffeemen.

Sunday, September 12

I was back at the internet cafe early doors (I really must get a better phone). Just below the cafe, there is the Body Shop. I considered a visit because I certainly needed a new body after 48 hours ravaging the one I had.

My study led me to having a £200 double on Liverpool to beat Birmingham at 6-5 and Leeds Rhinos to beat Wigan Warriors on the handicap (eight-point start) at even-money (on the advice of *Racing Post* rugby league sage Rod Studd), then we went for a tour of Anfield.

In the Anfield museum, I watched highlights of Liverpool's famous 2005 Champions League final triumph over Milan, where Didi Hamann's half-time introduction transformed the Reds from no-hopers to a dominant force. It made me proud to know the occasional *Racing Post* columnist and I sent him a picture text of the inside of the Liverpool changing rooms, where a photograph of Bill Shankly giving a team-talk adorns one of the walls, to perk him up. It must be so hard for sportsmen to adjust to a more humdrum existence (no disrespect to MK Dons) after playing at the highest level and it is no wonder the likes of Paul Gascoigne, Ricky Hatton, etc, have gone a bit off the rails.

I had my picture taken with the European Cup before leaving Anfield (as you do), then had a thorough check of the golf scores on Carl's phone. Horsey was bang in contention in the KLM Open, but Leishman had dropped away in the BMW Championship, so I reloaded the gun with Casey (£125 at 8-1).

Then it was time to get to Wigan for the Warriors' Super League clash with the Rhinos. The plan was to support the Rhinos if Liverpool beat Birmingham and my bet was still live, but to support the Warriors if the Reds failed to leave the Midlands with three points.

We watched the Liverpool game in a Wigan pub and, although I was disappointed to lose £200, my fatigue levels were so high I was quite pleased I didn't have to be part of a potentially rowdy away support at the DW Stadium. A nice bit of gentle encouragement for Wigan in a quiet section was what the doctor ordered.

Horsey finished tied for fourth in Holland to provide a small fillip, then we followed some Warrior-shirted characters to the DW. This would be both Carl and I's first live rugby match of any code and I approached the ticket office with trepidation.

"Two tickets for somewhere in the middle please?" was my opening gambit, before the woman behind the counter capitulated in laughter. I knew the accent of a southern softie might cause some surprise when I made my request, but I didn't expect full-blown ridicule.

The two junior assistants behind her also started sniggering and she chuckled back at them: "Oh, give over, you two!" before continuing to serve me. "What's so funny?" I asked, by now tiring at her lack of professionalism.

She pulled herself together, asked me if I had attended a Warriors game before, and then demanded to know my postcode and address, before finally issuing the tickets. I felt like throwing them back in her face and saying, "Is it any wonder no-one south of the Peak District gives a monkey's about this sport if this is the welcome they get when they try to watch it?" but instead I had a pint of Worthington's and tried to make myself look as northern as possible.

As instructed by Studd, I shouted "Geremonside" a few times during the match to fit in and tried to look angry when everyone else looked angry. At one point, I was about to apply some lip balm to my bone-dry mouth, but restrained myself in case that wasn't the done thing at Super League contests (you're one of us now son – you'll moisten those lips with Worthington's and nowt else).

Wigan got off to a flyer and I was pleased Liverpool had drawn, but Leeds fought back to win 27-26 and I was left looking wantonly in the direction of the away end at what might have been.

I was getting golf updates throughout – I was definitely the only person in the stadium more worried about the BMW Championship than the Super League – and Casey had gone two shots clear with a handful of holes to play. But by the time I was back in Liverpool, he had lost by a shot, the icing on the cake of an expensive weekend.

Monday, September 13

Up at 4am to make a flight from Manchester to Southampton. I hate taxi drivers that expect conversation whatever the hour.

Tuesday, September 14

Exhausted. What goes up must come down, I suppose. For the Austrian Open, I had £250 on Richard Green at 27-1, £180 on Jacquelin at 35-1, £120 on Goya at 45-1, £85 on Martin Wiegele at 64-1 and £65 on Kapur at 79-1.

Later, I had £100 on draw half-time, Man United full-time for their clash with Rangers at 4-1, laid £300 of Werder Bremen at even-money for Tottenham's visit and had a couple of Champions League outright investments (£150 on Barcelona at 4-1 and £50 on Milan at 22-1).

After a goalless first half at Old Trafford and with Spurs 2-1 up, I was long odds-on for a £700 fillip, but had to settle for £200 profit thanks to United misfiring.

Wednesday, September 15

Played golf and got about a minute's pleasure from a four-hour round (hit six very good shots and 80 terrible ones). Golf is a microcosm of life (utter despair for the vast majority of the time with a few precious moments of happiness thrown in to stop you giving up).

The evening was better thanks to a £300 double on Nicolas Anelka to score for Chelsea against Zilina at 21-20 and Zlatan Ibrahimovich to score for Milan against Auxerre at 13-10. I was toying with also throwing in Gonzalo Higuain to score for Real Madrid against Ajax, but he was only 8-11 with the firm who were best price on Anelka and Ibra (10-11 elsewhere), so I left him out.

I flicked between the Chelsea game and the Milan one until Anelka notched after 24 minutes, then focused on the San Siro until Ibrahimovich's breakthrough on 66 minutes.

I was delighted – it felt like the easiest £1,114.50 I had ever won – but my mood dipped just seven minutes later when I switched over to the Bernabeu to see Higuain tapping in from close range.

So that added up to eight minutes of happiness for the day. Yep, that's about average.

Thursday, September 16

Goya withdrew after nine holes of the Austrian Open with illness. You can't beat a good run for your money, eh?

Friday, September 17

Who have Everton got this weekend? Newcastle? I'll be at Weymouth versus Cambridge City, but from now on a small place in my heart will forever be reserved for the Toffeemen.

CHAPTER 24

HOUND HEROICS

Canine crusaders

Saturday, September 18

I spent the morning wringing moisture out of the shirt I had been wearing the previous night because a mate had just been dumped by his girlfriend of six years and he had been crying on my shoulder for several hours.

I'm getting fed up of seeing good pals of mine having their hearts ripped out by trigger-happy women – I'm sure females are getting more ruthless as society evolves – and my friend was in a completely bewildered state after his sudden dismissal. He had got home from a game of five-a-side football to be greeted by the line: "This is not working out, is it?"

It's not working out after six years? Was there a six-year probationary period before that conclusion could be reached? What was she thinking after five-and-a-half years? Hmmmm, I'm not quite sure whether this is working out yet – I'll give it another six months and see.

Well, my mate did what any self-respecting man does in this situation – he smoked a forest's worth of marijuana and drank a riverload of ale – and sought the advice of relationship expert Aunt Steve. As someone whose longest relationship lasted nine whole months, I'm supremely qualified in such matters.

I saw an opportunity to get him 'back in the saddle' in one club we were in when a girl came over to ask if one of us would tell her sister that she was beautiful "because she has just gone through a messy divorce and is feeling really low".

I offered my amigo the gig, but he ushered me on and it all kicked off when I did my bit to try to help the divorcee's morale. "Has my sister put you up to this? She has, hasn't she? I'm not falling for this."

I tried to convince her I had come of my own volition and merely spotted her beautiful face from the other side of the room, but she kept going bananas and I jumped ship back to my pals. I presumed I was at a safe distance in the crowded room, but two minutes later I was confronted by the raging divorcee with her burly father in tow!

He was wearing a Wolverhampton Wanderers shirt and barked: "I hear you've been upsetting my daughter."

A ridiculous situation had developed and it was time for us to make for the exit. I retreated straight to my flat, insisting I would have to think long and hard before considering a return to the outside world. It is just not safe anymore. You get asked to give a girl a compliment, you do it, then you get threatened with physical violence for doing it. How can that happen?

I stayed deep under my duvet to place £300 on Stoke to beat West Ham at 10-11 and settled back for 90 minutes of soothing lunchtime football, hoping to shake off the trauma of the previous night.

The Potters hit the woodwork about 500 times in a 1-1 draw, so it was not an entirely satisfying hour and a half, but Hamann (who is now a League One expert) texted to advise a loss-recovering trixie on Brighton to beat Carlisle, Southampton to beat Colchester and Swindon to beat Walsall.

I've always thought trixies sound a bit woofterish – too much like pixie – so I just had a £100 treble at 21-10, 8-11 and 13-8 respectively. Then I waited for the teams to drop in for the 3pm kick-offs, before having my main investments of the day (£400 on Everton to win to nil against Newcastle at 2-1 and £300 on Villa to win to nil against Bolton at the same price).

I felt confident enough to venture out for the Zamaretto League clash between Weymouth and Cambridge City (you don't get many mad divorcees at the Bob Lucas Stadium) and the Terras were soon losing to the table-toppers.

I found a spot in the sunshine near the tragic travelling party of five or six City fans, who were singing "We're top of the league, we're having a laugh, we're top of the league, we're having a laugh" while occasionally shouting: "How many more points have we got than you? Ha, ha, ha."

I'm pretty sure I've never seen anything quite as pathetic. I felt like explaining to the chief cheerleader that watching them 'having a laugh' made me want to have a cry at the sheer woefulness of the human race, but instead I just moved to a different section of the ground.

They switched to a rendition of: "City till I die." as I passed them. Any chance you could hurry up with that, lads?

More misery arrived at half-time when the Premier League scorelines were read out over the Tannoy. Bolton had scored (£600 down for the day). And Newcastle had scored (£1,000 down for the day).

By full-time, Weymouth had lost 3-0, Brighton had drawn (£1,100 down for the day) and I swiftly checked to see if any salvation was forthcoming on the Austrian Open golf. Jacquelin had been in contention when I left for the footy, but he had dropped five shots behind, so I reloaded the gun with £300 on McDowell at 7-2 and headed down to Coral.

I told the shop manager I had come to win back the bag of sand I lost on the football and he responded dismissively: "If you win £1,000 on the BAGS, I'll give you a medal."

Famous last words, sunshine, famous last words. I opened up with £30 on Trap One at 2-1 in the 7.52 at Sittingbourne and he blasted home in fine style. "Here we go," I chuckled at the cashier as I pocketed £30 of the return while having £60 on Trap Four in the 7.58 at Monmore.

It drifted from 5-2 to 4-1 after I had placed my bet, so I feared the worst, but it was in front from the boxes and never caught. "Keep pulling you bitch – oi, oi, oi!"

Races were coming thick and fast, so I was acting on impulse, and I quickly swapped my winning ticket for £300 on Trap Two in the 8.02 at Hove, which opened at 4-5 before drifting to even-money.

This was a ding-dong affair and he just got home, providing a wonderful buzz for his backers. "What a sport!" I commented to some strangers who were circling around the shop.

By now I was £600 up for the session and starting to believe the impossible was possible. I studied the formguide for the 8.07 at Sittingbourne with enormous relish and my *Racing Post* colleagues were confident that Trap Five could upset the Trap Two favourite. I wholeheartedly agreed and had £200 on Five, which was showing at 5-2 as they entered the traps. If this won, I would have expunged my £1,100 football losses.

I gave the TV screen a piercing David Moyes-style glare as the race began. Five flopped out the boxes and was finding plenty of trouble, but it was billed as a strong finisher, so I stayed positive.

Slowly but surely he crept back into contention and was swooping to conquer round the final bend. "Oi, oi, oi, oi, oi, oi, oi – call a copper!" He finished like a Trojan who was carrying a wet sail and I went bonkers. If I had been winning a grand on the golf or a conventional sport, there is no way I would have celebrated so hard. But the fact I had done so on the dogs, universally accepted as one of the toughest betting mediums of them all due to the poor percentages and unruly nature of the competitors, gave me a real thrill.

I felt a little aggrieved that Trap Five had been clipped late from 5-2 to 2-1, so I had won £1,000 rather than £1,100, but I had got the vast majority of my football losses back and immediately ended my session.

I waddled out of the shop with a wad in my trousers, soon swaggering around a pub with the confidence of a man who knew he could purchase 350 pints if he so wished, winking at any lucky ladies that caught my eye.

Is that a bag of sand in your pocket or are you just pleased to see me?

Well, there is a bag of sand in my pocket, but I'm also sporting a full erection. Is that the right answer?

Sunday, September 19

I laid £600 of Man United to beat Liverpool at 8-11 and watched the match up the local. Barmaid Sophie, who had been all sweetness and light the last time I visited the pub, was back to blanking me again. I find women are much like football referees – there is no consistency.

When United went 2-0 up, I got hold of the teams from the DW Stadium, having £500 on Man City to beat Wigan at 8-11, which proved a more solid wager. Liverpool and McDowell threatened to add to the booty at one stage, but there was no further joy, and when I found out Bet365 were offering 4-5 about Chelsea winning to nil against Blackpool I decided to stop messing about. It was the best football price I had seen all season, so I had £1,000 on, a wager that gave me few concerns.

Monday, September 20

Had a long sea-swim soon after eating three pots of out-of-date chocolate mousse. Big mistake.

Tuesday, September 21

I abandoned my policy of waiting for football line-ups before betting because I could not see how Tottenham could field a weaker team than Arsenal in their Carling Cup tie, so I had £400 on Spurs after they had drifted to 13-8 by late afternoon.

Whoopseedaisy. Tottenham were soon trading at 2-1 after the teams had been named and suddenly I was watching the game more in hope than expectation.

With full-time approaching, Spurs were out on their feet and hanging on at 1-1, and I was convinced Arsenal, who had brought some big guns off the bench, would progress in extra-time. There was not enough liquidity in the 'method-of-victory' market on the exchanges to justify that bet, though, so I had £400 on the visitors to qualify at 8-11 to get out of the game with a small loss.

Wednesday, September 22

For the Vivendi Cup, I had £180 on Bourdy at 22-1, £155 on Jacquelin at 26-1, £150 on Green at the same price, £75 on Garrido at 54-1 and £40 on Kenneth Ferrie at 99-1. For the Tour Championship, I had £410 on Mickelson at 15-2, £310 on Stricker at 11-1, £185 on Scott at 18-1, £170 on Els at 20-1 and £125 on Zach Johnson at 27-1.

On a visit to my flat, my nephew started fiddling with all the £20 notes that were sitting on my table (the greyhound winnings). "You've got lots of change," he said.

"If you think that is just 'change', pal," I replied. "Then you're destined to become an extremely successful businessman."

Thursday, September 23

Gosh, only eight days until the Ryder Cup. Shall I have £5,000 on Europe at 8-11 and then £8,636.36 on Phil Taylor to win the World Grand Prix arrers the following week? That would give me an interest in life, I suppose.

Friday, September 24

Or maybe I should get a new hobby. Anyone ever tried salsa dancing?

Saturday, September 25

Thank God (whoever he is) I only had £582.39 in my Betfair account when I woke up. I loved the Chelsea line-up that was taking to the pitch for the lunchtime kick-off at Eastlands and felt the only way they could possibly lose to Man City was through a freak goal in a 1-0 home win.

So I punted my entire balance on Chelsea to beat City at 8-13 on the draw no bet market, before settling down to watch Chelsea concede a freak goal in a 1-0 home win.

City fans may not agree with me that Carlos Tevez's goal was freakish – and I'll admit he took his chance well – but what in the name of sanity (as Victor Meldrew used to say) was Ashley Cole thinking as he ran away from the Argentinian like a frightened rabbit?

Oh, I'll only think about tackling this toothy little rascal when he gets close enough to goal to have a very good chance of scoring. The Chelsea left-back should have weighed in with a thunderous man-and-ball tackle as soon as Tevez got possession – with John Terry behind him it would never have resulted in a red card if he brought the striker down – but Cole gets paid millions of pounds for his footballing judgement, so I suppose he must know better than me.

I wonder if he used to sprint away from Cheryl like that when she came at him with a copy of the *News of the World* and a rolling pin?

Fuming that Cashley had cost me more than a monkey, I eagerly studied the teams for the 3pm kick-offs, a frenzied 20 minutes of betting action resulting in £350 on Liverpool half-time, Liverpool full-time at 11-8 for their clash with Sunderland, £100 each-way on Andrei Arshavin to score first for Arsenal against West Brom at 9-2, £200 on Everton to win to nil against Fulham at 7-2 and £150 on over 2.5 goals in the Blackpool versus Blackburn game at 4-5.

I needed a lie down at 3pm. My new policy of waiting for the team sheets before placing any football bets is probably sensible, but it does not leave much time to assess the line-ups, devise punting strategies and get the wagers in place, so I usually find myself on the phone to bookmakers while also frantically fiddling on the computer. I have not even decided on stakes when telephonists ask how much I want on – it is very much a case of flying by the seat of your pants (whatever that means) – so errors are entirely possible.

Well, I definitely made plenty of errors, and a nightmare afternoon followed. Blackburn scored a late goal to give me a small crumb of comfort, but by full-time I was well over a bag down for a footballing Saturday for the second week running.

Seven days earlier, I had conjured a miraculous turnaround on the Saturday-night greyhounds to get my losses back, but I reasoned that

£1,000 BAGS victories come once in a blue moon and a trip to Coral would almost certainly just add to my malaise.

Instead, I entertained my young nephew for the evening, trying to shrug off my punting problems. I explained to him why I'd had such a bad day and he did his best to console me. "Don't worry" seems to be his standard opening to everything he says to me now. "Don't worry – I give you this robot!" "Don't worry – I put your favourite dvd on!"

My supposed favourite dvd is, in fact, a nonsensical cartoon that is his favourite dvd. It wouldn't be in my top five million dvds. I could show him what is actually my favourite dvd, but I don't think that would go down too well with his parents.

Sunday, September 26

Trifleface has started going to the gym because his wife has been threatening to divorce him unless he loses some weight. Love can be a cruel game to play sometimes. He was trying to tempt me down there, but I needed to focus on launching a punting fightback, which I planned to start with £400 on Man United half-time, Man United full-time at 5-4 for their visit to Bolton.

The 1-1 half-time score at the Reebok thrust another emotional dagger through my skull and I reacted with £200 on Aston Villa to win to nil against Wolves at 7-2.

That wager was looking extremely promising until Wolves equalised on the hour mark, and Emile Heskey's last-gasp goal just added to my woes. A chunk on a Villa victory in a virtually your-choice match would have been enough to get me back on the winning trail, but I got too ambitious.

The Vivendi Cup golf leaderboard was not providing any solace either. All five of my players were up there, but as lunchbox-lacking men the world over often get told, they were not up enough. Green, on whom I added £100 at 15-2 going into the final round to bolster the £150 I originally had on at 26-1, dropped heartbreakingly from a close fourth to a distant eighth.

I had a roast in the local, cutting a forlorn figure, and the only way

I could take my mind off my problems was by having a ridiculous amount of horseradish sauce on my beef. It is impossible to think about anything else but horseradish sauce when you've got a large dollop of the stuff sizzling on your tongue. I might carry a pot of horseradish in my pocket at all times in future to whip out whenever I need to stop my brain thinking about bad things.

Mickelson was not doing quite enough to provide potential salvation in the Tour Championship, so I had £167.32 on Ogilvy at 12-1. The Aussie soon blew his chances too, though, and I lost more than two bags on the golf.

In full chase mode, I had £300 on one goal or fewer in Newcastle versus Stoke at 5-2, expecting a drab encounter, but in the 67th minute Kenwyne Jones used his massive hairy bonce to make it 1-1 and my weekend was an unqualified disaster. I had started it relatively rich. I ended it as a pauper.

To get over the anguish, I wrapped myself up in the two things that make me most happy at the moment, Guinness and pizza. Quaffing Guinness is such a lovely sensation, isn't it? And plopping the crust of a pizza into the garlic and herb dip that my friends at the pizzeria provide, then slowly making love to it with my lips, also provides deep satisfaction.

I'm considering devoting my entire life to Guinness and pizza, and not worrying about the consequences. So what if I get fat? What's wrong with being fat? Are you going to divorce me if I get fat? I'm not even married, so you can't divorce me. Ha, I win.

Monday, September 27

Ammunition supplies were too low to go crazy on the Ryder Cup, so I had £100 on McDowell to be top European points scorer at 8-1, £150 on Tiger Woods to be top US points scorer at 6-1, and £50 on McDowell to be top overall points scorer at 18-1.

Later I was astonished to discover Paddy Power had already paid out on Europe and I was very jealous of those who had won money on a risk-free wager. What a wonderful feeling that must have been.

Trouble is, I know what is going to happen now. In two years' time, I'll remember this moment and in the lead-up to the 2012 Ryder Cup, I will be throwing fortunes at Europe with Paddy Power, building up a stake of £15,000 by midnight on the Sunday prior in anticipation of free money.

Then I will wait, and wait, and wait, Power won't repeat the trick, the USA will triumph, and I will be forced on to the streets, eventually perishing from pneumonia around Christmas time.

Is that what you want, Paddy? Because that's what's going to happen.

Tuesday, September 28
Had £200 on Chelsea to win to nil against Marseille at 6-4 and £200 on Anelka to score anytime at 11-10. At last, I had stopped the bleeding.

Wednesday, September 29
With £1,000 cash of greyhound winnings still sitting on my table, it was time to use it, and I headed to a Betfred shop to have £200 on Woods to be top Ryder Cup wild-card at 9-4.

Unfortunately, the bloke behind the counter had the customer service skills of Jack The Ripper and growled at me: "Wild-card? Don't know what you're talking about."

Eventually he gave me the price, counting my £200 in dramatic fashion (not once but twice), before looking me up and down with suspicion, then finally releasing the betting slip.

He made me feel like a criminal. "Oh yeah, I've had the word mate. The Ryder Cup is fixed so that Woods ends up as top wild-card. I would have had a bit more on, but thought you would only accept £200, so went with that. All those notes are fake as well. Can you give me some real ones when I come in to collect on Monday? Cheers."

I popped down the road for £150 each-way on Toms for the Viking Classic at 22-1 in Coral, getting my usual exemplary service from the sweetheart called Kelly in there, then later I had some Champions League investments, £200 on Tottenham to beat Twente at 5-6 and

£200 on under 2.5 goals in Valencia versus Man United at 8-11. It was a solid two days of midweek footy punting.

Fiddling around on my computer, I made a late spot of a juicy Ryder Cup price, so dashed back down to Betfred to have £500 on their 2-5 about Jeff Overton scoring one point or less. Fortunately, The Ripper was off duty and I got a more helpful member of staff this time, but it made me chuckle that they had to ring through the wager before accepting. Fred Done, who once famously bet £1m with Victor Chandler that Man United would finish higher than Chelsea in the Premier League, now seemingly frets over £200 liabilities. Pah.

CHAPTER 25

TIGER TO THE RESCUE

Tiger Woods

Thursday, September 30

After the opening Ryder Cup pairings were announced, I had £200 on Harrington and Donald to beat Bubba Watson and Overton at 3-4, £200 on McDowell and McIlroy to beat Cink and Matt Kuchar at 10-11, £200 on Woods and Stricker to beat Poulter and Fisher at evens, and a £200 treble on my three fancies at 8-11, 10-11 and 4-5.

Friday, October 1

My Ryder Cup morning started with a daddy longlegs goading me in the kitchen by dancing in my face. I was so pumped up that I destroyed him dead with a single blow to the torso. He won't be goading me again in a hurry.

Then everything came to a grinding halt at Celtic Manor because the golf course had turned into a swimming pool. My word, I love my continent so much.

Saturday, October 2

Rain, eh? You'll miss it when it's gone.

It's all very well having a go at rain when it's holding up play in the Ryder Cup and your favourite golfers can't get their Titleists out, but let's see how you feel when Mr and Mrs Raincloud are murdered by global warming and we've all got to start drinking oil to survive because there's no water left.

You'll never catch me criticising rain. I love the stuff and am well aware that my grandchildren's grandchildren are probably going to be so thirsty in future that they will be sucking from the udders of cows every day if we don't do something to stop climate change soon.

But yeah, I'll admit it was a tad frustrating to be setting alarm clocks for 7.45am expecting to watch the greatest golfers in the world swinging their clubs and then instead having to watch the greatest greenkeepers in Wales wringing their mops.

Still, the session-two foursomes line-up provided a superb betting opportunity when it finally came round and, despite being short of gunpowder, I did not hesitate to have £600 on the formidable duo of Donald and Poulter to beat Overton and Watson at 10-11. Most of the moisture was at Celtic Manor, but there was also a puddle of excitement forming in my pants when I clocked eyes on that tasty price, and the Englishmen went on to claim the point with ease.

Fortunately, given my parlous financial position, I hardly fancied anything in the afternoon's football. I invested £150 on Stoke to beat Blackburn at 13-10 (winner) and the same stake on Weymouth to beat Chesham in the Zamaretto League at 4-1 (loser).

Later, I had a few pints of stout while putting the world to rights with a pal, a night that was marred by how many fight situations I witnessed while walking to and from my house. You are always put in such a difficult position when you walk past a fight, aren't you? Do you intervene or leave them to it? Is it serious enough to ring the authorities or is it about to fizzle out? Is that guy wielding an iron bar or is it merely an umbrella?

My standard policy is that if I was not present at the start of the fight and do not know the reasons for the conflict, then I am not qualified to judge on the various rights and wrongs, so if everyone is still conscious I will just glide past with a token "tut-tut" to show my disapproval of violence.

You may think that makes me a bad citizen who should do more to resolve fight situations, but I won't act unless I'm in possession of all the facts. The chap getting repeatedly smacked in the chops when you happen to walk past may have started the fight, initially dishing out 50 punches of his own, so natural justice may be prevailing. Or he may have mischievously put his hand up his mate's wife's jumper and be fully deserving of some punishment. Unless you know, you just don't know.

Of course, if there is a lady in peril during a fight, that obviously changes matters. We simply must protect the ladies of the world. As is the case with rain, the human race could not continue without ladies. These days you can squirt sperm that has been frozen for centuries into test tubes and it will still get the job done eventually, so men are becoming an increasingly less important cog on the reproduction merry-go-round.

But I'm afraid you can't squirt wombs into test tubes, my friends. It is imperative we look after the ladies.

Sunday, October 3

My £200 on the Molinari brothers to beat Cink and Matt Kuchar in the session-three fourballs at 6-4 disappeared when the match was halved, while my £300 on Man City to beat Newcastle to nil at 11-8 perished when prolific Toon midfielder Jonas Gutierrez (four goals in 81 appearances for the club) decided to upset the applecart at Eastlands.

My £150 on any unquoted scoreline in Liverpool versus Blackpool at 3-1 was equally foolish (I really fancied Blackpool to score four goals you see, but they managed only two) and I opted for a get-out-of-trouble £500 on Chelsea to beat Arsenal at 8-11.

Phew. The Blues got me back in the game, but my mood soon dipped again when Toms double-bogeyed his 71st hole in the Viking Classic to drop out of the places and deny me the best part of a bag of sand.

It was time to order another morale-boosting pizza.

Monday, October 4

Had a £250 accumulator (draw no bet) on Westwood to beat Stricker (8-11), Poulter to beat Kuchar (4-5), Woods to beat Francesco Molinari (4-7), and Edoardo Molinari to beat Fowler (4-5).

Westwood controlled his match early doors, but Stricker fought back to provide the one losing leg of the fourfold. Overton then beat Fisher to confirm the loss of that monkey I had with Betfred, but thankfully I had judged the timing of Tiger's return to form to perfection, his three-point haul enough to land dead-heat winners on top US scorer and top overall wild-card.

Tuesday, October 5

For the Dunhill Links Championship, I had £450 on Westwood at 12-1, £400 on McIlroy at 13-1 and £50 on Wood at 79-1, then I grabbed a spot of lunch at the chippy.

Misjudged banter syndrome. Are you a sufferer? I know I am. As the old woman behind the counter was wrapping up my battered sausage and chips, the sausage fell off the top of the chips and almost off the counter altogether, so I weighed in with: "Ooh, has my sausage slipped out again? My sausage is always slipping out. Naughty sausage!"

I don't know why I said it – I suppose I was just trying to make her feel better about her blunder – but it went down like a lead balloon full of jumbo sausages and she remained stony-faced throughout the transaction. My new tactic in life is to say nothing at all times unless it is absolutely necessary.

The Coral telephonist who took my next bet of the day – £150 on Jonathan Byrd to win the McGladrey Classic golf at 25-1 – will certainly not be joining me in a vow of silence. He was the chattiest, most cheerful character I've ever encountered and a credit to his company.

With the subject on golf, he told me all about his holiday to Florida, how he was instructed not to look for balls in the rough because of all the dangerous animals that were lurking, how his trip to the NASA Space Station went, how he suspects a certain professional golfer is homosexual (all the usual topics of conversation you expect when ringing up for a bet!).

I presumed all bet-takers were under strict orders to get transactions done as quickly as possible and get on to the next customer – when I was a child slave working as a general dogsbody in a toy shop my boss used to bark at me: "Time is money" while I struggled to lug boxes up from the store room – but the chief of Coral's telephone operation must be a pretty chilled-out dude.

Wednesday, October 6

A mate who lives in London owed me £20 for a losing wager I put on for him, so rather than get him to send me such a meagre amount, he placed a £20 Westwood-Byrd double for me at 10-1 and 22-1. Gosh, I hope a trustworthy postman is on duty when my pal mails me £5,060 next week.

Later in the day it emerged that I had forgotten it was my mother's birthday, but a swift charge to Betfred for a £15 each-way double on Westwood and Byrd at 11-1 and 20-1 (the best present I could muster with so little time to play with) repaired some of the damage.

"What's this?" she asked. "That is almost certainly £4,117 and 50 pence," I replied.

Thursday, October 7

I logged on to Betfair to be greeted by the news that I had been given a £15 free bet on 'arcades'. All that arcade nonsense fails to float my boat – it took me five minutes as a kid to work out that playing fruit machines was about as much fun as eating actual fruit – but I never turn down a free bet.

Virtual dogs was always going to be my 'arcade' of choice and I had my £15 on Trap One at 2-1. It was so far behind throughout the 'race' that you could only see his 'head' in the left of the screen, and the set of pixels carrying my hopes and dreams trailed home in last place.

I spotted a 'rate this game' option in the bottom left-hand corner, immediately informing the Betfair bosses it was 'very poor'. Had I won £30, it would obviously have been 'very good' and I would probably have been addicted to dangerous cartoon canines forever.

Friday, October 8

To paraphrase Sir Steven Redgrave, Atlanta, 1996: "If you ever see me logging on to arcade virtual greyhounds again, you have permission to shoot me."

Saturday, October 9

You can't beat an all-night lock-in at a public house, thrashing around the topics of the day with a few pals, can you?

My morale has plummeted significantly in the last few weeks – I can't wipe the grimace off my face – but chewing the fat (quite literally when the pork scratchings come out) with comrades in the wee small hours always has a soothing effect on me.

I don't know why so many publicans ignore the lock-in option. If you've got drinkers drinking in your pub (the whole idea of owning a pub) and they want to drink more drink (thus bolstering your coffers further), why chuck them out?

If I ever become a publican, my premises will be open 24 hours a day to properly cater for the drinking community. I'll have a mattress behind the bar on which I can occasionally sneak a little kip through the night, and a bell in position for patrons to wake me whenever they require service. My pub will be called the I'm Always Inn.

It is only natural for thirsty drinkers to make a dash to the bar when the scheduled closing time is imminent and it is a joy to behold the buzz that is generated when everyone realises a more flexible cut-off point is in the offing. "She's pulling the curtains, she's only pulling the ruddy curtains!"

Conversation typically gets more interesting the longer the night wears on. A couple of friends laid into me for lacking self-esteem and being too awe-struck when I'm around beautiful women. One used his heavily pregnant partner as an example to underline his point, graphically describing the trauma of being around a female who is in the latter stages of the gestation period.

"Every time she moves, the moody cow just farts all over me," he chirped. "It's disgusting, but they all get like that once you've planted the seed, no matter how good they looked in the first place. There's no point putting them up on a pedestal, Steve. They will only disappoint you."

Well, that's something to look forward to then, eh? A few hours later, I suggested my mate should apply for the role of advertising chief of Durex, then I got a taxi to the 'special bench' to spend some time in quiet contemplation.

Unsurprisingly, I awoke on Saturday afternoon lacking sharpness, making my appointment at the local salon by only a few seconds. The girl who used to cut my hair at her house has hung up her scissors, so I have been forced to seek out pastures new. Fortunately, a delightful little beauty called Gemma has taken the job on and immediately become my new No. 1 love interest.

I employed all my journalistic training to extract as much information as possible during my trim. Originally from Oxford, moved down to Weymouth with parents as a kid, lives by the train station ... Then I weighed in with the haymaker, "Are you single?", which drew the reply: "Well, yeah, sort of."

Sort of, eh? I know what that means, treacle. It means, I wish. It means, I wish a handsome lad called Steve would come into my salon to provide a wonderful alternative to the miserable relationship I'm suffering in at the moment (that journalistic training I was on about knows no bounds).

I'm definitely putting her up on a pedestal. She can fart over me as much as she likes. In fact, I'll positively encourage her to do so.

On leaving Gemma, I headed for another arranged rendevous with Trifleface at KFC. He asked me not to write about our binge-eating session because his wife has become a diary reader to check up on him, but I'm afraid this column has always prided itself on not keeping secrets.

Welcome to my world, Trifles. I've been living like that Jim Carrey character in The Truman Show for two and a half years, with my every move tracked. Not very nice, is it? You'll probably be thanking me, though, when Victoria bends you over and gives you a good, hard spanking today for being such a naughty boy.

Come the evening I was ready for some more Guinness and, even though I was short of ammunition, I convinced myself to have a bet on the darts and watched it in the local. I fancied Barneveld to make a fast start with the arrers in his World Grand Prix semi-final against Wade, so I had £120 at 5-6 on the Dutchman winning the first set.

Barney lost 3-2, but some solace soon arrived in the shape of Lewis beating Taylor in the other semi. I had been planning a chunky Europe (to win the Ryder Cup) and Taylor (to win the Grand Prix) double a little while ago, but could not muster enough funds to make it worthwhile. Thank goodness for that, eh? I would probably have drilled through my brain with a power tool had I watched The Power getting beaten by Jackpot with a few bags on the line.

On leaving, I went home to watch *Tyson: The Movie* while eating the pizzas and chicken strippers I had ordered en route. I was expecting to be delivered chickens that flounced around in thongs demanding £20 notes, but the strippers turned out to just be slices of dead chicken meat covered in breadcrumbs. How disappointing.

I think Mike Tyson has got serious mental problems. I wouldn't say it to his face though.

Sunday, October 10

I woke up flatter than the flattest pancake in the flat Michael Flatley uses to flatter his flat-tummied dancing girls. Or something. I had blown a fortune in the last few weeks and had nothing to show for it.

My life was as empty and as meaningless as ever.

Eager to get back on the front foot, I studied the McGladrey Classic leaderboard intensely for ten minutes and arrived at the conclusion that Heath Slocum would definitely win, so I had £200 on the third-round leader at 5-2.

There was also the chance Westwood could get me right back on track – my £450 at 12-1 on him winning the Links Championship was looking more promising as the week wore on – so I settled down for an afternoon following the pride of Worksop.

My dad wanted to play golf, but I told him I could not leave my house with Westwood still in contention. However, when the world No. 2 missed a two-foot putt (I don't think the ranking system is supposed to work like that) on the 11th hole, I knew all hope had gone.

I should never have attempted to play golf in such a bad mood. The course was crowded, we had a fourball in front, and after I fluffed a chip beside the third green I informed my father I physically could not continue, pocketing my ball and marching straight back to the car.

I have not got the temperament for golf anymore. I fear I've not got the temperament for anything anymore, but certainly not golf, so I won't be swinging a club again until 2011 at the earliest.

I strongly fancied Wade for the arrers final, so had £200 at 4-6 and £100 on him to hit the first 180 at 11-10. The Machine did the business and so did Slocum, securing some timely funds for the week ahead.

Monday, October 11

My cricket-loving colleague Max Oram rang up to advise me to lay the draw in the India versus Australia Test match, so I heeded with £150 at 1-3.

Tuesday, October 12

For the Portugal Masters I had £221 on Quiros at 16-1, £174 on Schwartzel at 20-1, £155 on Willett at 23-1 and £80 on Noren at 33-1, and for the Frys.com Open I had £265 on Fowler at 16-1, £55 on Troy

Matteson at 79-1, £50 on Sabbatini at 49-1, £40 on Romero at 64-1 and £25 on Webb Simpson at 99-1.

Then I visited the gym for the first time in a while, and possibly the last time ever. One of the 'instructor' women held some boxing pads for me to hit, but she seemed to be under the impression I was David Haye, demanding a ludicrous amount of punching and hand speed. "Come on – quicker, harder – what's wrong with you?" she kept barking.

I just flipped in the end because her tone was outrageously patronising. "I'm not very fit – that's what's wrong with me – that's why I come to the f****** gym isn't it?"

I threw the gloves down and walked out, the gym falling silent as I staggered to the administration office to sever my club membership.

A bubbly blonde called Clare was in position to calm me down. She told me she would devise a more exciting exercise programme for me that I would enjoy (oh, will you now?), so I agreed to sleep on my cancellation decision.

I immediately settled myself down with some stout and a burger, then popped into Ladbrokes to place a £135 double on Quiros and Fowler (both 16-1), fully anticipating a £39,015 return.

Then it was back to watch my dear country's football team. I wasn't going to get involved financially, but as Fabio had picked my two favourite wingers, Adam Johnson and Ashley Young, I felt almost contractually obliged to back England, so had £220 on us winning to nil at 10-11 and £80 on any unquoted scoreline at 4-1.

The match was so miserable that the pal who had come round my flat to watch it with me asked with genuine desire at one stage if I could switch over to Masterchef: The Professionals.

England till I die? More like England till they start serving up souffle with caramel sauce on BBC2.

Wednesday, October 13

Oi, oi, the Indians! Nice one Oramgutan.

Thursday, October 14

Willett withdrew, so I got £155 back but had only three strings to my Portugal Masters bow.

Friday, October 15

Payday. And breathe.

CHAPTER 26

MANASSERO MAGIC

Theo Walcott

Saturday, 16 October

Respite. No matter how much peril you are in, usually you will get a little respite at some point, even if you know it will probably be only a temporary cessation of terror.

Our soldiers during the Great War, fending off German attacks in the trenches, got their respite when the guns fell silent. A chance to gulp down a shot of rum and smoke a cigarette. But they knew that once the enemy had reloaded their heavy artillery, another bombardment of shells was coming at them.

A person getting stabbed to death by a frenzied psychopath gets their respite when the unstable aggressor tires enough to put the dagger down for a few seconds. An opportunity to look back on the good old days and beg an imaginary God to save a place in 'heaven'. But the victim knows that once his assailant has had a refreshing breather, the murderous formalities will be completed.

For a punter, respite often comes in the form of payday. You may have been spectacularly losing your battle against the bookmakers and not have a proverbial tin to tinkle in, but a pay packet provides instant ammunition with which to mount some sort of fightback.

The trouble is, like with trench warfare and knife crime, there is a strong possibility of the situation getting worse after the respite. Unsuccessfully invest too much of your wages too quickly in an attempt to reverse your slide and by the end of the month you will be hoping no-one is looking as you eat a daffodil in the park for your dinner.

My first financial manoeuvre of the day was to ring my bank, who had sent me a letter informing me I would soon be paying a £25 charge for exceeding my overdraft limit a couple of weeks ago. I presumed this was an outrageous error and demanded answers, but the lady at the end of the blower guided me through the hard facts, leaving me only to apologise for wasting her time. There is nothing worse than readying yourself for an argument you fully expect to win, then losing by half the track.

Bloodied but unbowed, I decided to top up my ante-post Fowler to win the Frys.com Open, remaining convinced the cocksure young buck was coming of age. I had £155 at 7-1 to bolster the £265 I had already placed at 16-1.

Later I dipped my toes into the choppy waters of horsey racing. A pal convinced me that a couple of our sugarlump-loving friends would run very fast at Cheltenham, so I had £95 on Royal Mix to win the 3.15 at 2-1 and £60 on Great Mates to win the 4.25 at 4-1.

Then the football line-ups started trickling in and I could not resist the 11-10 about Man United defeating West Brom to nil, having £250 on, and I also had £100 on Andrew Carroll to score for Newcastle against Wigan at 13-8.

By 5pm, both horses had lost, West Brom had scored twice at Old Trafford, Carroll had missed a hatful of chances to draw a blank at

St James's, and I had already frittered away a disappointing amount. How long till next payday? Oh, only 30 days.

I opted to have one last arrer on the late kick-off at Villa Park – £150 on Anelka to notch for Chelsea at 15-8.

Fool. After the bore draw in the Midlands, I knew this month was now going to become supremely challenging. To steal the words of the greatest living Englishman, Sir Graham Taylor: "Now then, this is a test. This is a real test."

I popped to the supermarket to purchase some cheap beverages to keep my pecker up, but this raid only served to batter my morale further. I bumped into Gemma the hairdresser and she introduced me to her mother. Terrible timing.

I'm sure "What have you been up to today?" is an easy question for normal people to answer, but I often find it so difficult. What reaction do you think I would have got if I had said: "Oh, I sat around in my pants doing my nuts on horses and football – those Baggies are a bunch of little tinkers – but Rickie is going to win the Frys, so it's all good eh?"

Blank expressions all round, I would imagine. I find the line "this and that" is always a much safer option than the bleak truth.

A few minutes later, my dropping of a set of Tuborg bottles in the beer aisle deepened my sense of despair. They smashed all over the floor, leaving me cringing with embarrassment. Fortunately, Gemma and Co were elsewhere, otherwise I would have had no choice but to use one of the broken bottles to slit my wrists.

I set about trying to resolve what I quickly realised was an unresolvable situation (I'm one of the vast majority of people who go shopping without a dustpan and brush in tow), then made an escape.

I darted straight around Trifleface's house to assist him with some baby-sitting. He calls looking after his own daughter baby-sitting (because his wife usually takes full control). Mrs Trifle was out at a social function, so we watched sport while eating Chinese cuisine.

There are lots of fancy manuals about how to look after a baby, but it really isn't that hard. Stick it in front of a Barcelona match followed by a few hours of golf, squirt some milk in its face every now and then, piece of cake.

Actually, don't feed them pieces of cake – they can't keep it down.

Sunday, October 17

I had a faint hope of getting a return from the Portugal Masters, with Schwartzel close enough to catch the leaders, but that dream rapidly faded. I felt that after a succession of setbacks, I could not afford an investment on Everton, who had drifted to 7-4 prior to kick-off for the Merseyside derby.

I resorted instead to a correct-score wager, having £90 on Everton to beat Liverpool 2-1 at 11-1, before entering a packed local to watch the game.

With Everton leading 2-0, things were looking promising, but a consolation goal never came and I made the decision that if Man City could not beat Blackpool to nil then I would end my football betting days forever.

I got a mate to put £250 on at 2-1 and after 77 minutes, with City leading 1-0, I turned to Trifleface and said: "Looks like I'm back in the game!"

Marlon Harewood then immediately punished my schoolboy-like naivety.

As I supped on some stout, I felt relieved the struggle was over. I was beaten. There would be no more worrying about team news, no more fretting about missing prices, no more weekends being punctuated by soul-destroying late goals. My white flag was out in no uncertain terms.

While I considered life without football betting, I got a text from a thrilled friend who had put a fiver on Cahill to score first and Everton to win 2-0 at 45-1. He had asked me earlier in the week if there was any way of backing such an eventuality and I introduced him to scorecast betting.

He concluded his text by asking how much I had won (I had told him previously that I would be having a chunk on Everton). I didn't bother informing him I had lost £90. If I explained I had just quit football betting, three months after winning £4,400 on Spain's World Cup victory, he would have thought I was winding him up. But that is the way it is – only a madman can bet seriously on this most unpredictable of sports.

I trudged home knowing only one person could haul me from the mire – go Rickie, go Rickie, go Rickie ... The boy wonder slowly elevated himself into a tie for the lead and it looked like a £5,745 cash injection was going to put me right back in business.

He missed makeable birdie putts at the 15th and 16th, to falter, opening the door to Van Pelt, who was facing a simple up-and-down from the side of the 15th green for birdie. At that point, I elected to do some aggressive hedging, as he was the only player I could see denying Fowler, so I had £250 on Van Pelt at 2-1.

Van Pelt made his birdie to go one clear, but Fowler birdied the 17th to tie at the top again, so I was in a fantastic position.

Then Rocco Mediate, whose very mention now makes me feel physically sick, birdied the 16th hole, before holing out from 116 yards for eagle on the 17th, leapfrogging ahead of both Fowler and Van Pelt.

The commentators were chuckling away like the ruddy Chuckle Brothers – it was the fourth time in the tournament that Mediate had holed out from distance – but I was stunned into silence. Fowler's hopes were suddenly in tatters and Van Pelt three-putted the 17th to blow his chance.

I felt like quitting betting altogether at that point, never mind just football. Rocco Mediate? For crying out loud.

Monday, October 18

I would like to have assumed the ostrich position for the week, but when I started getting my head into the Grand Slam of Golf, I ended up having £200 on Kaymer at 15-8.

I had some Castello Masters wagers too – £51 on Bourdy at 43-1, £45 on Soren Hansen at 49-1, £42 on Manassero at 54-1, £39 on Horsey at

54-1 and £30 on Bjorn at 74-1 – then researched the Justin Timberlake Open.

I thought the event was tantamount to a penalty kick for Fowler on his home track. I had some cover shots on two others – £50 on Charles Howell at 49-1 and £23 on Duval at 109-1 – and then debated how much I could afford to risk on Fowler.

At that point, my friend Keith rang to ask if I wanted to join him on a ramble, and off I trotted. Fowler was 14-1 with three firms and loads of others were yet to issue prices, so I did not fear missing any boats on a quick march around Weymouth.

Trouble is, the ramble turned into an epic, with me staggering through my front door three hours later in a state of exhaustion. I immediately turned on my computer to find all the 14-1 Fowler had been snapped up and he was no bigger than 12-1 anywhere. Devastation was etched across my face.

Tuesday, October 19

Failure to get the 14-1 was haunting me. I waited in desperation for one of the firms not yet up with prices to deliver some more 14-1, but even the 12-1 was disappearing fast. Bubbling over with frustration, I lost my rag, almost doubling the stake I had originally planned by throwing £420 at Hills. Death or glory.

Wednesday, October 20

Kaymer flopped in the Grand Slam as my head flopped into my hands.

Thursday, October 21

Maybe I could get a part-time job as a children's entertainer called Mr Floppy. No, that just sounds wrong, doesn't it?

Friday, October 22

Come on Rickie – do it for me. You've never met me and could not give a monkey's whether I live or die, but do it for me, eh?

Saturday, October 23

What is the world coming to?

Am I old enough to ask that question yet? Have I been alive a sufficient length of time to know what the world was like in the past, therefore having the right to be disturbed by what it may be coming to? Or have I got to wait until I am at least 40 before I can ask what the world is coming to?

Well, I don't care if I'm breaching damnation protocol. In fact, I'm going to weigh in with a few more haymakers. We're all heading to hell in a handcart, this planet is going to the dogs, etc.

I can certainly say with conviction that the evil concept of 'identity fraud' did not exist in what I consider to be the halcyon days of the early 1980s. But tragically, this is very much a part of modern society, and the fraudsters can strike in the oddest of places.

I was dumbfounded to discover someone, who can only be described as a professional weirdo, has been pretending to be me under the comments section of my blog on racingpost.com, employing slight variations of my username (stevenjohnpalmer) to banter with other contributors and, more annoyingly, to provide false golf tips in my name.

I can't believe what I'm seeing. What satisfaction could this character possibly be getting from assuming my identity? I can understand the motive of identity fraud when it results in draining someone's bank account (there is nothing in mine at the moment so he would be wasting his time with that), but what upside is there in playing the role of a little-known betting writer?

If you are a nutcase looking to adopt an exciting new identity for a while, at least find a worthwhile target who has a bit of status, eh? You're more than welcome to spend some time in my shoes, pal, but I'm guessing you'll be begging for your own shoes back once you've sampled life inside the torture chamber I carry between my ears.

Why don't you try to find a way of becoming Theo Walcott instead? If I could spend a day as anyone in the world, it would be Theo. It is nothing to do with playing for Arsenal – I would rather be a winger for Weymouth – but full access to Melanie Slade for 24 hours would be tremendous reward for successfully stealing Walcott's identity. Does he write a blog on the Gunners' website? Go on son – hack in there – live the dream!

I suppose I should take it as a compliment that this fruitcake wants to be me. His existence must be woefully lacking in sparkle and I greatly sympathise with him. I guess Theo would look at me in the same way. What about you, though? Who in the world would you most like to swap places with?

You're a liar if you answered: "No-one." So many people are full of bluster about how they wouldn't swap places with anyone because they're so wonderfully content. This is such blatant deception. There are almost seven billion people in the world and you think you're the happiest? Nonsense.

If you offered me five years as Theo now and then death, I would take it over another 50 years as Steve. That is what is known as honesty. I know it doesn't reflect well on me – nothing in this column ever does – but the "no-one" brigade are full of tosh in my opinion.

Anyway, I spent Saturday lunchtime watching Tottenham tackle the Toffeemen (I bet you can't say that after ten pints of Old Speckled Hen) with a friend in the local, the first match I had viewed since quitting football betting forever the previous weekend.

It was incredibly relaxing not really giving two hoots what happened at White Hart Lane and even with the ball in play I often found myself glancing out of the window to admire any birds who were frolicking outside. Ooh, a pied wagtail – haven't seen one of those for a while.

But my new-found abstinence was challenged when Leighton Baines curled a superb free-kick into the back of the net, a goal that won my mate across the table £330. He had wisely reacted to Arteta being missing from the Everton line-up by having £10 on Baines to score first at 33-1, knowing full well the left-back would be on duty for free-kicks and penalties.

I was obviously thrilled for my chum, but seeing a football betting coup landed was not exactly what the doctor ordered for a man going cold turkey.

I suppose small stakes at big prices can't do any harm, eh? It's a slippery slope, though, isn't it? A little first scorer bet, then a few quid on a correct score, a ton on over 2.5 goals and suddenly you're injecting heroin up your arse. Gosh, that slope is slippery.

With money tight, I spent the afternoon at my friend Satelliteface's house. He installs satellites and aerials for a living and has a big, round face, much like one of his products. In his front garden, he has got an enormous Nasa-style satellite that can pick up just about any televised football being shown anywhere in the solar system.

Satelliteface often rings up full of joy to inform me he is watching a live match which is beaming into his lounge from a far-flung location ("I've got Dynamo Moscow playing in the Russian Premier League if you fancy coming round"), failing to realise he is probably the only person in the British Isles who would choose to use valuable leisure time this way.

The chance to watch Chelsea versus Wolves while regularly flicking over to the Castello Masters golf, though, was an attractive enough package to lure me round, and the rise up the leaderboard of Manassero in Spain put me in high spirits.

Satelliteface's wife popped out to walk their dog just as the half-time whistle blew at Stamford Bridge, which gave him an opportunity to guide me through the 25 'secret channels' his remarkable satellite system allows him to enjoy during times of solitude.

I've seen some rather humdrum half-time entertainment in my time, but this did not fall into that category. I don't think the idea of the 'watershed' has reached continental Europe yet. If that is the material being served up in the middle of the afternoon, I dread to think what dizzying heights our liberal cousins across the channel take things to after dark. Jeepers creepers.

Back later in my own bolthole, I watched Fowler fail to improve on his position in the Justin Timberlake Open. He was only three off the lead going into the third round, but then slumped a further three shots behind.

My word, I was frustrated. Maybe I should have popped back round Satelliteface's house.

Sunday, October 24

I was in a deep financial pickle and my father, who had just read my latest diary in the *Racing Post*, texted to inform me that the Salvation Army runs an excellent soup kitchen five days a week in Weymouth town centre. How reassuring.

Rather than resign myself to a life eating flavoured water, I decided to be more pro-active, trying to turn the remaining few quid I had at my disposal into something more substantial. My horse source had told me Wishfull Thinking would be unbeatable in the 2.45 at Aintree, so I had £200 at 4-5, looking to eke out enough to survive until the next payday.

I spent most of the day following the progress of Manassero in Spain – he was jostling for the lead and threatening to provide a much-needed two-bag boost – but I popped to my favourite betting shop to watch what was supposed to be Wishfull Thinking's destruction of his three rivals at Aintree.

I rubbed my hands together with a grin as the horseys set off – it was an expression that said: "I know who is going to win, nah nah nah nah nah!" – but seconds later Wishfull Thinking fell at the first ruddy fence.

My eyes closed, my head lolled to one side and I struggled to generate sufficient enthusiasm for life to breathe. That's it, I said to myself. No more horse betting. I quit that too.

If there is such a thing as God, I believe he comes in the shape of a 17-year-old Italian called Matteo, who has every right to be wishfully thinking about becoming one of the best golfers in the world. Manassero forged clear over the final few holes, romping to a four-shot triumph, saving me from becoming a season-ticket holder at the Salvation Army soup kitchen. Phew.

In my post-victory haze, I pressed up on Fowler, with £150 at 33-1, gunning for a £10,000 jackpot, but he soon made a poor start to his final round. I jumped ship to Ryan Palmer, having £50 at 25-1, and he made much more positive strides.

Having done so little betting all weekend, though, I was over-eager for action, so I ended up throwing further coal at Palmer as if he was the engine of a steam-train, shovelling another £50 at 13-1, then £25 at 14-1 and finally £100 at 10-1. My namesake got into a tie for the lead and I had visions of a £5,000 profit from the golfing day, but a bogey at the par-five 13th hole derailed him.

Still, I was mightily relieved to be back in the game thanks to magnificent Matteo.

CHAPTER 27
THE QUITTING MACHINE

Susan Boyle

Monday, October 25

Infuriatingly, I fancied too many players to go well in the Asia Pacific Classic, having £236 on Els at 10-1, £178 on Retief Goosen at 14-1, £118 on Scott at 20-1, £90 on Noh at 28-1, £40 each-way on Arjun Atwal at 50-1, £40 each-way on Sim at 50-1 and £25 each-way on Leishman at 80-1.

For the Andalucia Masters, I had £112 on Francesco Molinari at 20-1, £73 on Hanson at 31-1, £62 on Simon Dyson at 39-1, £33 on Garrido at 69-1 and £26 on Bjorn at 89-1. Settle down Steve, settle down.

Tuesday, October 26

I watched a 16-1 Trap One finish first and a 12-1 Trap Three finish second in a greyhound race from Wimbledon on Sky Sports. How much would I have lost on that race if I had got involved? Right, add it to the list. I've quit dog betting.

Wednesday, October 27

Had a £62 double on Hanson (29-1) and Noh (26-1) that should return £50,220 for its sins.

Thursday, October 28

Molinari took an early lead in the Andalucia Masters before a three-putt double bogey at the 15th hole. I would now be in the Guinness Book of Records if they had a section reserved for the longest ever man-sigh.

Friday, October 29

What can I quit next? Deodorising?

Saturday, October 30

I made a point of entering the gymnasium for the final time looking as unhealthy (and happy) as possible. I had finally come to my senses and decided to officially hand in my membership resignation, so with an enormous hangover, bloodshot eyes, unkempt hair and looking like I was en route to an early Halloween party, I swaggered in purposefully to explain why I have gyms second only to concentration camps on my list of places I least like to frequent.

The usual sickening scene greeted me. A dead-eyed beefcake was grimacing while lifting weights in front of a mirror at one end of the gym, desperately trying to add extra bulk to his muscles in the hope that large arms will compensate in some way for a pea-sized personality.

And at the other end, a chubby young girl, who no doubt spends nights wantonly staring at pictures in glossy magazines of matchstick women like Victoria Beckham and Paris Hilton, was sweating buckets on various machines in a frantic quest to defy the laws of genetics.

Misery. That is all you find in gyms – miserable people seeking solutions to unconquerable problems through a dumbbell or an exercise bike. Well I wasn't going to be a dumbo any longer – it was time to get on my bike – so I launched my membership card at the 'fitness instructor' and demanded the termination of my £33-a-month contract.

Nothing is ever straightforward, is it? I had to fill out a cancellation form detailing my reasons for quitting before I could be set free. I didn't think I should have to justify my decision – it was none of their business – so, to use General Election parlance, I opted to 'spoil my paper'. I ticked the 'pregnancy' box and then wrote 'also having a gastric band fitted' in the comments section. Take that, you profiteers of misery.

Back in the safety of my bunker, £33 a month richer, I admired the huge amount of chocolate in my fridge while sucking on a Fudge Finger. I found the Andalucia Valderrama Masters leaderboard less alluring, though, with only Bjorn threatening to bring home any bacon.

I added Jimenez to my stable after round two (£180 at 13-1), as well as bolstering my Bjorn investment with a further £20 at 74-1, but McDowell was keeping them both at a safe distance.

My morale failed to improve during Match Of The Day in the evening as one of the commentators used the single most annoying line in the history of football coverage: "The crossbar comes to their rescue!"

The crossbar never comes to anyone's rescue. The crossbar does not stretch out a hand to deflect a shot away. The crossbar remains completely still, at the height and width outlined by the rules of association football, and can play no part in deciding the outcome of matches.

That commentator ruined my night and should be sacked forthwith.

Sunday, October 31

The Asia Pacific Classic was an unqualified disaster. Els closed with four birdies to finish fifth, but that was very much a case of too little too late, so it was all down to Bjorn and Jimenez in Spain to rescue my betting week.

I had another £60 on Jimenez at 18-1 after a flash of foolish optimism during the final round, but unfortunately he and Bjorn could only rescue me in the style of a crossbar (they hardly moved on the leaderboard, finishing fifth and seventh respectively).

Oh well, there it is. Having trousered £2,000 from Manassero's heartwarming Castello Masters triumph, I had blown nearly all the winnings seven days later. Am I allowed to use the word penis in a family newspaper? Penis.

With spirits low, I needed some sort of distraction and Satelliteface's suggestion that we go on a night-time Halloween witchhunt in a wood in deepest Dorset was just what the doctor ordered. He claimed that as a teenager he went to this wood with a few pals on Halloween night and they found a small church, inside of which (if you'll pardon the pun) were ten or so white-cloaked Pagans burning a witch (and several pigs) while chanting strange songs.

My natural scepticism kicked in – I know Satelliteface had a penchant for strong cider as a youngster and may have been hallucinating – but I was eager for adventure, so we set off in the GTI.

I must admit I almost bottled out of our mission completely when we parked up on the edge of the wood, turned off the engine and sat in pitch black silence, fumbling for our torches. What would the Pagans do if they saw us, I wondered? Burn us too? I don't look much like a witch, but I could easily be mistaken for a pig.

I steeled myself and we searched for several hours, slowly working our way around the wood, my tour guide trying manfully to call upon a 15-year-old memory to locate the church.

But sadly, the closest thing we got to a witch was when Satelliteface's wife rang up to ask why he hadn't yet walked their dog, so we were forced to abandon our church chase.

It was a massive disappointment. Trifleface, who had said he was too scared to join us on the witchhunt, texted me: 'Are you dead yet? If so, can I have your dartboard?'

Nope, sorry mate. Still alive. Still ruddy alive.

Monday, November 1

I squeezed the last few beans out of my bank account to get some wagers on the HSBC Champions event, having £116 on Casey at 20-1, £100 on Els at 23-1, £56 on Scott at 41-1, £43 on Ross Fisher at 59-1 and £35 on Villegas at 74-1.

Everything went swimmingly later – I beat Trifles 10-9 in a 'chicken-wing-off' at KFC, compiled a 32 break at the snooker club, then nailed a 180 on the arrers board at home. Win your small battles and the war will take care of itself, eh?

Tuesday, November 2

A woman from HSBC rang up to "discuss what improvements we could make to your account", an expression I felt was rather taking the piddle considering my parlous financial position. How about I back a couple of winners, eh? That might improve it.

I knew straight away that nothing could be gained from the conversation, so I took her as far off official business as possible for my own entertainment. I first requested a new overdraft limit of £500,000, which she told me, in all seriousness, was not possible.

I then asked her who was going to win the HSBC Champions – "Your employers sponsor the tournament, so you must have the inside track" – but all I gleaned from that chit-chat was that she doesn't like Tiger Woods.

Further into our entirely pointless dialogue, I established that her finances were in an excellent state because she has got "a rich husband". "Where can I get one of them from?" I asked. "Maybe that's where I have been going wrong all these years."

In the evening a friend rang to say he had popped up the local to watch Tottenham versus Inter but had got roped into doing the pub quiz instead, so he asked me to join him in a two-man team. I've made some poor decisions in my time, but agreeing to this is right up there with the worst of them.

When I arrived to discover my pal had been drinking since high noon and the question 'What is your name?' would have severely challenged him, I knew the chances of quiz success were slim.

After three rounds, we were doing surprisingly well, storming the sports section, but then we both failed to hear the instruction to exchange sheets with another team for marking purposes. When the quizmaster began reading out the answers at pace, we realised our blunder, suffering immediate disqualification.

We reacted by storming to another pub, imbibing heavily and debating the most frightening subject matter of them all. Death. The end of everything you have ever known. We then concluded the night with a less disturbing but infinitely more bemusing topic. Life. What is the meaning of life?

I think every pub quiz should consist of just one question: 'What is the meaning of life?' The most illuminating essay presented to the quizmaster should be rewarded with the prize money.

Wednesday, November 3

I have now got a photograph of a graveyard as my screensaver on my mobile phone to provide a constant reminder of how lucky I am to be alive. I recommend you do the same.

Thursday, November 4

The family who live in the flat below me are starting to drive me bonkers. The mother, who like most of the ruddy world seems to be unemployed and on benefits, has taken to singing loudly like a poor man's Susan Boyle throughout the day. It's unbearable. I've resorted to singing: "You're s*** and you know you are" in response, but she just doesn't take the hint.

Then when her army of children get back from school, they spend all night playing some sort of Star Wars computer game at high volume, with light-sabre noises piercing my ears for hours on end.

I want to get rich from betting for so many reasons, but being able to buy a detached house (maybe on the moon) in which I can enjoy 24-hours-a-day peace would be one of the greatest consequences of prosperity.

Friday, November 5

"You're doing my head in, you're doing my head in, you cow" (to the tune of 'Walking In The Air' by Aled Jones).

Saturday, November 6

What time is it? What day is it? Who are you? Who am I? What am I? Where am I? What is that? How is Ernie Els getting on?

When there is live European Tour golf being screened in the middle of the night, which is often the case now that so many events are played in the Far East, a man can find himself drifting in and out of consciousness during the coverage, struggling to get his head around the world at a time usually reserved for sleep.

I knew following the HSBC Champions event from China in the early hours of Saturday morning would be particularly tricky given I had spent the previous evening inhaling fumes at a Ministry of Defence bonfire party. I had devoted half an hour to getting up close and personal with the fire, drowning my eyes in the enchanting flames, admiring the awesome power of fire.

I reckon I might become a twisted firestarter if my life doesn't take a significant turn for the better in the next couple of years. There is just something about fire, isn't there? Imagine bowling around with spiky hair, setting fire to anything you didn't like the look of and telling everyone you were the firestarter (the twisted firestarter). That would be a tremendous giggle, wouldn't it?

I felt a little sorry for the MoD boys who were in attendance at the party. A fireworks display, combined with a great big fire, had to be something of a busman's holiday for these chaps. If you've just come home from fighting the war on terror in Afghanistan, having spent months battling insurgents in Helmand province, you're surely not going to be too excited by the prospect of bangers and burning.

Maybe they only turned up for the burgers that came free with every ticket. You can't beat a good burger, can you? When I went to get my burger, I was disappointed with the enormous size of the queue to the sauce table, but patiently waited ten minutes to reach the front. What happened when I finally got to the head of affairs made me realise just how much my luck is out at the moment and how this is probably not a good time to be betting.

There was no tomato sauce left, you see. The lad immediately ahead of me had polished off the last of the ketchup. I made do with the far less satisfying mayo, but by the time I had finished applying it, the chef arrived to replenish the giant bowl of tomato sauce. So, out of about 250 people, I was the only one at the function who didn't have the opportunity to have tomato sauce on his burger. God Almighty, give me a ruddy break.

Hearty cheers rang out when Guy Fawkes, perched on a stick at the top of the bonfire, perished in spectacular fashion. As his head toppled into the heart of the blaze, I overheard a father explaining to his daughter how Fawkes tried to blow up the Houses of Parliament, therefore making him the arch villain.

Isn't it curious how everyone suddenly rallies around Parliament and politicians on Guy Fawkes Night, having spent the rest of the year abusing them? Clearly, it is okay to to be angry with politicians ("that Nick Clegg is a bit of a wally, eh?") but it is not okay to be really angry with them ("I'm gonna blow up Nick Clegg with lashings of gunpowder"). Where do you draw the line, eh?

Three of my HSBC hopefuls were in the mix (£116 on Casey at 20-1, £100 on Els at 23-1 and £43 on Ross Fisher at 59-1) but Francesco Molinari and Westwood had gone clear at the top of the leaderboard after round three, so the chances of a Chinese takeaway were slim. I dozed in the afternoon with the agitated snore of a doomed man.

In the evening, I was reunited with Simon The Stalker, who had made another raid to Weymouth from Torquay, this time bringing his mother and father (who could easily get work as Roy Hodgson's stunt double), along with his new girlfriend Emma.

A jolly time was had by all, although an unsavoury incident with a pool cue seemed to put the frighteners up Emma, bringing their night to a close. A pool cue can be an extremely dangerous weapon if it falls into the wrong hands.

Sunday, November 7

I was violently ill for much of the day. Molinari triumphed in China, so my bank balance remained in woeful condition, while I was downing ibuprofen as if they were sweeties in an attempt to exterminate the most horrific headache I had ever encountered.

I have quit many things in the last few weeks, but this was a big one. It was time to quit alcohol, which was once described to me by a learned friend as "the devil's sperm". I think I've finally worked out what he means.

CHAPTER 28

GREAT SCOTT

David Haye and Audley Harrison

Monday, November 8

It was time to lose what little self-respect I had left and get out the begging bowl. I'm a big fan of Buddhism and 'no ego, no problems' is a mantra I like. Lots of people can't face the indignity of begging so they go hungry, but no ego, no problems. Beg and eat. Or, in this case, beg and bet.

Week-long loans from richer pals secured me £65 on Poulter to win the Singapore Open at 18-1, £60 on Scott at 20-1, £45 on Schwartzel at 26-1 and £20 each-way on Bourdy at 100-1. For the JBWere Masters, I had £40 each-way on Rumford at 50-1 and £105 on Allenby at 9-1.

Tuesday, November 9

I dangled my bowl elsewhere and got some Children's Miracle Network Classic wagers placed, having £43.24 on Cink at 24-1, £35 on Holmes at 27-1, £30 on Howell at 33-1, £23 on Vijay Singh at 45-1 and £18 on Davis Love at 54-1, then I had a £10 treble on Allenby (9-1), Scott (16-1) and Cink (25-1) with a view to a £44,200 coup.

I had lunch on my tab at my mate's cafe and I noticed the Thai girl who works there was in floods of tears in the corner of the kitchen when I placed my order. I'm not sure what was bothering her, but she looked so sad. When you think about, every second of every day, millions of people across the globe are crying. So if you're not crying, you're not doing that bad in the grand scheme of things.

If you're laughing, then you're doing incredibly well. My mate just hired an Eastern European cleaner and it took her seven days to hoover his house. Turns out she was a Slovak.

Go on – have a ruddy good laugh!

Wednesday, November 10

I believe lacking a worthwhile cause is the key to human unhappiness.

My Everton-supporting pal had been devoting his life to the Toffeemen winning the Premier League this season – he was bursting with optimism that this could be the campaign when they really make their mark – but after the 1-1 Goodison draw against Bolton he has officially resigned himself to the fact that it is not going to happen. In the vice of depression, he has sought an alternative cause, and he texted me: "I'm now focusing all attention on saving the polar bear instead."

Helping polar bears avoid extinction is the cause now keeping him going. When he dies, he wants to have 'He saved the polar bear' on his gravestone. Fair enough, eh?

I've been trying to work out what cause I can have to give me a bit of direction too, and I'm thinking about doing my best to save the whales. I'm not that bothered about saving the Wales – I've only been there once and I got headbutted by a Newport County fan during a ding-dong FA Cup tie – but I've always been very fond of whales.

As it turns out, polar bears actually eat some types of whale, so saving the whales will, in turn, help save the bears. My friend and I have got a new motto that is giving us plenty of motivation to get up in the morning: Bear there's a will, there's a whale.

We know it doesn't make much sense, but it keeps us happy, and that's the main ruddy thing isn't it?

Thursday, November 11

The sperm whale has got a funny name, hasn't it? If I ever switch careers to the pornography business, I think I'll call myself Stefano 'The Sperm Whale' Palmaro whenever I'm in front of the cameras.

Friday, November 12

The humpback whale has also got a peculiar denomination. Sperms and humpbacks? These randy rascals can't be an endangered species – they must be reproducing at a rate of knots. I don't think they need my help after all.

Saturday, November 13

Oh well, you've still got your health.

That is a line often trotted out by humans who are looking to give other humans something positive to concentrate on during times of struggle. Your health is the most important thing, eh?

But what if you haven't got your health? What can be said to you then to provide some cheer when morale is in short supply?

Nothing. That's what. Nothing can be said. And with illness overwhelming me heading into the weekend, I was bedridden, inconsolable and on complete mental lockdown. I only showed signs of life as each wave of autumn germination lodged itself in my nostrils, forcing me into a series of hysterical sneezes that threatened to snap my head from my neck.

We don't fully appreciate health when we've got it. Only when we are at death's door do we realise how wonderful it is to be free of any significant physical suffering. If I ever make it back to relative fitness, I'm going to make sure I spend every day marvelling at my body's immune system, staring at myself naked in the mirror for at least seven hours a week.

Getting no sleep was not aiding my condition. Another 'European Tour' event was being played in the middle of the night about a million miles from Europe and following the progress of Poulter and Scott in the Singapore Open was putting an extra strain on my snot-caked carcass.

Too ill to do anything but open my eyes, I ended up watching some rugby union in the afternoon, as England were demolishing Australia at Twickenham.

The performance of Martin Johnson's charges was a fillip. England were wearing all black and were playing like the All Blacks, and I texted my rugby-loving pal Graham Woods to wax lyrical about the scoreline. He was trying to watch the game on his iphone while playing 'What's the time Mr Wolf?' in the park with his daughters.

I texted back: 'What's the time Mr Wallaby? It's time to eat our s***!' There is nothing quite like the sight of humbled Australians to make an unwell Englishman feel a bit better.

Humbled Australians and hot chocolate is the perfect remedy recipe, but I could not make the latter due to having no drinkable milk. Milk goes off so ruddy quickly, doesn't it? You would think in the year 2010 we might have somehow developed cows that can squirt milk which lasts a month or so, but we clearly haven't. Maybe farmers should store all cows in giant blocks of ice to keep the milk fresh. Would that work? Never mind Friesian cows, how about freezing cows? I'd vote for it.

Desperate for a hot chocolate, I drove to my local Coral shop to get one of the complimentary cups they always happily serve up for me. It was delicious. It comes to something, though, when your life is in such disarray that you have to go to a betting shop to have a hot chocolate. No doubt I'll get confused soon and end up asking the girl in Costa Coffee for £50 on Trap One.

Back in my bunker, the tonic of my hot chocolate soon wore off and my condition worsened. What to do? Feed a fever, starve a cold, or is it the other way around? I didn't even know whether I had a fever or a cold anyway. What's the difference? I decided to feed whatever it was (because feeding is more enjoyable than starving), so Trifleface came round and we pooled resources to purchase an extreme amount of pizza and some cookies.

Neither of us could move after the session, but I'm certain we would still have been better equipped than Audley Harrison to compete in a Manchester ring with David Haye, the 'fight' I sadly invested £14.95 to view.

I should have asked for my money back as soon as I saw Harrison waddle to the ring in a 'Keep Stonebridge Adventure Playground Open' T-shirt. What a fearsome message that sent out to his opponent.

If he had worn a T-shirt that read 'I'm Gonna Knock Your Ruddy Block Off' then he might have got the favourite fretting. But arriving for combat saying: 'I'm more worried than anything else about little people not having little swings to play on in their little park' hardly conveyed the impression of a warrior.

Your destiny, Audley? My arse.

Sunday, November 14

Scott was leading from Poulter in Singapore, so I was in a strong position, but a disappointing weather delay meant the tournament could not be finished until Monday morning. I still had no money to bet (or do anything else) with.

The great Raymond van Barneveld was a mouthwateringly big 5-4 with one firm to beat an opponent called Tricia 5-0 in the Grand Slam of Darts – it was an unbelievable price – but I had no ammunition. Deeply frustrating. And I probably would have had a couple of quid on the Nedum Onuoha, 3-0 Sunderland scorecast at 10,000,000-1 for their Stamford Bridge trip, too!

All my Network Classic golfers were on the edge of the leaderboard without seriously contending, although I got some cheer from the tournament when the triumphant Robert Garrigus credited his victory to 'The Lord'.

Super stuff, Robert. It had nothing to do with you then, mate? Nothing to do with your powerful driving and a superb week of putting? Nope, you were just a puppet on strings being dangled down by The Lord, eh? Amazing.

I went back to bed dosed up to the eyeballs on Night Nurse, craving an actual night nurse. Why does sex have to get in the way of everything all the time? If I put an advert in the local paper requesting a night nurse, everyone would presume I was a deviant seeking a sex worker to indulge in nocturnal horseplay between the sheets. In fact, all I wanted was a night nurse to stroke me till morning and mop sweat off my ailing brow, and there is nothing deviant about that.

Would a sex worker provide that service for a discount price? Or do they cater only for hammer-and-tongs action? I must make some tentative inquiries.

Monday, November 15

Thankfully, The Lord made sure Scott cruised to victory. I endured a few nervous moments as Poulter dropped out of the running and Anders Hansen applied some pressure, but a bonus bag of sand was eventually banked on payday.

I approached the week's golf with confidence. I've been in some deep financial trouble through the years, but I always break free with a golf wager. It just always happens. I'm invincible. When I really need to focus and deliver, I usually do. Looking to build momentum, I had £100 on Schwartzel to win the Hong Kong Open at 27-1, £85 on Thongchai Jaidee at 30-1, £40 each-way on Bourdy at 50-1, £30 each-way on Maybin at 66-1 and £20 each-way on Horsey at 100-1.

Despite my upturn in fortunes, my illness was still keeping spirits low and my dissatisfaction with the human race increased when I popped into town for some dinner. I did not have any change for the car park and ran into the neighbouring newsagents, explaining my plight to the cashier and buying some chewing gum with a £5 note.

Just as he was typing 45p into the till, I said: "Some 20-pence pieces would be really useful, thanks."

He promptly handed me back four pound coins, a 50-pence piece and a five-pence piece.

I thought that just about summed up the selfishness that festers through modern society in this part of the world. Would it really have put this chap out so much to have given me five 20-pence pieces rather than one of the £1 coins? Or even just two 20-pence pieces and a ten rather than the 50?

But no, he stuck rigidly to the company policy of providing change in as small a number of coins as possible, despite the customer having only been attracted to the shop in the first place to garner as many coins as possible.

I'm definitely going to have to emigrate soon – I'm sure there is not as much evil around on mainland Europe.

Tuesday, November 16
Had £205 on Ryo Ishikawa to win the Dunlop Phoenix Open at 10-1, £20 each-way on Taichi Teshima at 50-1, along with a £40 Schwartzel (25-1) and Ishikawa (10-1) double, seeking an £11,440 injection.

Wednesday, November 17
My nephew tripped over a beanbag and smashed his head against a wall on a visit to my flat, and as I tried to find a way of calming his delirious wailing, he actually used the words: "I want my mummy!"

I virtually disowned him at that point. I didn't realise children actually used that line. You're not going to survive five minutes in the playgrounds of broken Britain with an attitude like that, buster.

Thursday, November 18
With the Grand Slam of Darts knockout draw complete, I had £111 on James Wade to lift the trophy at 9-1, fancying The Machine to be too strong for Taylor should they meet in the final.

Friday, November 19

A baby shark swimming up the coast asks his dad: "Why do we circle people in the water with our fins showing before we eat them? Why don't we just attack and eat them straight away?"

The wise old father shark replies: "Come on son, don't be silly. They taste much better without the crap inside them."

CHAPTER 29

BEANPOLE BOB WALKS TALL

Robert Karlsson and Martin Kaymer

Saturday, November 20

Oh, golf. If I watch any more golf, I'm going to end up looking like a ruddy golf ball. The only fortnight of the year I don't watch golf is the one that includes Christmas Day, and what does that Claus character usually throw down my chimney as my main Yuletide present? A shiny set of golf balls.

You definitely can get too much of a good thing. I love watching golf, but these late-season through-the-night tournaments from the Far East result in overkill. Making love to Kelly Brook for 15 hours would be wonderful, but if she then immediately spreadeagled herself in anticipation of another round of action, you would probably be dreaming of a nice sit-down, a cup of tea and a tub of Sudocrem. The golf season, like an insatiable Brook, goes on a tad too long.

After three nights following golf balls in Hong Kong, my only real hopes of getting any return were from each-way investments on Bourdy and Maybin, as Poulter looked certain to claim victory.

In the other event, the Dunlop Phoenix Open, handy Japanese ace Yuta Ikeda was well clear at the end of day three and I was expecting him to be a best price of around 1-3. Extrabet were going a stand-out 8-11, though, which had me foaming at the mouth.

I rarely feel the need to open new accounts, but was hooked by the 8-11 Ikeda (and the free £25 bet offered to new Extrabet customers). All went smoothly at first and I got an email straight away saying I could start betting, but then when I tried to log in, the message 'Your account has been suspended from online dealing' flashed up.

Bloody Nora. The classic line 'We apologise for any inconvenience this may cause' was also on show. It is the word 'any' that really gets my goat at times like this. Any inconvenience? Not 'the inconvenience'? The most inconvenient thing possible has happened for someone hoping to place a bet (not being allowed to place a bet), so I think that might just sneak into the 'any inconvenience' category.

I rang up customer services, presuming there was a technical gremlin halting my progress, but I was told that I needed to send a copy of my driving licence, utility bill, etc, to verify my account before I could start betting. God, I wish I had been born in caveman times – I'm sure no-one had to send around copies of their utility bills in caveman times.

I decided it was far too much effort to get the account going and it was with relief that I found Ikeda trading at the same price on the betting exchanges. I got £203.77 on at 8-11, before heading off to watch my local football team.

Weymouth converted an early penalty to take the lead against Bedford, but then one of the linesmen pulled a hamstring and had to go off, putting the match in jeopardy. A Tannoy announcement was made asking any qualified referees in the ground to go to the dugout and I immediately strode purposefully in the direction of the remaining officials as if I had Fifa badges coming out of my arse.

I thought if I got a flag in my hand, I could perform the most biased piece of linesmanship in the history of football, but unfortunately they had ways of checking your credentials through a computer database and I had to skulk off shame-faced.

After a 20-minute delay, a genuinely certificated candidate had got the gig, but even without the assistance of a dodgy referee's assistant, the home team triumphed 3-1 with two of the greatest goals I have ever witnessed at any level of association football.

If Lionel Messi had scored them, the whole world would still be talking about them now. But, then again, I suppose if Lionel Messi had scored them, the whole world would be so concerned with why Lionel Messi was playing in the Zamaretto League, they probably wouldn't have taken much notice of the two wonder goals he had just scored. I'm going to stop thinking about this now.

In the evening, trying to get through day 13 of my self-imposed drinking ban, I had a good, old-fashioned smoke. Is smoking worse for you than drinking? If it stops you drinking, is it worth smoking? Starting smoking at the age of 32 is not standard procedure, but I was desperately doing anything to stop me falling off the drinking wagon.

A couple of hours later, though, I tumbled off all wagons, ending up smoking and drinking, but it was tough to stay level-headed when news reached me that Steve Beaton had defeated Taylor in the Grand Slam of Darts.

With my £111 on Wade to win the tournament at 9-1 suddenly looking a terrific wager, I was buzzing, happily bringing complete strangers up to speed about Beaton's heroics. A shock loss for The Power is always a great topic with which to break the ice at a busy set of public house urinals and the news that "Beaton's beaten Taylor" raised plenty of eyebrows.

The gents cleared quickly for some reason, though, when I went on to passionately express my deep admiration for the Bronzed Adonis.

Sunday, November 21

The Hong Kong Open provided no joy – Maybin finished seventh and Bourdy finished 11th – but Ikeda got the job done with ease.

My afternoon was spent rambling deep in the Dorset countryside

– so deep, in fact, my pals and I came across some old, abandoned tanks. Wow. The kid in me came roaring out with the chance to play on actual tanks. They are majestic beasts. I would obviously love to see a war-free world dominated by peace, pansies and pixies, but I have to admit I would miss the tank.

As we left the detritus of war behind and returned to a designated coastal path, we frightened a pair of old ladies with our presence, despite attempting to appear as unthreatening as possible. When you are literally in the middle of nowhere, the arrival of others is a concern. You just don't expect to see anyone else in such remote pastures and these two veteran ramblers looked petrified to find three unshaven thirty-somethings approaching them.

I suppose we could have easily overpowered them, taken all their money, thrown them into the sea and gone on our way safe in the knowledge that all the crimes would go unpunished, but that would not have been a very nice thing to do. I think it's a great shame that elderly folk have to view their youngers (that should be a word, even if it isn't) with such suspicion these days. I blame that Crimewatch programme.

Keith had packed a superb lunch for our rambling party and I was left absolutely stunned by the magnificence of his thermos flask. I had never seen a thermos flask in action before, and when he offered me some tea, I told him I didn't drink the iced variety. When he insisted the tea would be piping hot, I was awash with scepticism and thought I was being subjected to some sort of prank. But, amazingly, I almost burned my lip when I took a gulp of the thermos flask conditioned tea.

What an invention. We had been on the move for hours, yet the tea was still hot. Whoever invented the thermos flask is a genius. It is the most impressive thing I have ever encountered.

As our ramble concluded, my mind turned to Wade and how The Machine was getting on in his semi-final against Wayne Jones, but I was in a pub in Worth Matravers, the sort of far-flung Dorset village where chickens roam freely among drinkers, and I could not get any reception on my phone.

By the time I was back in proper civilisation, Wade had won 16-6 and booked his place in the final with ease, so I was looking good for a £1,110 return. Even more so later when he cruised to an 8-0 lead in the first-to-16-legs final.

Scott Waites pulled it back to 8-4, but I still didn't fret. The Machine was slightly malfunctioning, but would surely be back online soon enough. 9-8? Oh Christ, The Machine is crashing. 11-14? The Machine has turned into The Muppet. Why won't you work, you so-called Machine?

Monday, November 22

Still shaken by Wade's capitulation, I placed some tentative Dubai World Championship wagers, having £83 on Ross Fisher at 39-1, £59 on Robert Karlsson at 54-1, the same stake at the same price on Schwartzel, £47 on Peter Hanson at 69-1 and £37 on Quiros at 89-1.

Later, after a large pizza, I watched a programme called 'Inside Britain's Fattest Man'. It was about a lad called Barry, who is 50 stone, can drink 40 pints of lager in a single sitting and typically consumes 29,000 calories a day.

Barry was as happy as Larry, tucking into a delicious fried breakfast each morning, watching his beloved Birmingham City every weekend, with his voluptuous girlfriend eagerly rubbing cream on to his leg ulcers whenever they needed tending.

There is no evidence that thin people are any happier than fat ones. In fact, it may even be the opposite. My new motto is: Being thin is a sin – being fat is where it's at.

Tuesday, November 23

I popped out for a bacon roll in the morning and a black cat walked beside me for several yards. It refused to actually cross my path, though, so I don't think I will get any luck out of it. I turned towards it after a minute or so and demanded: "Cross my ruddy path, you little teaser!" but it freaked out and ran off.

Just before going to bed at night, I watched a programme about piranhas on Discovery, which featured the story of a three-year-old Amazonian boy who fell into a lake and was nothing but a set of bones within a few seconds.

I got a poor night's sleep after that, believing I was about to be gobbled to death by a swarm of carnivorous fish at any moment. The half-hour before you intend to go to sleep is crucial if you plan to actually sleep. Reading a book before intercourse with Brook is probably the best route to perfect sleep. Learning about piranhas before going bananas is probably the worst.

Wednesday, November 24

Had £125 at 7-1 on the Ashes series score being 2-2. As much as I would love to see the tourists triumph outright, I think an urn-keeping draw is the best we can hope for.

Thursday, November 25

Having made a disappointing trip to the bank to discover a winner was urgently required, I had £200 on O'Sullivan to claim Premier League snooker glory at 11-10.

Friday, November 26

Karlsson had the lead in Dubai, then lost it, then Fisher took over at the top as I rode another golfing rollercoaster. The constant rollercoasters are making me sick. Can't I just have a snooze on the Ferris wheel occasionally? Oh yeah, I can do that when there is no golf in the last two weeks of the year.

When does the darts World Championship start? December 16? Oh, just get me a bucket.

Saturday, November 27

The last thing I need is another addiction – my list of dependencies is already long and alarming – but I almost added to my mental malaise during an afternoon visit to my local pub.

I have tried to avoid computer games since passing through puberty.

A lot of people I know spend plenty of time these days banging on about COD, which is a nice fish in my book but an abbreviation for a war game called Call of Duty in theirs, and they often try to convince me of the merits of 'gaming'.

But I can't help feeling there is something rather tragic about a grown man sitting at home pretending to be a soldier (I expect some really serious COD gamers play while dressed in full camouflage), so I have always resisted.

Playing a computer game at the pub with a beer in your hand, though, is slightly more acceptable, and while short of stimulation during a moment of solitude, I got lured into a session of Premier League Darts on the boozer's multi-purpose gaming machine. If you beat every member of the league in a one-leg virtual arrers match, you win £10, with lesser prizes for a shorter sequence of victories.

As a total novice, I was finding it tough, and throwing 50-pence pieces into the machine at regular intervals. I twice drew Taylor out of the hat first and got a pasting, and was even thrashed by Jelle Klaasen. But I eventually got the hang of the aiming technique, nailing my first maximum to defeat Terry Jenkins! It was such a rush – I had slayed The Bull and could feel the addiction lodge itself deep into my brain – and I looked forward to round two with confidence.

But then I found the aiming device suddenly going round at 500 miles per hour. No such thing as a free lunch, eh? Getting through to round three required the hand-eye co-ordination of a Top Gun pilot and I sat back down at my table, disgusted with myself for being so naive. Gaming, shmaming.

A great tit (not a pretty bird, but a stupid human) was adding to my air of discontentment. He was watching the England versus South Africa rugby union match, making a huge song and dance about everything that happened, shouting with an accent that even Hugh Grant would describe as posh.

His favourite player was Mark Cueto. In fact, if you put Mark Cueto in the same room as this fella, I think Mark Cueto's face would be covered in slobber within seconds. "Go on Cueto, go on Cueto," he chirped every time the apple of his eye got within 20 yards of the ball. And anything remotely positive England did was followed by the stomach-churning sight of Cueto's biggest fan clapping his hands like a demented seal.

I felt like asking him: For whose benefit is this clapping? How is anything positive coming from this clapping? By all means clap if you're at Twickenham – the players like a spot of encouragement from the stands – but you're in a public house 100 ruddy miles away!

His moaning about the refereeing was even more sickening. "He's coming from the other side!" he bleated, desperately trying to impress his glassy-eyed girlfriend with his knowledge of the RFU rule book. At that point even the landlady, desperate for business during the cold snap, was casting dagger-like glances in his direction.

I tried to ignore this vile character by reading the paper, but that just served to annoy me too. There was a letter to the agony aunt that read: Dear Deidre, can you catch HIV through jeans?

Oh, for crying out loud, I feel so alone on this planet sometimes. I threw the paper down and left Cueto's biggest fan to it, marching home to fulfil my promise to Bruce Millington by joining Twitter.

Bruce and other colleagues had been trying to convince me that Twitter was worthwhile, but I was full of scepticism, as I have always been with Myspace, Facebook and the like. "My mates have got my phone number," was my standard response to the topic of social networking sites. With Tiger Woods, Lee Westwood and other superstar golfers now 'tweeting', though, I mustered sufficient interest to get involved.

Before long, I had sent a tweet to Karlsson, trying to pump him up for the final round of the Dubai World Championship, then I logged off to enjoy watching O'Sullivan crush Robertson in their Premier League semi-final.

Sunday, November 28

I thought I was on for a tricast in Dubai, with Fisher, Karlsson and Quiros bang in contention, but Fisher soon dropped away. The event was turning into a two-horse race between Karlsson and Poulter, with

Quiros and Westwood the only others having any hope, and I was sniffing around Betfair with view to a chunk on Poulter at around the even-money mark.

My financial position demanded some sort of trading. Despite backing Manassero for the Castello Masters and Scott for the Singapore Open in recent weeks, the winnings were paying off debts more than anything and I could not risk getting nothing from Dubai. I'll just see Poulter through the difficult par-four 12th, I said to myself. He might drop a shot there and I'll get a bigger price.

The plan looked to be coming together nicely when his ball careered through the green in two, leaving him a tricky up-and-down, but the cocky rascal then holed his chip. I picked up my phone to find Millington, who was clearly concerned that I had already lost interest in Twitter, had texted prior to Poulter's chip-in: Your army of Twitter followers are wondering how you're feeling.

Tell them I'm weeping, I replied. At the same time as Poulter was killing me, the freak who lives in the flat below me continued her one-woman assault on the ears of the nation by singing at the top of her voice. She has now brought some sort of karaoke machine into play to provide a musical accompaniment to her glass-shattering voice.

You would think she would rein herself in a bit on a Sunday, the traditional day of rest, but she clearly doesn't enjoy resting. And she seems to specialise in songs where you have to hold the final note for ages. While Karlsson was making a disappointing par five at the 14th hole, she was belting out the Queen classic, I Want To Break Free. You took the words right out of my mouth, love. I want to break free from your incessant wailing.

My first in-running wager was £500 on Poulter at 1-2 in the aftermath of his birdie at the 12th, but I laid the monkey back at the same price after his shocking approach to the 15th, at the same time as having £100 on the fast-finishing Westwood at 4-1. Then after Westwood hit his second shot into the water at the 18th, I laid £250 of Karlsson at 2-1 and had £400 on Poulter at 1-5.

I now wish I had not bothered with any of this trading. Beanpole

Bob birdied the 18th before beating Poulter in a play-off. I should have won three bags, which would have given me a delightful financial boost, but traded like a girl and only won two.

Monday, November 29

I had another look at Twitter and found out that John Daly was one of my 'followers'. I thought he must have wanted to chat to a gambling soul-mate who had similar interests to him, but then I discovered he follows about 90,000 people, so didn't feel quite so special.

Seeking betting clues, I asked Westwood how his troublesome calf was feeling. No response. I asked Justin Rose if his swing was rusty after his long break. No response. Bob Karlsson had not replied to thank me for my Saturday night rallying cry and even my old mucker Rory McIlroy, who I had spent a day with in Dublin just a few months ago, was not up for communicating.

Fast losing interest in Twitter, I set my sights lower, asking US Tour journeyman Kris Blanks, who was practising (but not competing) at the Q-School venue, if anyone looked in top form. No response. This was an all-time low for my self-esteem levels – being blanked by Kris Blanks!

Without any Twitter assistance, I got all my golf wagers in place by the end of the evening. For the Chevron World Challenge I had £260 on Tiger at 9-2, £90 on Casey at 14-1 and £42 on Villegas at 33-1. For the Nedbank Challenge I had £528 on Westwood at 7-2 and £265 on Els at 6-1. For the Australian Open I had £110 on Ogilvy at 9-1, and for the Nippon Series JT Cup I had £130 on Ryo Ishikawa at 15-2. I threw in a £65 Woods (4-1) and Westwood (7-2) double and a £10 Woods (4-1), Westwood (10-3), Ogilvy (8-1) and Ishikawa (7-1) four-fold for good measure.

The nominations for Sports Personality of the Year were announced on the One Show and I was angry with myself for letting it catch me on the hop. Still, once Taylor was named on the shortlist, it was obvious where the value lay and I had £30 on Europe's finest sportsman at 16-1. I backed The Power with Paddy Power, so if I was a complete dick, I think this would be my cue to say: Ooh, is that an omen then?

Tuesday, November 30
She was singing at 7.30am! Unbelievable. If she is still warbling away come 2011, my plan is to shove a soiled sock through her letterbox every time she starts crooning (put one in it, eh?).

Fortunately, in the evening my Twitter experience improved greatly to perk me up. Tiger came on, so I gave him a pep talk for the Chevron, then I asked The Power whether a chunk on England to win the darts World Cup was sensible and he warned me that the format was a bit dodgy. Rory told me he thought Jose Mourinho should be the next Man United manager, then I had some banter with Troy Merritt, who finished 125th on the US Tour money list, about him narrowly avoiding Q-School.

Merritt also informed me he has never touched LPGA princess Natalie Gulbis (well, you've got to ask, haven't you?) and I was warming to Twitter.

Wednesday, December 1
Taylor tweeted to say he is watching Homes Under The Hammer as my love affair with Twitter intensified.

Thursday, December 2
Had my first investment on the PDC World Darts Championship – £40 each-way on Mervyn King at 50-1, a disrespectful quote for a recent semi-finalist with an excellent draw. Also had £100 on England to win the arrers World Cup at 2-5 and £200 on Ali Carter to win the UK Championship snooker at 18-1.

Friday, December 3
England (Taylor and Wade) lost to Spain in the World Cup. That just shouldn't happen in the real world.

CHAPTER 30
THE WOODS WOBBLE

Tiger Woods and Graeme McDowell

Saturday, December 4

I woke up in the morning to find my sofa adorned with 30 packets of Royster's T-bone steak flavour crisps, a fresh loaf of bread and a pair of knickers, and I had no idea how any of these items had made it into my establishment.

This is the kind of thing that happens when you have got money on the leader of three golf tournaments simultaneously – it is very easy to get carried away with life.

With Westwood in full control of the Nedbank Challenge, Ogilvy proving an equally dominant force in the Australian Open and Woods out in front in the Chevron World Challenge, I was convinced a serious payday was in store and was letting my hair down in spectacular fashion.

I had not given up on Ishikawa either, who could still win the JT Cup with a fast finish, and a £65 Westwood-Woods double, along with a £10 Westwood, Ogilvy, Woods, Ishikawa four-fold (which returned £15,600) had me dreaming of the crown jewels.

I was looking at almost £23,000 coming back my way if all four of these superstars triumphed and wondering whether I could be happily retired in time for Christmas. Ishikawa had some hard work to do if he was to keep up his part of the bargain, but it was odds-on that I would be getting a return of more than £6,000 from Westwood, Ogilvy and Woods.

Some fresh afternoon air was just what the doctor ordered to get my head together after an extremely late night, but I regretted my decision to watch Weymouth FC after just four minutes of their crunch Zamaretto clash with the mighty Banbury.

A deliberate handball on the goalline gifted Banbury a penalty, and put Weymouth down to ten men after a red card was brandished, and by half-time the score was three-nil to the visitors. I was fearing a rendition of "We can see you sneaking out" as I scuttled off to my car during the interval, but fortunately Banbury's away support was not exactly on a par with Manchester United's, so I managed to escape without any ridicule.

In the evening, I had £50 on Wales to beat Scotland in the World Cup of arrers quarter-finals at a generous 3-1, then watched Tiger stretch his lead in the Chevron to four shots. Casey was one of the biggest threats to Woods, but I had him covered ante-post too, so I went for another night on the tiles to celebrate the impending joy.

I remember giving my taxi driver home, a pleasant Hungarian chap, a £10 tip "because all my golfers are going to win tomorrow". He looked bemused and happy in equal measure.

Sunday, December 5

Ogilvy won by four shots to bank me £1,100 and Westwood delivered £2,270 with an eight-shot cruise. Ishikawa finished seventh, so the really big potatoes stayed in the sack, but another £2,866 would be coming my way once Tiger had put the finishing touches to victory in California.

Exhausted from a weekend of hedonism, a Woods wobble was the last thing I needed, but he missed some early tiddlers and let McDowell join the party.

A brilliant approach to the 18th hole left a tap-in birdie for Tiger, which would have been enough to seal a one-shot triumph if McDowell missed his birdie putt from much longer range, but the gutsy Northern Irishman stroked his home too. Europe's Ryder Cup hero, probably the best holer of clutch putts in the world at the moment, then nailed another left-to-right slider in the resulting play-off to poop all over Woods's party.

I'm so used to the heat of the golf-betting battle now – gunning for retirement on the Rory McIlroy St Andrews rollercoaster in July has made everything that has followed pale into insignificance – so it did not take me long to get over the disappointment of Tiger's surrender.

If you do something long enough, you get immune to it. Bash your head against a brick wall for 10,000 times a day every day for a calendar year, and come December you will hardly feel a thing each time you bash your head against that brick wall.

I've suffered so much Sunday golf-betting trauma through the years, I don't think any possible scenario can faze me any longer. I remember being in floods of tears when Jonathan Kaye blew a great winning opportunity in the 2001 BC Open. Almost ten years later, I think I've seen it all.

McDowell's heroics merely made me reconsider my Sports Personality of the Year plans. I had £30 on Taylor at 16-1 after he made the shortlist, but since then he has been part of an England World Cup flop, while the golfer of the year has humbled Woods in front of partisan American galleries.

I had £105 on McDowell at 4-1 in the wake of his Chevron magnificence. What more could he have done to convince floating voters? I now think the genial Northern Irishman might just pip Taylor. G-Mac first, Power second, AP third is my idea of the first three.

Monday, December 6

My pal at what was once called the Goalmouth Scramble cafe (he has since changed the name to the Sausage Locker) put "a pot of complimentary fresh cream" into my daily pint of banana milkshake. It was a kind gesture, but it only served to make me fit to explode at any moment, and the rest of my day was a challenge.

Carter's defeat to Mark Joyce in the UK Championship (£200 loss) added to my problems and I was starting to question snooker as a betting medium. O'Sullivan landed me a nice touch by winning the Premier League in style the previous weekend, but only a few days later he performed abysmally in a 9-6 defeat to Stuart Bingham. It was time to ignore the green baize for a bit and line some more golf tanks on the lawn.

For the Alfred Dunhill Championship, I had £350 on Schwartzel at 7-1 and £100 on Thomas Aiken at 22-1. For the Australian PGA Championship, I had £310 on Ogilvy at 6-1, £50 each-way on Leishman at 40-1 and £30 each-way on Rumford at 66-1. And for the Shark Shootout, I had £350 on Rickie Fowler/Bubba Watson at 6-1 and £85 on David Duval/Davis Love at 27-1.

To add fuel to the flames, I had a £100 double on Schwartzel and Ogilvy at 13-2 apiece, along with a £45 treble on Schwartzel, Ogilvy and the Fowler/Watson partnership, all at 6-1.

While settling down to watch England go 1-0 up in the Ashes, I reassessed the UK Championship while revelling in Australia's demise, having £150 on Mark Allen at 11-1, along with £35 each-way on Judd Trump at 33-1.

I then completed my PDC World Championship arrers outright portfolio, with £80 on Adrian Lewis at 37-1 and £170 on Whitlock at 16-1.

The late-night betting frenzy closed with me having £170 on Barcelona to win the Champions League at 5-2, bolstering the £150 I placed ante-post at 3-1. My plan at the start of the season was to keep topping up on Barca whenever I had some spare wedge, but this is the first time I have had the opportunity since the competition started.

Hopefully there will be enough coal on the fire come May 28 for me to justify buying an expensive ticket for the Wembley final to watch Barca's coronation as Europe's elite club side.

Tuesday, December 7

Shall I have some more on Barca then? Settle down, Steven, you restless plonker.

Wednesday, December 8

I saw a father dip his baby daughter's dummy into his Guinness before putting it into her mouth. Scandalous parenting. Is it any wonder we are a nation of binge drinkers?

Thursday, December 9

With the UK Championship semi-finals line-up complete and Allen still a runner, I had £275 on Shaun Murphy at 9-4, anticipating an Allen-Murphy finale.

Friday, December 10

I slumped into a depression for some reason, but a spot of CPR lifted me out of it. Many people require cardio-pulmonary resuscitation (CPR) to come back to life, but all I need is a Chinese, an episode of Peep Show and a drop of Radiohead (CPR) to revive me.

Saturday, December 11

Did you know that televisions can turn themselves on if they fancy doing so? I didn't either until a rather frightening incident in the middle of the night had me reaching for my five-iron. It was about 3.30am when the TV in my office sparked into life, blaring out at high volume, leaving me to fret that an intruder had entered my flat.

Quite why an intruder would want to reveal himself by switching on a TV, I did not factor into my calculations, but I prepared for combat with golf club in hand.

A slow prowl around my premises resulted in the all-clear, though, and it became obvious that the TV had powers of its own. Astonishing.

My betting day did not run smoothly either. Murphy was defeated by Mark Williams in a final-frame decider in their UK Championship semi-final, and my Shark Shootout wagers were failing to make an impact. I invested £200 on Dustin Johnson and Poulter at 9-4, believing the pre-tournament favourites were now in a position to justify that status.

Sunday, December 12

I had a good chance of success in the Alfred Dunhill Championship golf, with Schwartzel and Aiken in the mix. Charl finished second and Thomas finished fifth, though, so the tournament ultimately ended in disappointment.

I headed to the local for a roast to raise my spirits and the generous landlord provided the largest helping of brussels sprouts I had ever encountered. I got 28 sprouts inside me and then watched as my half of the pub started clearing at pace. Other patrons obviously feared the worst in terms of the gasses that were set to be emitted from my backside.

Afterwards I popped into my favourite betting shop to find the manager under fire because Coral TV had been waxing lyrical about their 'best on the high-street' 13-2 on Didier Drogba scoring the first goal in the Chelsea match. "He's not even f****** playing," barked the seething skinhead at the poor cashier. The manager tried his best to explain that Drogba backers would get their money back if the first goal was scored before he came on to the pitch, but this did little to calm the fury of Mr Angry.

I watched a dog win the 4.08 at Oxford having drifted in the betting from 5-1 to 12-1, then I headed back home to follow my golfers. Johnson and Poulter won with a degree of comfort to limit some of the damage, then Ogilvy started his final round of the Australian PGA in superb fashion.

Ogilvy claimed the clubhouse lead at 12 under par and looked to have secured back-to-back wins, but Peter Senior birdied the hardest hole on the course (the 18th) to force a play-off. Ogilvy then three-putted at the second extra hole to gift the veteran victory and deny me the best part of two bags.

Still, I finished the day with a winner, having had £49.23 on John Higgins to win the UK Championship at 4-1 when he was 8-5 behind to Williams in the final.

Monday, December 13

I got straight back down to business, hunting for value prior to the final golf event of the year, the South African Open. I quickly devoured the 12-1 about Tim Clark, having £400, then got £100 on Schwartzel at 14-1 and a further £200 at 12-1.

I briefly switched my attentions to the World Championship arrers, having a £350 cover shot on an all-English final at evens. I don't fancy Taylor this year, but with him odds-on to win the tournament, and Wade and King among the English stars in the other half of the draw, I thought evens was too big to ignore.

Tuesday, December 14

Had to venture north to London for various meetings and to attend the *Racing Post* Christmas Party in the evening. A free bar is always a dangerous beast to put near me and with a magnificent waiter quick to replace my empty pint glass with a full one whenever required, I soon found myself inebriated.

It was a good job I was, though, because the gathering turned into groundhog party for me near the end, a man who was eager to abuse Kevin Pullein and I 12 months earlier electing to repeat the trick. Having told Kevin last year that he was 'an idiot' because he did not rate Zlatan Ibrahimovich the best footballer in the world, this aggressive character rounded on the pair of us again because we didn't know who he was.

"You're Steve Palmer, aren't you? You're Steve Palmer – everyone knows Steve Palmer – but you don't know me," he bleated. The assertion that Kevin and I act as RP big shots could not be further from the truth – it is ridiculous – but it seems we now have to face the accusation on an annual basis. Never mind having a chip on his shoulder – this bloke carries a ruddy potato factory around with him. I still don't know who he is, so I guess we'll be doing it all again next year. Can't wait.

Wednesday, December 15

The temperature of the room at my Travelodge was nothing short of scandalous and at about 6.30am I was in the process of vomiting through chattering teeth. There was no point in going back to bed – getting any sleep in this icebox was impossible – so I headed to reception and ordered a taxi to Waterloo station.

I got on famously with the Polish driver, nailed a quick breakfast at McDonald's and then had to quickly assess whether there was any value in saving 17 pounds to stay another half an hour in London. It would cost me £50 to travel on the 9.35am to Weymouth, you see, but only £33 on the 10.05am. It was an easy decision to make – I was in a terrible condition and needed to escape – so I leapt aboard the earlier rattler.

Thursday, December 16

My illness intensified as time went by, the agony increasing as whooping cough was added to the mix of flu-like symptoms and a throat so sore that even eating ice cream was difficult.

Friday, December 17

Help me. Oh God, help me.

CHAPTER 31

ENDING WITH A WHIMPER

Phil Taylor

Saturday, December 18

Agony. Consistent, unrelenting, 24-hours-a-day agony. Flu is such a little word – it seems so harmless when popped on a page – but it packs plenty of punch when you're carrying a strain of flu inside you that could fell a woolly mammoth.

It has been a while since I've experienced pain as severe as this and even maximum dosages of the most powerful remedies I could get my hands on were failing to make any impact. I would go from sweating to freezing in seconds, poison oozing from every pore, and my coughing was so intense that I felt it was only a matter of time before pieces of ribcage started emerging from my mouth.

This was the day I was supposed to be making a pilgrimage to Alexandra Palace for a night of top-class arrers action, but I could not move a yard, let alone battle through snow to Muswell Hill.

It was with great sadness that I watched the darts from my bed and my misery peaked when the cameras trained on Hayley Turner, who was enjoying a night of tungsten pyrotechnics. My big chance to meet Hayley Turner had gone. We probably would have got on like a house on fire, would have immediately started courting and would have gone on to live happily ever after in a nice house in the country, playing with our ponies, watching darts, etc.

But now none of that is going to happen because I got the ruddy flu. Jesus Christ.

Sunday, December 19

Enough was enough. At the beginning of my fifth consecutive day of pure torture, with no signs of improvement, I decided I needed to visit a medical professional to see what the future held (if anything at all). It was Sunday, though – the day of The Lord – so I couldn't see a doctor. Get ill on the day of The Lord and you're in trouble. No doctors, so just pray a bit more, eh? Prayers count double on the day of The Lord (like away goals in many football cup competitions).

No, sod praying. I don't believe in The Lord anyway. The Lord wouldn't have ruined the Hayley-Steve love story. I'm going to the hospital to demand medical attention.

I obviously didn't want to stop people with broken necks or heart attacks from being treated, but I couldn't imagine 8am on a Sunday morning being much of an emergency hotspot, so I waddled into the hospital.

Fortunately, I was made very welcome and a nurse called Elaine was eager to assist me when I informed her I had endured a temperature of 104F for several days. That stat, coupled with a cough that had tears streaming down my face after every flurry, was enough to justify my presence.

Elaine was magnificent. She told me she could fry an egg on my forehead (that surely would have contravened NHS health and safety guidelines), but sorted me some magic pills and wished me well.

The South African Open golf could have provided another fillip, with Clark and Schwartzel close enough if good enough, but they finished ninth and fourth. The Sports Personality of the Year result was my only remaining chance of a winner, with Taylor and McDowell running for me.

Taylor finished runner-up, McDowell didn't even get a place, and my fragile mental state regressed further. The worst aspect of having a high temperature is the delirium that accompanies it, particularly when you attempt to sleep. You suffer the weirdest dreams of your life when you've got a fever and there is nothing you can do to stop them.

I spent the vast majority of the night convinced Paul Casey had won SPOTY. I was on the phone to the BBC in my mind-frazzled slumber going bananas about Casey's victory because he had not been on the shortlist of potential winners. The woman on the other end of the phone explained that because Casey looked a bit like Mark Cavendish they let people vote for him. I had almost drowned in my own sweat when I woke and rediscovered AP McCoy, not Casey, had succeeded.

Monday, December 20

I decided to have a football bet to distract me from my condition. It didn't count as a proper football bet – this was just like buying a sedative. I had £50 on no goalscorer at 10-1 for Manchester City versus Everton.

Four minutes in, 1-0 Everton. Four minutes of distraction (£12.50 a minute).

Tuesday, December 21

Finally felt well enough to type, so dipped back into Twitter. I was thrilled to see former world No. 3 snooker player Neal Foulds had become one of my 'followers'. My nan would be so proud if she was looking down on me now. She used to watch even more snooker than me in her last few years before succumbing to cancer. Now her grandson is friends (well, sort of) with Neal Foulds. Funny old world.

Wednesday, December 22

I was virtually on a Diet Coke drip, the tasty brown fluid the only thing capable of raising my spirits. I had great sympathy with John McCririck when he was denied his Diet Coke in Celebrity Big Brother. It is a substance on which many a man can become dependent. I could not live without Diet Coke and during times of sickness it is the single most satisfying thing I can feel on my tongue. If you offered my illness-riddled tongue one of Holly Willoughby's nipples or a mouthful of Diet Coke, it would definitely go for the latter.

Thursday, December 23

Lollipops are also excellent healing tools. The biggest laughs I've had during a dismal week or so have been when I have approached the fridge pretending to be the Lollipop Monster. Try it. Aggressively attack your fridge, growling: "Give me a lollipop, give me a f****** lollipop, you ****" while pawing wildly at the freezer compartment and ripping lollipops from the packet.

Maybe it's the heavy medication I'm on, but I'm getting an awful lot out of pretending to be the Lollipop Monster.

Friday, December 24

Time to start Christmas shopping. My three arrowsmiths are safely through to round two, so I can afford to be generous. Chocolate Orange for him, Chocolate Orange for her, Chocolate Orange for him . . .

Saturday, December 25

Christmas Day. The most overrated day of the year bar none. I don't think anyone actually enjoys themselves, do they? That Christ has got a lot to answer for.

I know one chap who certainly didn't have much fun on Christmas Day. My father and I walked to the pub as soon as it opened and came across a man lying still on the pavement en route. We were concerned our Christmas Day had got off to the worst possible start (discovering a dead body), but fortunately he was still in the land of the living.

Clearly inebriated, he had taken a tumble in the icy conditions and injured himself badly enough to find getting up impossible. We assured him everything was going to be alright (goodwill to all men, etc) and called an ambulance.

There was no evidence of unbridled Christmas joy in the pub, either. The first thing my pal Keith said to me was: "It's no fun for the IBS sufferer." Keith's irritable bowels become an even bigger burden than usual at this time of the year and the prospect of Christmas dinner with his wife's family was filling him with dread.

My old man and I had our enjoyment cut short by my sister arriving at the pub to force us back for lunch – she expertly used her upset son as a bargaining tool – so the Guinness quaffing was over and the day could only go downhill from there.

The Queen was busy banging on about how sport can bring everyone together. Not when Daddy's done his conkers punting on the football it doesn't, I mused to myself.

In the evening Stacey Slater's departure from EastEnders was a savage blow to morale – I don't know quite how I'm going to be able to live without her – and then another Christmas Day came to a close.

Sunday, December 26

Why is there never any darts on Boxing Day? If slimline footballers can digest their turkey in 24 hours, then roly-poly arrowsmiths should have no problem either.

Monday, December 27

Yes. Arrers is back. I had £200 on Mark Webster to beat Ronnie Baxter at 1-2 to nail an early ton, but £195.20 on Colin Lloyd to beat Mark Hylton at 2-5 undid that good work. A token ton on Adrian Lewis to beat Mark Dudbridge at 2-7 limited the damage.

I watched Arsenal versus Chelsea in the local and the place looked like a drop-in centre for the homeless. The pub comprised ten men, including the barman, and no women. Lonely old men seeking solace in football to get through the Christmas period. Ten men largely sat in silence staring at the screen. Society's rejects.

When football pundits talk about the Premier League having a winter break, I think they need to consider the impact it would have on life's losers. What would we do? I suppose we would all end up in church. Church and Christmas? No, they don't really go together, do they?

Tuesday, December 28

I had £327.61 on Wes Newton to beat Brendan Dolan at 2-5. The plan was to reinvest all the pot if Newton won on Whitlock to beat Dennis Ovens, but I was in the pub by 5.30pm to watch West Ham versus Everton, so had no access to a computer.

I was thinking about backing Everton (I've decided small 'fun' football bets can be introduced into my punting), but David Moyes had named Saha, Yakubu and Beckford on the bench and put Tim Cahill on his own up front. A barmy decision that was enough for me to keep my powder dry.

As Birmingham versus Man United started, I was having a good chin-wag with the landlord and urging him to back United to win 1-0, a scoreline that should have been about 1-5 in my eyes. I decided to put my money where my mouth is (dangerous business that – those coins don't taste very nice) and had £150 on United to win 1-0 at 9-2.

The game was going just as anticipated – hard-working Birmingham were making life tough for the visitors but offering nothing going forward – and when Berbatov made the breakthrough on the hour-mark everything was looking rosy.

Five minutes later, United were swarming all over their hosts and I decided to have a cover shot on 2-0, confident that Birmingham wouldn't score in a month of Sundays (whatever that means). I had £175 on United to win 2-0 at 9-4 to secure a tidy return on either scoreline.

After 88 minutes, I had £825 coming back from my 1-0 wager. But then a 'goal', which featured a foul by the attacking side, followed by a handball by the attacking side, followed by an offside by the attacking side, was registered. The attacking side was Birmingham and I lost £325 on the match. Was that a 'fun' football bet? I'm not so sure.

Wednesday, December 29

Had £125 on Barneveld to beat Kevin McDine 4-0 at 7-4. King's 4-3 defeat to Andy Smith was a blow and I reacted by having £135.48 on Barneveld outright at 10-1, his path to the final looking relatively straightforward.

Barney's 4-1 victory was not enough to land any correct-score booty and my £42 on Webster to beat Hylton 4-0 at 3-1 went the same way. I had £220 on Webster to win the match at 1-3 after he had lost the second set, which salvaged some sterling, but £300 on Taylor to beat Peter Wright 4-0 at 1-2 made it an expensive night.

The Power allowed a man with some sort of green vegetable growing out of the back of his head to take a set off him, much to my chagrin.

Thursday, December 30

I played my recording of Steve Farmer's World Championship first-round match against Paul Nicholson while throwing darts myself. Every time the commentators say Steve Farmer it sounds just like Steve Palmer, so I can pretend I'm in World Championship action.

Escaping the real world at every opportunity is my New Year's resolution.

Friday, December 31

Oh, sorry, did I say Christmas Day is the most overrated day of the year? How could I forget New Year's Eve?

I headed up the local looking to talk about proper things (the amazingness of a man called Arsene managing Arsenal, the amazingness of a man called Mancini managing Man City, etc), but New Year's Eve is all about 'fancy' dress and what not, isn't it?

I spent the night mulling over another year in which I had aggressively tried to punt my way to freedom and ended it as skint as when I started. I'm beginning to think the all guns blazing approach may not work in the betting game and it is time for me to drastically reduce the amount of wagers I have. Slowly, slowly, catchy monkey, as a wise man once said.

Hmmmm, midnight on December 31 – by far the most agonising time of the year for a single man. Kiss anyone? Oh, I'll just kiss my hand instead. Happy New Year, hand.

LOOKING TO THE FUTURE

I was asked by a lady the other day: How long are you going to keep trying?

As long as it takes, I replied. Or until I die. Or until I find happiness some way else.

"You're never going to give up?" she queried.

With a 33rd birthday looming, the pressure to successfully punt my way to freedom is intensifying. There is not long left to make it count. I'm not a very healthy person – I don't envisage lasting far beyond my 60th birthday even if all runs relatively smoothly – so I won't have a great deal of time to enjoy the pro punter's lifestyle unless I get my act together very quickly.

I could take the advice of many of my peers and try to accumulate wealth slowly – winning a bit here and a bit there is a lot easier than hitting the jackpot – but is there any point in reaching a magical financial figure just at the point you start going senile?

I have been eager to claim a retirement-clinching return (or the facespitter as it has become widely known) sooner rather than later. Whatever I win has just become ammunition for more substantial bets – it has been that way for a while – with the idea being to bag enough booty to walk away from full-time employment.

A wise man called Wayne Dyer once put it so well: Freedom means you are unobstructed in living your life as you choose. Anything less is a form of slavery.

I've spent several years trying to free myself of all shackles – if Tim Clark hadn't laid up in the Bob Hope Classic I may have done so in February last year – but to no avail. I'm as skint now as when I started this mission.

Maybe it is time to do what the lady suggested. Maybe it is time to surrender. Tragically few people get to taste true freedom and it may be time to accept I'm not going to be one of them.

Oh, fiddlesticks.